JAN 15

D0863832

Thomas Hauser on Boxing

Books by Thomas Hauser

General Non-Fiction

Missing
The Trial of Patrolman Thomas Shea
For Our Children (with Frank Macchiarola)
The Family Legal Companion
Final Warning: The Legacy of Chernobyl (with Dr. Robert Gale)
Arnold Palmer: A Personal Journey
Confronting America's Moral Crisis (with Frank Macchiarola)
Healing: A Journal of Tolerance and Understanding
With This Ring (with Frank Macchiarola)
Thomas Hauser on Sports
Reflections

Boxing Non-Fiction

The Black Lights: Inside the World of Professional Boxing
Muhammad Ali: His Life and Times
Muhammad Ali: Memories
Muhammad Ali: In Perspective
Muhammad Ali & Company
A Beautiful Sickness
A Year At The Fights
Brutal Artistry
The View From Ringside
Chaos, Corruption, Courage, and Glory
The Lost Legacy of Muhammad Ali
I Don't Believe It, But It's True
Knockout (with Vikki LaMotta)
The Greatest Sport of All
The Boxing Scene
An Unforgiving Sport
Boxing Is . . .
Box: The Face of Boxing
The Legend of Muhammad Ali (with Bart Barry)
Winks and Daggers
And the New . . .
Straight Writes and Jabs
Thomas Hauser on Boxing

Fiction

Ashworth & Palmer
Agatha's Friends
The Beethoven Conspiracy
Hanneman's War
The Fantasy
Dear Hannah
The Hawthorne Group
Mark Twain Remembers
Finding The Princess
Waiting For Carver Boyd
The Final Recollections of Charles Dickens

For Children

Martin Bear & Friends

Thomas Hauser on Boxing

Another Year inside the Sweet Science

Thomas Hauser

The University of Arkansas Press
Fayetteville
2014

Copyright © 2014 by Thomas Hauser

All rights reserved
Manufactured in the United States of America

ISBN 978-1-55728-667-3
e-ISBN: 978-1-61075-547-4

18   17   16   15   14   5   4   3   2   1

∞ The paper used in this publication meets the minimum requirements of the
American National Standard for Permanence of Paper for Printed Library Materials
Z39.48-1984.

Library of Congress Control Number: 2014939432

For Don Turner, Bruce Trampler, Steve Farhood, and Tom Gerbasi,
four good boxing guys who've shared the journey

Contents

Author's Note

Thomas Hauser on Boxing contains the articles about professional boxing that I authored in 2013. The articles I wrote about the sweet science prior to that date have been published in *Muhammad Ali & Company*; *A Beautiful Sickness*; *A Year at the Fights*; *The View From Ringside*; *Chaos, Corruption, Courage, and Glory*; *The Lost Legacy of Muhammad Ali*; *I Don't Believe It, But It's True*; *The Greatest Sport of All, The Boxing Scene, An Unforgiving Sport, Boxing Is, Winks and Daggers, And the New*, and *Straight Writes and Jabs*.

Fighters and Fights

Don King and I have had our differences over the years. And at times, they've been heated. I'm grateful that he allowed me to share the night of March 9, 2013, with him.

Don King in the Twilight

Don King arrived at Barclays Center for the March 9, 2013, IBF 175-pound title fight between Bernard Hopkins and Tavoris Cloud shortly after 8:00 PM.

King will be eighty-two years old on August 20, but he has the physical presence and vitality of a man half his age. His large bulky frame, Cheshire Cat grin, booming voice, and high-pitched laugh suggest a force of nature.

Wherever King goes, he's encapsulated in a bubble of public attention. Everyone, from high-ranking corporate executives to men and women on the street, stop and stare and are drawn to his side.

In the September 2, 1974, issue of *Sports Illustrated*, Mark Kram wrote, "Don King is big, black, and hardly beautiful, a 50-carat setting of sparkling vulgarity and raw energy, a man who wants to swallow mountains, walk on oceans, and sleep on clouds."

That was mainstream America's introduction to King. Two months later, Muhammad Ali dethroned George Foreman in Zaire with Don playing a key role in the promotion. In the decades that followed, King promoted more than five hundred world championship fights. At one point, Don King Productions could lay claim to promoting seven of the ten largest pay-per-view fights in history (as gauged by total buys) and twelve of the top twenty highest-grossing live boxing gates in the history of Nevada.

King has promoted Ali, Foreman, Joe Frazier, Larry Holmes, Mike Tyson, Evander Holyfield, Ray Leonard, Roberto Duran, Julio Cesar Chavez, Felix Trinidad, Roy Jones, and dozens of other Hall of Fame fighters. He's one of the few people in boxing today who transcend the sport. His name and face are more recognizable than those of Floyd Mayweather Jr or any other active fighter.

"People come up to me all the time, put their babies in my arms, and ask me to kiss them." King chortles. "That doesn't happen to Bob Arum or Richard Schaefer."

Boxing fans are used to seeing King in a tuxedo on fight night; a shining apparition draped in bling that seems to reflect off everything from the top of his hair down to his black patent-leather shoes.

At Barclays Center, King had a different look. The promoter was wearing red-white-and-blue jogging shoes, maroon corduroy pants, a blue shirt, an American-flag-themed tie, and a rhinestone-studded blue-denim jacket accessorized by three "Obama" buttons. The jacket (one of three celebrating America that the promoter owns) was badly frayed. By contrast, King's fingernails were impeccably manicured. He had an unlit cigar in one hand and miniature flags representing two dozen nations in the other. The name of each country was written at the base of its respective flagstick.

There was a time when it didn't matter a whole lot to King who won or lost a big fight because he controlled both fighters. That time is long gone. Now it's rare for Don to control even one combatant in a major bout. Cloud was under contract to King, but the Hopkins fight was the last under their promotional agreement. It was also possible that this would be King's last fight on HBO.

What happened to King's power?

For starters, he was a prisoner of his own success. What had worked in the past stopped working as well as it had before. But King had enough money and enough trappings from the glory years that he wasn't forced to adapt. The times changed and he didn't change with them.

King is into control. He has always been hands-on in every area of his business. He likes everything to run through him and chooses not to share his tricks of the trade with anyone. Thus, he never had a strong number two to help with the heavy lifting or guide him in new directions.

Don had always played leverage to the hilt. For years, control of the heavyweight champion (Ali, Holmes, Tyson) and the heavyweights beneath them was his most valuable asset. Then he lost that control. He managed to thrive afterward with lighter-weight fighters like Felix Trinidad and Julio Cesar Chavez. But the power dynamic in boxing was shifting to favor the premium cable television networks. Network executives found other promoters easier to deal with than King. After Don took Mike Tyson to Showtime in the mid-1990s, HBO made a decision to license fewer fights from him. Then King lost Tyson, and Showtime moved away from him too. Eventually, King no longer had a fighter that network executives felt they absolutely needed, and HBO begin the process of helping to build Golden Boy as a countervailing promotional power.

Also, whatever corners King had cut as part of his business model (and there were many), other promoters began cutting with an even sharper razor. The world sanctioning organizations found new suitors to occupy the place on their balance sheets where King had once been. The tentacles of these promoters soon reached throughout the boxing industry as Don's once had.

Meanwhile, King's reputation was catching up with him. National attention focused on him in a critical way. Elite fighters became wary of signing with him. He was subjected to closer legal scrutiny than other promoters and, in some instances, held to a higher standard.

And finally, Don got old. People slow down at a certain age. There are no eighty-year-old international chess champions. At a certain age, men and women think one fewer move ahead than they used to.

"I'm like Churchill," King says. "I'll never surrender."

But one had the feeling at Barclays Center that King is nearing the end of an extraordinary journey. Indeed, although his fighter was the champion, it was Bernard Hopkins (promoted by Golden Boy) who had been listed first in pre-fight promotional material. Cloud was fungible, a guy with a belt. Hopkins vs. Cloud was about Hopkins.

The defining feature of Bernard's career has been his longevity. As noted by Tom Gerbasi, "He took the time when boxers' legacies get destroyed or at least tarnished and made his even greater."

Hopkins ascended to stardom with a twelfth-round knockout of Felix Trinidad on September 29, 2001. He was thirty-six years old, and the assumption was that his days in boxing were numbered.

Big number.

Over the next forty-one months, Bernard recorded victories over Carl Daniels, Morrade Hakkar, William Joppy, Robert Allen, Oscar De La Hoya, and Howard Eastman. Then, at age forty, he lost twice to Jermain Taylor. Now, surely, the end was near.

Hopkins's record has been uneven since then. Prior to facing Cloud, he hadn't scored a knockout since stopping De La Hoya in 2004. Over the previous eight years, he'd recorded 6 wins, 4 losses, and 1 draw with 1 no contest. He had won only one fight in the preceding thirty-five months. But he'd been competitive every time out. And what makes Bernard's ledger so impressive is his age. He's now forty-eight years old.

Margaret Goodman (former chief ringside physician for the Nevada State Athletic Commission) says, "If a fighter is old enough to need Viagra, he shouldn't be boxing."

Hopkins says, "I'm a fighter. This is what I do. Age is not my enemy. Don't look at the number. Look at the man. I'm not counting age. Everybody else is counting it. I'll stop when I want to stop."

Hopkins has superb footwork, great balance, and a rock-solid chin. He comes into fights in the best condition possible and is a master of ring generalship.

"No fight is about yesterday," Bernard says. "Every fight is about now. I take every fight like the building block of another generation of what I need to do."

His mindset also includes a healthy respect for the traditions of boxing.

"I don't know that I could have survived in a time like the 1940s," Hopkins acknowledged several years ago. "Fighting three, maybe four times a year, I think I would have been competitive with the best in that era. But physically and mentally, it would have been hard for me to fight fourteen or fifteen times a year like those guys did."

Hopkins-Cloud was Bernard's first fight in New York since 2001. There were the usual mind games such as Hopkins showing up at the final pre-fight press conference wearing a black hoodie with sunglasses and a mask across his face and refusing to speak.

"I'd be a fool to get caught up in Bernard Hopkins's mind games," Cloud told the media. "That's a fool's game, buying into those traps. You can't lollygag and bullshit because that's his game. He's in his own world, so I'll let him be until March the ninth."

Cloud was a 3-to-2 favorite, based largely on the seventeen-year age differential between the fighters. When Bernard turned pro in 1988, Tavoris was six years old. Cloud's own pro debut hadn't come until thirty months after "Old Man Hopkins" beat Trinidad in 2001.

"I don't think any fighter can stay young forever, no matter how hard they try," Tavoris said. "And it's evident that he slowed down in the last couple of years."

But the feeling among the boxing intelligentsia was that youth was Cloud's only edge. Tavoris's record was 24 and 0, but there wasn't much on his résumé. He'd had only two fights since 2010. The only slick boxer of note he'd fought was Gabriel Campillo. Campillo was the better fighter that night, although two of the three judges gave the nod to Cloud. The other "names" on Tavoris's curriculum vitae were Clinton Woods and Glen Johnson. Other than Yusaf Mack (who has been knocked out in three of six fights during the past forty-five months), Cloud hadn't stopped an opponent since 2008.

Moreover, the fighters who have given Hopkins the most trouble over the years (Roy Jones when he was young, Jermain Taylor, Joe Calzaghe, and Chad Dawson) all had speed on him. Cloud is slow on his feet and slow to pull the trigger.

Much of the pre-fight activity was focused, not on Hopkins vs. Cloud, but on Hopkins vs. Don King. They've had a long and often contentious relationship.

King promoted Hopkins for much of Bernard's middleweight title reign, and the fighter (like many of his brethren) bridled at what he perceived as exploitation at Don's hands. Bernard exacted a measure of revenge in 2001, knocking out Felix Trinidad to derail the promoter's plans for a megafight at Yankee Stadium between Trinidad and Roy Jones. But he was still contractually bound to King for three additional fights that covered two more years.

King, of course, was supportive of Cloud in the upcoming battle against Hopkins.

"Tavoris Cloud will beat Bernard Hopkins," Don proclaimed at the January 15 kickoff press conference (held on Bernard's forty-eighth birthday). "That's not a guess or speculation or prognostication. It's a promise." On the same occasion, King turned to Hopkins and noted, "You're smart. When Tavoris knocks you out, you'll know it's time to quit."

But for the most part, King kept the rhetoric down. "I love the man," he said of Bernard. "I have no problem at all with him."

Hopkins took a contrary view.

"I don't like Don King," the fighter declared. "And I made it clear I don't like Don King. Tavoris Cloud is Don's last horse. There ain't no stable. When Don's last horse breaks his leg, Don will be done. Whoever thought that Bernard Hopkins—not the mob, not the street people, not the fighters who threatened him over the years, not other promoters—whoever thought that it would be me that shut him down? Everybody that Don threw at me, I knocked out. I'm 15 and 0 against him. I understand my biggest motivation. Don King, willingly or unwillingly, helped me build my legacy, and I've been beating him ever since. To put the last nail in the coffin, it's an honor."

To that, Richard Schaefer added, "I guess he [King] enjoys what he's doing, walking around in his jean jacket with the flags and yelling 'Puerto Rico.' He doesn't even have a Puerto Rican fighter anymore. He's living in the past."

King took it all in stride.

"I'm very delighted to have listened to some of the comments that Mr. Hopkins made," Don said during a February 27 teleconference call. "I thought he was just par excellence. Bernard is doing a great job of promoting, and I just want to say that he's not a nemesis to me. I think it's really wonderful that he's had such a unique grand wonderful career. There's nobody that can take that away from him. I love Bernard. Both of us are alumni from the penitentiary. He's a fraternity brother."

In truth, there are many similarities between the two men. Like King, Hopkins (whether he admits it or not) has become part of the boxing establishment. Like King, Hopkins has defied age and uses words as a battering ram. There was a time when King was the hardest working man in boxing and also the hardest man working in boxing. That mantle arguably now belongs to Hopkins. Each man has a take-no-prisoners mentality and wants all the toys for himself.

Listen to Bernard Hopkins speak:

★ "It's not luck. Luck didn't get me out of the penitentiary without getting killed, stabbed, raped, or whatever. Luck didn't get me out of the ghetto and turn my life around. Hard work creates luck."

★ "The rules are different for Bernard Hopkins. The rules should be different for Bernard Hopkins because I've made them that way."

★ "I'm doing something that ain't supposed to be done. Now it becomes something different, and that's what I am. Different."

★ "I do it my way."

King laughs when Bernard's words are brought to his attention.

"Bernard wants to be like me," the promoter says. "But he's got a long way to go."

★   ★   ★

When Don King arrived at Barclays Center on fight night, he went directly to Tavoris Cloud's dressing room.

"Let's get ready to rumble," he told the fighter. "Do your business. Then we'll go home and eat a steak."

In years past, most likely that would have been followed by a pre-fight victory tour of the arena. Tonight, King settled on a folding cushioned chair, where he would remain until Cloud walked to the ring two-and-a-half hours later. It was more comfortable for Don in the dressing room, and less energy was required of him there.

The room was quiet and would remain so for most of the evening. There was no music, little conversation within the fighter's camp, and virtually no interaction between any member of Team Cloud and King.

Unprompted, the promoter took a smart phone out of his pocket and began brushing his finger across the screen to move from photo to photo.

"That's me with Jimmy Carter. This is me with the first President Bush . . . Bill Clinton . . . George W. Bush . . . Mobutu . . . Coretta Scott King . . . Ferdinand Marcos . . . Nelson Mandela. He's the most interesting person I've ever met."

Abel Sanchez (Cloud's trainer) drew the attention of New York State Athletic Commission inspector Mike Paz to a cut on Tavoris Cloud's right index finger that hadn't fully healed.

"Can we put a piece of tape over the cut to protect it before we wrap."

The answer was no.

"Hugo Chavez. I loved that man. He was like a brother to me . . . Silvio Berlesconi . . . Jacques Chirac at the French White House."

That was followed by photos of King with a parade of boxing luminaries.

"Muhammad Ali. Me and him; we changed history . . . Joe Frazier . . . Mike Tyson . . . Larry Holmes . . . George Foreman . . . Roberto Duran . . . Felix Trinidad . . . The big fights bring people together. It's not just about two men fighting. It's about bringing people of the same culture and different cultures together. It's a happening that people feel in their hearts and talk about for years. I didn't just promote fights. I promoted cultures and people. When I wave the Puerto Rican flag and shout 'Viva, Puerto Rico,' all of Puerto Rico gets involved."

More photos. Then King paused to gaze at an image of his younger self standing next to his wife of five decades.

Henrietta King died in December 2010.

"My wonderful wife, Henrietta. I miss her dearly. Everything I accomplished in life, I owe to her."

The viewing continued.

"Pope Benedict. He just resigned . . . This is a picture of a painting that the Pope gave me. It's worth a million dollars That's me at the United Nations . . . Henry Kissinger . . . Here's some more presidents. I forget what countries they're from . . . Shimon Peres at the Wailing Wall . . . That's with a giant panda in China . . . This is with some troops. I support the troops wherever I go."

"Michael Jackson . . . Janet Jackson . . . Christie Brinkley . . . Celine Dion . . . Danny Glover . . . Natalie Cole . . . This is some hip-hop stars . . . LeBron James . . . Martina Navratilova . . . Roger Federer . . . Rafael Nadal . . . All these people, and I came out of the ghetto in Cleveland."

Then a photo of King embracing a gray-haired woman with her head pressed against his chest.

"My sister Evelyn. There were seven of us. Six boys and a girl. We're the only two left."

King looked at photos for well over an hour. One can surmise that virtually every person whose photo is on his smart phone remembers meeting Don too.

"The reward is in the journey," King said. "And I've had a wonderful journey."

At 9:30 PM, Cloud stood up and began shadow boxing.

Another hour passed.

"I get anxious sometimes before a fight," King admitted. "But you don't want to show that to the fighter."

Then King began talking about Bernard Hopkins vs. Felix Trinidad and how fate had conspired to deny Trinidad his due. Team Cloud couldn't have cared less about what had happened in a boxing ring more than a decade ago.

Don waved his miniature Puerto Rican flag and called out "Viva, Puerto Rico."

Silence.

King refocused his attention on the fighter in front of him.

"Mr. Thunder," he roared. "The storm is coming. Let the warm air come in and mix with the cold air and we'll have ourselves a storm. God parted the waters for Moses. We're gonna part the waters tonight. This man is gonna strike a blow that will free us all. The walls of Jericho came tumbling down. You got to land that thunderous blow for all mankind."

At 10:50 PM, Cloud left his dressing room and walked to the ring with King behind him.

The fighters were introduced to the crowd. Hopkins didn't look at King and refused to come to ring center for referee Earl Brown's final instructions until Don had stepped outside the ropes and begun moving toward his seat in the front row facing the main television camera.

The bell rang. The fight was on.

Before the bout, Cloud had said, "If you look at Bernard Hopkins fight, he doesn't fight the whole round. You just gotta go in there and make him fight. You can't let him tie you up and start all that bullshit. You have to be really blunt with your fighting style. You just gotta go in there and beat his ass."

"I know I'm the better fighter," Hopkins had responded. "I know I have the better fighter's IQ, and I'm also the better-conditioned fighter. Cloud is one-dimensional. I love his style. He'll be coming right at me."

The fight was fought at Bernard's pace. Jimmy Tobin summed it up nicely for TheCruelestSport.com.

"Gabriel Campillo had already skywritten Cloud's limitations," Tobin wrote. "And Hopkins had read the message. This was an impressive performance primarily because of Hopkins's age, not because of his opponent.

With a combination of feints, purposeful movement, and a handful of discouraging punches, Hopkins physically and psychologically wedded Cloud to his own inactivity. Cloud spent long stretches of the fight harmlessly following Hopkins as the latter slid along the ropes. He should have forced the fight against Hopkins, thereby increasing his chances to land something withering enough to remind Hopkins of his age. He should have played to his strengths, abandoned thinking, and tried to whale on the only other person in the ring not wearing a striped shirt. But this fervent attack never materialized. Even when in range, Cloud largely kept his guns holstered."

King knows what he's watching. He didn't say much as the fight progressed, but what he said was on the mark.

"Veteran moves from Bernard . . . See how he throws the elbow . . . He did it again just then . . . Whenever Cloud gets inside, Bernard ties him up but he doesn't do it the way most fighters do. He locks Cloud's head in with his arm, pushes down, and twists. That weakens a man, but you do it as long as the referee lets you."

There were moments of hope.

"That's it. Give it to the body. That got Bernard's attention and spread his legs . . . Bernard has a great poker face. He never shows when he's hurt, but he was hurt then . . . Cloud has to step it up and take the fight to him."

In round six, Hopkins opened a cut on Cloud's left eyelid. As the rounds went by, he continued to dictate the pace and terms of engagement. By round ten, there was a look of resignation on King's face. Midway through the twelfth round, he looked up at the giant screen overhead to see how much time was left.

"Bernard's got it . . . Great job. He's a good fighter."

The reading of the judges' scorecards was anti-climactic: 116-112, 116-112, and 117-111 for Hopkins.

Don King has had many critics over the years, and I've been one of them. But this is a time to praise Caesar, not bury him.

King was capable of sitting down with professionals on the opposite side of the negotiating table (whether it was Seth Abraham at HBO or Bob Arum at Top Rank) and doing what had to be done to make the big fights that the public wanted to see. Historic co-promotions like Ali-Frazier III, Holmes-Cooney, and Trinidad-De La Hoya bear his imprint. His showmanship put 132,247 fans in seats for Julio Cesar Chavez vs. Greg Haugen in Azteca Stadium in Mexico City. And for those who think that anyone could have sold tickets for Chavez in Mexico, King also sold out the Savvis Center in St. Louis for Cory Spinks vs. Zab Judah. If Don had been calling the shots, Manny Pacquiao vs. Floyd Mayweather would have happened.

"Everybody is trying to do what I've already done," King said three days before Hopkins-Cloud. "Ain't nobody can touch me here, not in this lifetime."

So for the moment, let's put the bad aside and celebrate the excitement and energy that Don King has brought to boxing over the past forty years.

"You'll never be able to replace boxing as a sport," King has said.

Boxing won't be able to replace Don King either. He'll leave a global footprint when he has gone.

Seanie Monaghan embodies a lot of what's good about boxing.

Seanie Monaghan Loves to Fight

Seanie Monaghan is a "throwback fighter." In the 1940s, he would have been a neighborhood fight-club headliner and local hero.

Seanie is the oldest of four children. His parents immigrated to the United States from Ireland and settled in Long Beach; a town of 33,000 located on a barrier island east of New York City. Long Beach faces the Atlantic Ocean. There was a time when it styled itself as "the Riviera of the east" and vied with Atlantic City as a tourist destination for New Yorkers during the hot summer months. That time is long gone. In recent decades, the town has gone through cycles of urban decay and renewal. Last October, it felt the full force of Hurricane Sandy.

Seanie grew up in Long Beach and still lives there. His father runs an upholstering business. His mother is a physical therapist. His paternal grandmother was one of seventeen children, so he has a large family, many of whom still live in Ireland. His wife, Beverly, earned a master's degree in special education from Hofstra. Together, they have a twenty-two-month-old son, Sammy.

But there's a painful backstory.

"I was a lost teenager," Seanie acknowledges. "I had no ambition or direction. Everything was short-term. I didn't care where I was going. I smoked weed every day. I wrestled a bit in high school and played some sports like football and lacrosse. But the other guys were better than me. And if I wasn't good at something right away, instead of working to get better, I gave up on it."

Seanie graduated from Long Beach High School in 1999. "Barely," he says.

But trouble was brewing.

"There was an unhealthy culture in Long Beach and I got caught up in it," Seanie recalls. "I wasn't a bad kid. My mother and father are good hard-working people. I came from a decent home. I wasn't a street guy. I never stole anything or sold drugs. But a lot of people in my family have had drinking problems. I was drunk a lot, and I tried just about every drug there was except heroin."

"Around the time I was fifteen," Seanie continues, "I started getting into bar fights. I was working as a barback [a bartender's assistant] and was surrounded by grown men who were drinking, and I'd try to keep up with them. A fight would start; sometimes with me. Or if it started with someone else, I'd jump in. People would crowd around and cheer. I'd always wanted to be really really good at something. And there it was. Knocking guys out. It felt so good. There were a lot of fights; fifty or sixty over the years. My nose got broken. I was constantly hurting my hands. I'd come home with a black eye or cuts and try to hide it from my mother. I look back on it all now and say, 'Forget about everything else. Look at the stress I put my mother through.' I wasn't a bad kid. I got along with people, all kinds of people, when I wasn't fighting. But it was like, if there was a problem, I was the Long Beach representative. One time in a bar fight, I got stabbed in the throat and needed thirty or forty stitches. I was arrested a few times. The last time was for assaulting a police officer who was trying to break up one of the fights. I didn't know he was a police officer. He grabbed me from behind and I threw him off. The judge gave me a break. He put me on probation and told me, 'If I see you in my courtroom again, you're doing five years hard time.' That straightened me out. I stopped drinking and doing drugs. I don't drink or smoke at all now. I haven't had a drink in more than ten years. Casual drinking is okay if you can do it, but I couldn't."

As part of Seanie's probation, he was required to attend meetings at Alcoholics Anonymous and Narcotics Anonymous and also attend an anger-management course.

"The anger-management course really pissed me off," Seanie says. "I didn't think I needed to be there. But over time, I realized that little things were making me furious, and I was getting mad for no reason. Even though I might not have been starting the fights, I was looking for them. It took me a while, but finally I understood that I had to change. I learned to take a step back when there was a problem and how to control my emotions. I had relatives in Ireland who were telling me, 'You're on probation. Come back here before they throw you in jail.' But the problem wasn't that I was in Long Beach. The problem was me."

"Then I looked at my life as a whole. I hadn't built anything. All I was doing was drifting from day to day. I was in danger of losing any chance I had for a good future. My whole personality is different now. I've learned discipline and how to dedicate myself to things that are important to me. I'm a much better husband and father than I could possibly have been back then. I'm much happier than I used to be. I'm not an aggressive person anymore except when I'm in the ring."

After Seanie stopped drinking, a friend named Bobby Calabrese suggested that he try his hand at boxing. That sounded like a good idea, so he went to the PAL gym in Freeport, which had a boxing club run by a now-retired firefighter named Joe Higgins.

"Two guys were in the ring, sparring," Seanie remembers. "I liked what I saw. There was a trainer there. I told him, 'I'm Seanie Monaghan from Long Beach. I want to be a boxer.'"

"He was a real character," Higgins recalls. "A kid off the street with a chip on his shoulder. He told me he wanted to spar that day, and I started laughing. He said, 'I knock guys out on the street.' And I said, 'Yeah; but this ain't the street.'"

The next six weeks were about footwork, balance, head movement, and how to throw a jab.

"Finally, Joe said I could spar," Seanie says with a smile. "And the first punch I got hit with, I went down on my butt."

Seanie had fifteen amateur fights starting at age twenty-six and turned pro on May 21, 2010. He's now thirty-one years old and has had eighteen pro fights in less than three years. His trainer is still Joe Higgins. His manager is P. J. Kavanagh.

"I'm usually the aggressor," Seanie says of his fighting style. "I come at you, go to the body a lot, and don't stop coming. Getting hit doesn't bother me that much. I kind of zone out when I'm in a fight. The biggest problem I have is that I cut too easily. My biggest fear is that I'll be in a fight I know I can win and it's stopped on cuts. And I have to get past my natural instinct to try to just smash everybody."

"Seanie works so freakin' hard," Higgins says. "He takes a week or two off from the gym after a fight; but even then, he runs. And outside of those breaks, he hasn't missed a day in the gym since I started with him. He does everything I ask him to do. He's in monster shape every time he fights. He makes my job easy. I tell the other guys in the gym, 'Study this guy. Be like him.'"

The downside to it all is that Seanie started boxing late in life, has limited ring experience, and is relatively slow in a sport where speed kills.

Top Rank matchmaker Brad Goodman has taken a special interest in Seanie and notes, "The first time I saw him, he had no technical skills. But he had some natural ability, and I'm impressed with how much he has improved since then. It's our job as matchmakers to see that he isn't in with an opponent who's too advanced for him at this stage of his career because Seanie has a warrior mentality. He'll fight anyone you put in front of him."

In a similar vein, Steve Farhood (who has watched the evolution of Seanie's career while behind the microphone for Lou DiBella's Broadway Boxing series) observes, "Seanie is a good example of a fighter who started out with limited skills and has made something of himself through determination and hard work. He's always in better shape than his opponent. There was, and still is, a lot of room for improvement. But Seanie has improved a lot. He's now a competent fighter. He's also one of those guys who's easy to root for. He's very likeable and unpretentious. You hope he succeeds."

"Seanie will never be on a pound-for-pound list," opines Lou DiBella. "He'll probably never be a world champion. But he's a guy who deserves to be seen. He's a blood-and-guts warrior. His arsenal consists of heart and balls. And he's also a good guy. If I'm going to war, he's one of the guys I'd want in a foxhole with me. And I'd sure as hell rather watch Seanie in a good club fight than a lot of so-called world-class fighters."

"Seanie is the quintessential club fighter," adds Top Rank matchmaker Bruce Trampler. "He's the kind of guy you want to put on your show if you're a promoter. He maximizes his talents. He gives you his best effort every time out. He energizes the crowd. And there aren't many fighters who sell tickets like he does."

There's a buzz in the room when Seanie fights. And more important, there are asses in seats.

Seanie started out as a Long Beach attraction. His fights were like a high school reunion for a dozen classes at the same time. And his fan base has grown since then. That appeal has enabled him to remain a promotional free agent. Because he's a ticket-seller, promoters like Top Rank, DiBella Entertainment, and Star Boxing are willing to use him on a fight-by-fight basis.

Seanie generally receives a fixed purse for each fight plus a percentage of the proceeds from each ticket that Team Monaghan sells.

"When there are four hundred people from your hometown watching you fight," Seanie says, "you have to look good."

Indeed, there's a school of thought that Seanie would be more disappointed if he let his fans down than if he didn't get paid.

If that sounds far-fetched, consider the events of January 19, 2013. Seanie had signed to fight Roger Cantrell at Madison Square Garden on the undercard of Orlando Salido vs. Mikey Garcia. Cantrell had been out of action for almost three years but sported a 15-and-2 record. One day before the bout, he weighed in at 184 1/2 pounds; well over the 178-pound contract weight.

Brad Goodman takes up the narrative from there.

"We told Seanie, 'You don't have to fight. We'll pay you your purse anyway.' And Seanie said, 'No, I'll fight him.'"

"We'd sold a thousand tickets," Seanie said afterward. "It was too late not to take the fight. It would have hurt my ticket sales for the next one. And I had family and friends who'd come over from Ireland. I couldn't send them home without seeing me fight."

It helped that Cantrell was required to forfeit half of his purse to Seanie. Be that as it may, the fight was a war. Seanie won a hard-fought eight-round decision but came out of the bout with an ugly cut above his left eye and a large welt beneath his right one.

Beating Cantrell brought Seanie's record to 17 and 0 with 10 knockouts. "We figured we owed him a soft opponent for his next fight," Goodman says. That led to Seanie vs. Rex Stanley on the undercard of the April 13 title bout between Nonito Donaire and Guillermo Rigondeaux at Radio City Music Hall.

Stanley is thirty-six years old. Prior to the fight, his record stood at 11 and 4 with 7 knockouts. But he'd won only once in the previous thirty-five months (a four-round decision over Andrew Keehn, whose record was 0 and 1 at the time). That was in May 2011, and Stanley hadn't fought since then.

Radio City Music Hall bills itself as "the biggest stage in New York." It's a long way from fighting on the street outside a bar in Long Beach.

Seanie had spent the day at a hotel in Manhattan and arrived at his dressing room in Radio City Music Hall at 8:00 PM. Higgins and cutman George Mitchell were already there. Joe had put in a full day at the gym in Freeport before driving to Manhattan for the fight.

Team Monaghan was sharing the dressing room with seven other undercard fighters. This was the "red corner" dressing room. All eight of the fighters were expected to win. The "blue corner" dressing room was within shouting distance down the corridor.

Donaire and Rigondeaux each had his own dressing room where they could dictate the mood; whether or not there was music, who said what. Undercard fighters can't control their surroundings. They coexist with other fighters and their teams.

Some of the fighters near Seanie were sitting quietly. Others were laughing and talking loudly.

The room was hot and stuffy with a claustrophobic feel; long and narrow with a low ceiling and thirteen vanity mirrors. Fifty people, many of them physically active men, were crammed into a space designed for thirteen chorus girls.

Seanie was weaing faded blue jeans, a black T-shirt, and blue sweatshirt. His fight was scheduled for ten o'clock. For a while, he talked quietly with Higgins, sipping occasionally from a bottle of water.

At 8:20 PM, Juan Perez of Top Rank came into the room and told Seanie, "Your opponent's not here yet. I hope he comes."

"Me too," Seanie said.

The undercard bouts were visible on a television monitor at the far end of the room. In the third fight of the evening, Tyler Canning (who'd been flown in from Wyoming on the assumption that he'd lose to prospect Dario Soccia) scored an upset decision triumph. Cheers erupted in the "blue" dressing room down the corridor.

Seanie lay down on the carpet in a corner of the room and closed his eyes.

Soccia returned, angry. "Un-fucking-believable," he said to no one in particular. "What the fuck were the judges looking at?" Then he picked up his cellphone and started texting.

Other fighters fought and returned, some with their faces bruised and swollen. In boxing, even winning takes a toll.

At nine o'clock, Seanie got up from the floor and sat on a chair. Higgins began taping his hands. P. J. Kavanagh came in to wish his fighter well. When the taping was done, Seanie put on his shoes and trunks. At 9:45 PM, trainer and fighter went into the corridor and began working the pads.

"Start with the jab," Higgins instructed. "That's it . . . Work with the jab from the opening bell. Then go after his body . . . Turn the hook over . . . Good. That's what I'm looking for. Show me that again . . ."

Down the corridor in full view, Rex Stanley and his trainer were engaged in a similar exercise.

"One-two," Higgins continued. "Again . . . One more . . . Jab . . . Hook . . . Keep everything nice and short. No gorilla punches . . . Beautiful . . . Nice deep breath."

When they were done, Seanie sat on a stool in the corridor and closed his eyes.

"I was thinking about my son," he said later. "Sammy is going to see this fight someday, and I wanted it to look good for him. And I was thinking, I can do all the work in the world in the gym, but it doesn't mean anything if I don't perform when it counts."

Moments before leaving for the ring, Seanie put on his last piece of clothing; a faded kelly-green sweatshirt that he'd worn for his first pro fight. There had been a problem on that night in 2010. Once Seanie had gloved up, the sweatshirt wouldn't fit over his gloves and Higgins had to cut a slit in each cuff to get it on.

"People tell me all the time that I should get a fancy robe," Seanie says now. "But why change what works."

This was the second fight card in the history of Radio City Music Hall. Roy Jones vs. David Telesco on January 15, 2000, had headlined the first. Like its predecessor, this card sold out. Seanie's purse was $20,000. Team Monaghan would also receive 20 percent of the revenue from the tickets it sold. Seanie had sold five hundred tickets and come back for more, but none were available.

There were cheers from the crowd as Seanie made his way to the ring.

"This place is so big that they were a little far away this time," he said afterward. "It means a lot to me that they're there. But to be honest—and this is no disrespect to my people; I love them—I used to think about my fans during a fight. Then I realized that my mind can't be in two places, so I kind of block them out once I get to the ring."

Radio City Music Hall was built for large stage spectacles, not boxing. The sight lines are good, but most of the seats are far away from the action. For most of the night, the capacity crowd of 6,145 relied on four large video screens to see what the two small figures in the ring were doing.

Seanie versus Rex Stanley was scheduled for eight rounds but was much shorter than that. Stanley has some skills but he doesn't have a chin, which is a prerequisite for a professional fighter. Seanie fought like a professional and did what he had to do, taking his time and moving forward behind a stiff jab. Midway into the first round, he backed his opponent into a corner and landed an overhand right flush. Stanley dropped to the canvas and rose on wobbly legs. He might have twisted an ankle, but the rest of him didn't look so good either. Referee Harvey Dock appropriately halted the bout before another punch was thrown. The time was 1:51 of round one.

Seanie Monaghan is now 18 and 0. Where does he go from here?

"I want to be a world champion," Seanie says. "That's my goal and dream. I get a sense of accomplishment from being a fighter. And boxing is an opportunity for me to do something big with my life, for me and for my family. I was a bricklayer before I turned pro. Believe it or not, I enjoyed laying bricks. I could do it again if I have to. But I feel like I'm getting better every day as a fighter. I take a lot of pride in what I do. If I stop getting better, I'll call it quits. But so far, that hasn't happened. I've sparred with guys like Tony Bellew and Isaac Chilemba. I get my respect from them."

"Seanie keeps getting better," Joe Higgins posits. "His boxing skills have improved a lot. He's sparring with top guys now and holding his own against them. He's number fifteen in the IBF rankings, and there's some other guys in the top fifteen we'd like to fight."

The people in a fighter's camp want to believe. What do more objective observers think?

"Let's be honest," says Ron Katz (who selected some of Seanie's early opponents for Star Boxing and is one of the best matchmakers in the business). "The best light-heavyweights—guys like Chad Dawson and Sergey Kovalev—would destroy Seanie. But he's better than a lot of people think he is. He's a top-fifty fighter for sure. And there are ranked fighters —guys like Tony Bellew and Andrzej Fonfara—who I think he'd be competitive against."

"Seanie believes in himself, and that's important for a fighter," adds Brad Goodman. "He's moving up in the rankings now. Maybe a champion will be looking for a soft touch and figure Seanie for an easy mark. It would be a nice payday for Seanie. And let me tell you something; Seanie is not soft. Seanie would be in shape. He'd fight his heart out. And this is boxing. On a given night, anything can happen. One thing I know for sure; a lot of people would be rooting for him."

In sum; everyone knows that there's room for improvement. The question is, "Given the fact that Seanie is thirty-one years old, how much time is there for improvement?"

That, in turn, leads to the big "what if?"

What if Seanie had started boxing when he was sixteen instead of twenty-six?

"I started late," Seanie acknowledges. "I know that. If I'd started boxing when I was sixteen instead of twenty-six, I'd be a lot further along than I am now. But I was so immature and undisciplined when I was young that it probably wouldn't have worked out. And you can't change what happened yesterday. So when people tell me I'm old, I say to myself, 'Look at what Bernard Hopkins is doing at forty-eight.' I don't want to be fighting when I'm forty-eight. But that tells me there's still time for me to do what I want to do."

Meanwhile, regardless of what happens next in his career, Seanie Monaghan is a boxing success story.

"There was always a big crowd cheering when I was fighting in the street," Seanie says. "Now I get paid, and I don't have to run away from the cops."

At the start of 2013, Gennady Golovkin was widely regarded as a star in the making.

A Note on Gennady Golovkin vs. Gabriel Rosado

"How do you fight someone you cannot beat?"

Hamilton Nolan of Deadspin posed that question not long ago and answered, "You simply do your best. That's all that can be done. You cannot win, but you can try your very best. Some people are more suited to this task than others."

Gabriel Rosado is suited to the task.

Rosado, age twenty-seven, fights out of Philadelphia. When he entered the ring at Madison Square Garden to face WBA 160-pound champion Gennady Golovkin on January 19, 2013, Gabriel's record stood at 21 wins and 5 losses with 13 knockouts and 1 KO by.

Rosado looks like the leader of a biker gang. He's heavily tattooed over virtually every part of his chest and arms with artwork on his neck for good measure. The images include Jesus on the cross, boxing gloves, a tiger, the Puerto Rican flag, quotes from the Bible, and a pit bull wearing handwraps.

"My mother hates it," Gabriel admits. "She cries every time I come home with a new one."

The losses on Rosado's ledger are explained in part by the fact that he had only eleven amateur fights and, until recently, held a full-time manual-labor job.

Golovkin, by contrast, had more than three hundred amateur fights in his native Kazakhstan. He won a silver medal at the 2004 Olympics and a World Amateur Boxing Championship the year before. At age thirty with a young face and soft gentle demeanor, he doesn't look like a fighter. But he fights like one.

Golovkin is undefeated in the professional ranks. He has good balance, a good chin, and has never been knocked down as an amateur or pro. He also has heavy hands. Twenty-two of his twenty-five victories for pay have come by way of knockout.

If someone saw Golovkin and Rosado at a staredown and knew nothing about either man, someone's money would be on Rosado. Someone would be wrong. Fighters at the elite level don't get there by accident.

Given the politics of boxing, Rosado had become the #1 challenger for Cornelius Bundrage's IBF 154-pound crown. He relinquished that opportunity to fight Golovkin on HBO.

"I like taking chances," Rosado said of his decision. "I dare to be great."

He also liked the fact that he stood to make good money fighting Golovkin on HBO as opposed to waiting around for a smaller purse against Bundrage in a bout that might never materialize.

Ron Stander was a heavyweight club fighter from Council Bluffs, Iowa, who was given a shot against Joe Frazier in 1972, took many shots in return, and was knocked out by Smokin' Joe in the fourth round. Before the bout, Stander's wife, Darlene, presciently noted, "You don't take a Volkswagen into the Indianapolis 500 unless you know a shortcut."

Rosado came in against Golovkin with the proper mindset. But he was competing against a different class of car. Or as former WBO heavyweight champion Lamon Brewster observed after disposing of hopelessly overmatched 309-pound Joe Lenhardt, "It's like when you look at a lion and he's about to eat you. It's not about what you're thinking. It's what the lion is thinking."

There's a line between confidence and wishful thinking. The overwhelming pre-fight sentiment was that Gabriel wasn't coming to lose but would. Golovkin-Rosado shaped up as a contest between a straight-ahead brawler and a fighter who could box better, hit harder, and take a better punch.

On fight night, Rosado's dreams quickly turned into a nightmare. The bout began with Golovkin coming out hard to establish dominance early and Gabriel in uncharacteristic retreat. Gennady fights with the confidence of a man who has never been on the canvas, and that translates into relentless aggression. Rosado had his moments. But when he hit Golovkin cleanly, which happened from time to time, Gennady walked through the punches. It was the hunter versus the hunted.

Midway through round two, Rosado was cut on the left eyelid. By round four, he was bleeding from the nose and his face looked like raw steak. He fought bravely and as well as he could. But there was too much mega-tonnage in the champion's arsenal.

It was a brutal beatdown. As the bout wore on, the cut around Rosado's eye worsened and the ring doctor began visiting his corner on a regular basis. Gabriel kept pleading to be allowed to continue. He fought bravely and as well as he could. But halfway through the scheduled twelve rounds, he looked as though he'd been on the receiving end of a grenade attack. He was being beaten up, badly. At the 2:46 mark of round seven, trainer Billy Briscoe wisely threw in the towel. Golovkin won every minute of every round.

Gennady now has a string of twelve consecutive knockouts and is widely regarded as the second-best middleweight in the world. The first best (Sergio Martinez) has shown little interest in fighting him. If there's a fly in the ointment, it's that Golovkin still hasn't fought a world-class fighter.

As for Rosado; he's definitely worth seeing again. Unlike many of the fighters who now receive large checks courtesy of the boxing establishment, he's willing to go in tough and he comes to fight every time out. Despite taking horrific punishment against Golovkin, he never went down.

Golovkin-Rosado was a lesson in courage, determination, and the brutal realities of prizefighting. In a just world, Gabriel's next fight would be against an opponent he has a more realistic chance of beating.

There's a maxim in boxing: "Win this one; look good next time." But is that always right?

Donaire-Rigondeaux and What's Expected of a Professional Fighter

On April 13, 2013, Nonito Donaire and Guillermo Rigondeaux met at Radio City Music Hall in New York in a 122-pound title unification bout.

Donaire, age thirty, entered the ring with a 31-1 (20 KOs) record. His sole loss came twelve years ago in his second pro fight. Nonito was ranked on most "pound-for-pound" lists. At various times, he'd won WBA, WBC, WBO, and *Ring Magazine* belts. Two nights earlier, the Boxing Writers Association of America had honored him as its 2012 "Fighter of the Year".

Rigondeaux, age thirty-two, has an outstanding amateur pedigree. He's a two-time Olympic gold-medal winner (2000 and 2004), two-time world amateur champion (2001 and 2005), and two-time Pan American Games gold medalist (2003 and 2005). He defected from Cuba in 2009 and turned pro several months later. His record was 11-0 (8 KOs), and he had won the WBA 122-pound belt with a sixth-round knockout of Rico Ramos on January 20, 2012.

Prior to Donaire-Rigondeaux, there were rumors (confirmed after the bout) that Donaire had suffered an injury to his right shoulder in training and also that he was taking long weekends off from the gym to be with his pregnant wife.

There was also a school of thought that Nonito was tailor-made for Guillermo.

Rigondeaux has superb footwork, adequate power, and superior tactical skills. At his best, he's an artist at work.

Donaire has prodigious physical gifts but is technically flawed. Those flaws showed against Rigondeaux. Nonito kept trying to engage, but it wasn't effective aggression. All of his shortcomings came back to haunt him. He was unable to cut off the ring, failed to effectively set up his punches, and over-reached on power shots, which left him vulnerable to counters. The only issues were whether Rigondeaux would tire (he did, but not much) and what would happen if Nonito hit Guillermo flush on the chin. That eventuality came to pass in round ten, when Rigondeaux went down from a left hook to the chin. But he got up.

This writer scored the bout 115-112 for Rigondeaux. The judges favored him by a 116-111, 115-112, 114-113 margin.

Now we come to a thorny issue.

When Frank Sinatra graced the stage at Radio City Music Hall, he sang that New York is "the city that never sleeps."

Sinatra didn't see Donaire-Rigondeaux. In a word, the fight was "boring." In two words, it was "very boring."

After three moderately entertaining rounds in which Rigondeaux got off first with straight lefts and crisp right hooks up top, he proceeded to stink out the joint . . . Run out the clock . . . Go into a four corners offense . . . Choose your metaphor.

Before long, Donaire was frustrated and the fans were angry. There was sustained booing for much of the night. What made it particularly unsatisfying was that Guillermo (unlike Pernell Whitaker, who was praised as a defensive master) didn't throw jabs as he moved. There were long periods of time when he all but ran away from the action. Fighting like that might play well in the amateurs but not in the pro ranks. It's one of the reasons why virtually no one in the United States watches amateur boxing anymore.

Donaire was gracious after the fight.

"There's no excuse," Nonito said. "He beat me tonight. I only have respect for Rigondeaux and the beautiful boxing he gave me."

The object of the game is to hit and not get hit. Trying to hit Rigondeaux was like trying to hit a moving nail with a hammer. His tactics won the fight. The sport is called boxing, not fighting; isn't it?

"No ! ! !," thunders Larry Merchant. "It's prizefighting, not boxing. The Rockettes are supposed to be the dancers at Radio City Music Hall, not the fighters."

Merchant has a point. And then he makes another one.

"Rigondeaux was skimming the money that real fighters generate for the sport," Larry declares. "If every fighter fought like Rigondeaux, there would be no money for anyone in boxing."

Agreed.

Rigondeaux fought within the rules and won the fight. It was his prerogative to fight the way he wanted to fight. But television network executives and fans have the right to say that seeing him fight again is a low priority.

Famed matchmaker Teddy Brenner once sat ringside at Madison Square Garden and watched a stylish avoid-getting-hit-at-any-cost boxer put round after round in the bank while a disgruntled crowd grew more and more restless. Midway through the bout, Brenner visited the fighter's corner and told his trainer, "If your guy doesn't start fighting, he'll never fight at The Garden again."

The pacifist won every round. True to his word, Brenner never used him at The Garden again.

A fighter who calls himself a "champion" owes the fans more than Guillermo Rigondeaux gave them on April 13.

Tyson Fury vs. Steve Cunningham brought a touch of professional wrestling to Madison Square Garden.

Reflections on Tyson Fury vs. Steve Cunningham

Tyson Fury makes a good villain.

Fury is a braggart who calls himself "the best fighter in the world." To the casual observer, he comes across as an obnoxious big-mouthed lout. As of this writing, the 6-foot-9-inch Brit (or is he is bit shorter than he claims?) has compiled a 21-0 (15 KOs) record against mostly club-fight-level opposition. On April 20, 2013, he made his American debut in New York.

Fury's latest designated victim, Steve Cunningham, was three months shy of his thirty-seventh birthday. Cunningham has now lost four of his last five fights and hasn't beaten a credible opponent since toppling cruiserweight Marco Huck in 2007.

Fury tipped the scales at 254 and outweighed Cunningham by 44 pounds.

The bout was in The Theater at Madison Square Garden. Main Events (Cunningham's promoter) kept the NBC license fee. Team Fury got the British TV money (which explained why the fight was scheduled for 4:00 PM instead of that night). The costs associated with renting The Garden were split evenly between the two camps.

It was an exciting fight. An inartful first round saw Cunningham missing with wild overhand rights and Fury bringing his jab back slowly and low. As the fighters made their way to their respective corners at the close of the stanza, Tyson conspicuously and gratuitously shoved Cunningham. It wasn't a bump; it was a shove. A hard one. Referee Eddie Cotton should have taken a point away on the spot. Instead, he let the matter pass, which was a clear signal to Fury that the rules didn't fully apply to him.

Prior to the bout, Fury had come across like a high-school bully who torments smaller boys in school. One hoped that Little Steve would punch the bully in the nose and make him run away.

Ten seconds into round two, that seemed possible. Fury threw a sloppy jab, and Cunningham responded with a right that was straight enough to land flush on the big man's jaw.

Fury went down flat on his back with a thud.

"What were you thinking when you got knocked down?" he was asked afterward.

"You don't think of things when you're lying flat in your back," Fury answered. "You get back up."

At the count of six, he did just that.

Thereafter, Fury used his size well and turned the bout into a brawl. His constant aggression and wild swinging punches forced Cunningham to trade with him to the smaller man's disadvantage. Equally important, Eddie Cotton allowed Tyson to lead with his shoulder, forearm, and elbow; push down on the back of Cunningham's head; and otherwise illegally rough Steve up (headlocks are illegal in boxing).

In sum; Cotton lost control of the fight. Although if one were being cynical, one might say that the referee was controlling the fight precisely the way he wanted to. Indeed, at one point when Fury seemed a bit buzzed by another blow, Cotton stopped the action to give him an inappropriately timed warning for fouling (which afforded Tyson time to recover).

In round five, a head butt by Fury cost him a one-point deduction. But by then, Cunningham was weakening and the momentum of the bout had shifted irrevocably in Tyson's favor. Whatever modicum of respect he might have had for Cunningham's punching power was gone, and he was firing his own punches with abandon.

The start of round six was delayed while trainer Naazim Richardson sloooowwwly repaired some loose tape on Cunningham's glove. That confirmed the obvious; that Steve was exhausted and would have a hard time surviving the second half of the fight.

The end came in round seven. With forty seconds left in the stanza, a paralyzing right uppercut to the body forced Cunningham to the ropes. Fury then moved in and finished his opponent off, setting up a final crushing right hand by jamming his left forearm into the smaller man's throat and pushing his head directly into the line of fire.

Two judges had Cunningham ahead on points 57-55 at the time of the stoppage. The third judge had matters even.

"I hunted him down like a lion hunts down a deer," Fury proclaimed afterward. "In a dog fight, the bigger stronger dog always wins."

"He did what he was supposed to do," Cunningham acknowledged. "He put his weight on me. He kept leaning on me and leaning on me. It felt like I was fighting two people." Then Cunningham added, "He can fight, but he did it dirty."

So . . . What should we make of Tyson Fury?

First, give Fury credit for getting in the ring. All fighters deserve that. He was in good condition against Cunningham, fought a physical fight at a fast pace, and showed a fighting spirit. He's fun to watch, less so to listen to. It would be interesting to know whether he's a jerk in person or if his public persona is just an act. Perhaps it's a bit of both.

Meanwhile, the heavyweight division is thin enough that Fury stands a reasonable chance of becoming a beltholder some day. Whether he can become a champion is another matter.

Fury's partisans would like to see their man in the ring against Wladimir Klitschko. In their view, Tyson's size, free-swinging style, and roughhouse tactics would bother Wladimir. It's likely that Wladimir's skill and punching power would bother Fury more.

Either way, Fury versus Klitschko would be fun to watch while it lasted. If Fury got blasted out, that would be entertaining too.

Zab Judah's April, 27, 2013, fight against Danny Garcia offered Zab a chance for redemption.

Zab Judah Comes Up Short Again

On November 3, 2001, Zab Judah fought Kostya Tszyu in a much-anticipated 140-pound title-unification bout.

Judah had turned pro in 1996 as an eighteen-year-old phenom with sparkling amateur credentials. He was 27 and 0 in the pay ranks with six title-fight victories and ranked in the top ten on most pound-for-pound lists. Power, speed, boxing savvy; Zab had it all. Some experts likened him to Pernell Whitaker, only Judah had more power.

"If you come down to 140 pounds, I'll knock you out," Zab told his friend, Mike Tyson.

Tszyu had some impressive victories on his ledger, but he'd been stopped by Vince Phillips. The assumption was that Judah would be too much for him.

A few fighters at Gleason's Gym in Brooklyn where Zab trained had a contrary view. Local boxers tend to support and believe in their own. But Judah was flawed, those fighters said. When he got hit hard in sparring, he spent the rest of the session on the run. Not just that one round, the entire session.

Sugar Ray Robinson was once asked what he liked least about boxing.

"Getting hit," the greatest fighter of all time answered.

That said; fighters get hit. It's how they respond that separates legends from also-rans.

"Tszyu will hit Zab with something hard," those fighters at Gleason's said. "And when that happens, the fight will turn."

Judah dominated round one. Then, in round two, Kostya hit him with "something hard" and knocked Zab out.

In the eleven years since then, Judah's record has been 15 and 8 with one no contest. During that time, he has lost eight of thirteen title bouts and been a poster boy for unfulfilled potential. When people think of Zab, they're more likely to think of his defeats at the hands of Tszyu, Floyd

Mayweather, Miguel Cotto, Carlos Baldomir, and Amir Khan than his victory over Junior Witter. He has signature losses, not signature triumphs.

Judah is no longer fighting for greatness. He's fighting for money. He's thirty-five years old, and boxing is the only job he has ever known.

"I wish things had happened a little different," Zab said last year. "But we can't change the past."

Zab's latest "last chance" to regain a lofty standing in the boxing community came on April 27, 2013, against Danny Garcia at Barclays Center in Brooklyn.

Garcia, a Philadelphia native, came into the bout with a 25-and-0 record and two of the four major 140-pound belts. He also brought his father, Angel, who has graduated from provocateur to embarrassment.

Angel, who trains his son, has a penchant for making racist comments and engaging in other unsportsmanlike conduct. He shoots his mouth off, and Danny has to back it up.

The low point of the December 1, 2012, kick-off press conference for Garcia-Judah was an ugly pushing and shouting match that ensued when Angel told the assembled media, "Every time Zab has stepped up, he lost. I figure this will go four or five rounds because he's a four-round fighter."

Zab, as expected, took exception.

There were more pre-fight confrontations at various promotional events leading up to the final pre-fight press conference at Barclays Center on April 25. Then things turned bizarre.

The press conference was scheduled for 1:00 PM and began with the undercard fighters. Contrary to the norm, no one from the Garcia or Judah camps was on the dais. Once the undercard fighters had their say, the dais was cleared and Danny Garcia came out with his father.

"I'm going to take Zab into deep water, drown him, and beat the shit out of him," Danny proclaimed.

Angel kept saying, "This is bigger than New York or Philly. This is about king of the east coast."

That said everything one needs to know about today's so-called "world" championship belts.

Why wasn't Team Judah present?

Golden Boy (which was promoting the fight and had a vested interest in Danny winning) had made a decision in tandem with the Garcias to present the fighters to the media separately (Danny first) without consulting the Judahs.

After Danny and Angel finished with the media, there was a problem. Zab had left the premises. Twenty minutes later, following some frantic telephone calls, he returned and strode to the dais.

Zab was pissed. He'd been sitting in the basement when he was told that the press conference had started without him and that he wasn't welcome to address the media until after the Garcias were done. That angered him sufficiently that he'd walked out of the building. Now he was back.

"This is crazy," Zab declared. "Insane. I've been here since eleven o'clock in the basement downstairs, no water, no food, locked in a little room because of Danny Garcia and his insecurities. My call time was eleven. I've been in boxing seventeen years and I've never seen anything like this."

After predicting victory, Judah voiced more indignation and closed with the thought, "Angel Garcia is a dopehead. He must be a dope addict or crackhead because he can't control himself. He's a customer. After he gets his check on Saturday night, they'll be lining up on the street to sell to him."

As for clues regarding the outcome of the fight, Zab's partisans noted that Garcia had a limited résumé. Also, Zab's split-decision victory over Lucas Matthysse gave his backers hope. Matthysse is a good fighter who can whack.

But Judah-Matthysse had been thirty months earlier. A more appropriate measuring stick seemed to be how each fighter had fared against Amir Khan.

Nine months ago, Garcia was getting beaten up by Khan. But he kept punching with the faster sharper puncher until he landed a hard left hook on the Brit's neck that led to a fourth-round knockout.

One year before that, Judah had fought Khan, was getting beaten up, and submitted. The Khan fight was a low point for Zab. He did virtually nothing for five rounds before being stopped by what appeared to be a low blow. But he'd fought so poorly that there was little sense of injustice among fans or media regarding the foul.

Judah tends to fade in the second half of fights. And he's thirty-five years old. The feeling was that Danny could deflate Zab and turn the fight around with one punch. And when it came, that turn would be irrevocable because, once Judah stands down, he doesn't step back up. From that point on, it's just a question of whether he can hang on until the end of the fight.

"I've got it all," Zab told the media at the final pre-fight press conference. "Handspeed, style, power, defense. The Zab Judah you guys fell in love with is back."

He didn't mention heart.

When fight night arrived, a crowd of 13,048 was on hand to witness the proceedings. Because of the bad blood between the fighters' camps, there was a lot of negative energy in the arena. The boos were louder than the cheers during the ringwalk and introduction for each combatant.

The bout began with Judah, a southpaw, throwing jabs but showing reluctance to let his left hand go. Garcia threw occasional rights but had trouble pinning Zab down because of the latter's speed and movement. Danny wanted to mix it up. Judah wanted to box.

In round three, Garcia took control of the fight. He won the next six stanzas on the strength of his right hand. Too often, he throws it in a wide looping arc. When straightened out, it's effective. Most of the rights that Danny landed were above the belt. But enough of them were low that it was a problem.

Meanwhile, Zab was fighting a safety-first fight, which meant that he wasn't giving Garcia a reason to stop coming forward and throwing punches.

In round five, a big right hand wobbled Judah. That was the point at which he has been known to deflate and mail in the rest of the fight. Garcia knew it and went after Zab, wobbling him twice in round six with big right hands. Judah survived. But one could have made the case that it was a 10-8 round for Garcia. And Zab had six long rounds ahead of him. If history was a guide, he was toast.

Round seven was more of the same. Judah couldn't get out of the way of right hands. In round eight, Garcia appeared to seal the deal. Zab landed a sharp left. Garcia doesn't throw combinations as much as he throws one punch at a time. But there are times when he pulls the trigger quickly, particularly when countering. This time, he fired back with a straight right that deposited Judah on the canvas and opened an ugly gash beneath Zab's left eye.

Then the unexpected happened. Zab, who had come to box, started fighting.

Garcia has a good chin. For the rest of the night, he needed it.

In round nine, Judah landed some hard shots. Twenty seconds into round ten, a straight left hurt Garcia and forced him to back off. Zab took his time going after his foe; more time than he should have. But a minute later, another straight left wobbled Danny and he was staggered again just before the bell.

Zab was doing something that he'd never done before in a big fight. He was coming back from adversity. He had two rounds left to knock Garcia out. It seemed possible.

But instead of fighting with the desperation of a man who needed a knockout to win, Zab fought like a man who needed simply to put the last two rounds in the bank. He won the rounds, but it wasn't enough.

The judges gave the nod to Garcia by a 115-112, 114-112, 116-111 margin. This writer scored it 115-111 in Garcia's favor.

And now, one final thought.

In recent years, a culture of disrespect has taken root in boxing at all levels of the sport. Instead of being embarrassed by bad behavior, promoters and television executives have embraced it as a marketing tool.

Because of Angel Garcia's pre-fight antics and the bad blood between the fighters' camps, it was deemed necessary for Garcia and Judah to weigh in separately. On the night of the fight, six security guards divided the ring diagonally to keep the fighters apart before the opening bell.

Can anyone imagine the National Football League saying, "We're going to skip the ritual pre-game coin toss because the coaches and captains might get into a fistfight."

The fact that it was considered dangerous for the Garcia and Judah camps to be together at the final pre-fight press conference and weigh-in spoke volumes for the idiocy of those involved. If no one else can enforce order, the governing state athletic commission should take the lead in these situations.

Allow the fighters—and only the fighters—onto the platform for the weigh-in. Warn them that any antics will result in a huge fine. Stop allowing thirty people in the ring before a fight.

The pre-fight histrionics before Garcia-Judah tarnished boxing. The fight itself redeemed the sport.

Fans watch a fight and, except on rare occasions, don't think much about it afterward. For the fighters, the fight lingers in memory.

Paulie Malignaggi: Three Days After

Portobello's is a pizzeria in lower Manhattan. Entering the restaurant, patrons pass a long glass-partitioned counter that displays pies with a dozen different toppings. There's a large soda refrigeration case and two more counters where hot entrees and deli sandwiches are served. But the pizza is the main draw.

Part of a wall toward the back of the restaurant is covered with photos and press clippings that recount Paulie Malignaggi's ring exploits. Anthony Catanzaro (one of Portobello's owners) is Paulie's business adviser and friend. They've known each other since the fighter was sixteen years old.

At 1:00 PM on Tuesday, June 25, 2013, Malignaggi walked into Portobello's. Three nights earlier, he'd fought to defend his 147-pound title against Adrien Broner at Barclays Center in Brooklyn.

"This is my moment," Paulie had told writer Tom Gerbasi shortly before the bout. "Coming into my hometown as a world champion, defending my world championship in front of a packed arena against a guy that people think is the next big thing. These are the kind of opportunities you dream of when you're a kid and you put on that first pair of boxing gloves and you're hitting the bag and you're in awe of the big fighters training alongside you like I was when I was in Gleason's Gym at sixteen years old. This is why I was boxing to begin with. I intend to make it my best moment, a career moment, a trademark moment. I'm going to look back at this fight with a smile on my face when my career is over."

When the bell for round one rang, Malignaggi started well against Broner. Moving, jabbing, and counter-intuitively going to the body, he won four of the first five stanzas on most scorecards. But while he was able to frustrate Broner, he couldn't hurt him ("hurt" being a relative term in boxing). In the middle rounds, the momentum shifted. Paulie tired a bit and Adrien began stalking his foe. From that point on, Broner landed the harder punches and more of them. But he was inactive at times. And when he landed, Paulie handled his power without serious incident.

Judge Tom Miller scored the bout 115-113 in Malignaggi's favor. Glenn Feldman (115-113) and Tom Schreck (117-111) gave the nod to Broner.

Inside Portobello's, Paulie sat at one of the formica-topped tables spread around the black terrazzo tile floor. There was a bruise beneath his right eye and a welt on the right side of his neck. Otherwise, he was unmarked, although the palm of his right hand was swollen.

"I hurt it when I hit him on the elbow," Paulie said. "There's some tissue damage but it didn't affect the fight."

The red stripe that had adorned his hair on fight night was gone. He was casually dressed with six days growth of beard on his face.

"Last Saturday was the first time in my career that I didn't shave on the day of a fight," Paulie noted. "I shaved three days before the fight. Then I decided to leave it at that, so it would get in Broner's head that he was fighting a grown man."

"How much do you weigh now?"

"One-sixty-three, maybe 164 pounds. But I'm in good shape." Paulie lifted up his shirt to show his abs. "I'll put on a few more pounds, but I'm not one of those guys who balloons up after a fight."

Malignaggi is thirty-two years old now. He has earned everything that he has gotten from boxing. Like most fighters, he has earned it the hard way.

Paulie turned pro in 2001 after a decorated amateur career that saw him win a national amateur championship at 132 pounds. He won his first twenty-one pro fights, rebounded from a brutal loss to Miguel Cotto, and, in 2007, pitched a twelve-round shutout against Lovemore N'dou to capture the IBF 140-pound crown. After two successful title defenses, he was dethroned by Ricky Hatton. Forty-one months after that, Malignaggi traveled to Ukraine and stopped Vyacheslav Senchenko to annex the WBA 147-pound belt. A narrow points win over Pablo Cesar Cano on the first-ever fight card at Barclays Center followed.

In early 2013, Team Malignaggi began negotiations with Golden Boy (his current promoter) for a title defense against Shane Mosley. Paulie didn't have a win over a Hall of Fame fighter on his résumé. The Mosley fight could have changed that.

"It's a coin flip," Naazim Richardson (Mosley's former trainer) said of the proposed match-up. "Either guy could win, and it would be a good win for either guy."

But the fight fell through. Malignaggi's promotional contract with Golden Boy called for him to receive a guaranteed purse against a percentage of certain adjusted revenue streams from each fight. Golden Boy CEO Richard Schaefer wanted to limit Paulie's payment for Malignaggi-Mosley to a flat (albeit generous) purse. Team Malignaggi objected. Rather than try to work through the issue, Schaefer terminated negotiations. He had another opponent in mind.

The essence of boxing in it's purest form is truth. Stripped of phony belts, corrupt officiating, and other maladies, it's the most honest of all sports. But in recent years, a tidal wave of hype has washed over the sweet science.

Enter Adrien Broner.

Broner is a talented young fighter, who won his first twenty-six fights and had knocked out sixteen of his last seventeen opponents. During that time, he'd been anointed by the powers that be as the next great fighter in boxing. His résumé was thin, but the manner in which he'd devastated a series of carefully chosen foes was impressive.

Broner's chosen nickname is "The Problem." Outside the ring, that certainly has been the case. As an adolescent, Adrien was often on the wrong side of the law. "I did everything," he told reporters earlier this year. "You name it, I did it. I owned a couple of guns in my day."

He was also incarcerated for beating up someone and leaving the victim in critical condition.

"I got into some trouble, some big trouble," Adrien admitted at a media sit down last November. "They tried to give me some football numbers; you know, receiver-like numbers, like eighty-five years. I was in for about a year and two months. The first day out, I went to the gym, and they all said I looked better than before I left."

At last count, the twenty-three-year-old Broner had five children by four different women. In March of this year, a video surfaced that purported to show him at an adult club, administering oral sex to a stripper onstage.

"I'm not a villain," Broner says. "I'm just being me. I don't care where I am, I'm going to be me. I'm going to do what I do. I know it can rub off on some people the wrong way. This guy is too cocky or he's too arrogant or this or that. But once you get to know Adrien Broner, people just fall in love with me."

Broner's rise to prominence was nurtured by HBO. Last July, he weighed in 3 1/2 pounds over the 130-pound limit for a title defense against Vicente Escobedo, refused thereafter to try to make weight, and tipped the scales at 148 pounds at 6:00 PM on fight night. At the post-fight press conference, after stopping Escobedo in five rounds, he told reporters, "They [HBO] really ought to change the logo to my face."

Seven months later, Broner defeated an overmatched Gavin Rees and told the media, "I'm a legal bank robber. I just robbed the bank tonight. As long as HBO keeps paying me to fight these lightweights; I ain't never been on the farm but I'm milking the cow real good."

After the Rees fight, Broner moved to Showtime with the rest of the Golden Boy roster. But his self-reverence remained: "I'm trying to be the best boxer who ever laced on a pair of gloves. That's my goal . . . I'll make any fight look easy . . . The difference between me and other fighters is, they do what they can; I do what I want . . . You can't really do nothing for power. You're either born with it or you aren't. It's just something that God blessed me with. I'm God's gift to boxing."

The promotion of Malignaggi-Broner was largely about Broner.

"I knew going in that it was going to be that way," Paulie says. "It was all about him getting another belt. Even though I was the champion, the first contract Golden Boy gave me to sign had Broner going to the ring last and being introduced last. I wouldn't sign it."

Broner was a prohibitive favorite with the odds running as high as 15 to 1. He has speed, reflexes, skill, and power. Malignaggi never had power and, it was thought, no longer had the speed and reflexes to implement his skills. One was hard-pressed to find a knowledgeable boxing insider without a stake in the promotion who thought that the fight would be competitive.

"Broner changes men, professional fighting men, from aggressors to targets," Bart Barry wrote.

Adam Berlin was more expansive, extolling, "Broner has it all. He's a boxer and a puncher. He can fight outside and inside. He's a master of ring geography. He's acutely aware of his opponent's condition, sensing fear and fatigue and hurt. And he possesses the kind of cold killer instinct that's far more effective than its hotter-tempered versions. There is a rare breed of men born to box, who are so in control inside the ring, so at home in harm's way, they seem unhurtable. Broner comes to inflict pain. Watch him between rounds and you'll forget about his clownish pre- and post-fight antics. As with all artists, we should judge Broner on his work. And when he's working, he's the opposite of frivolity. Sitting on his stool, waiting for the bell to ring, Broner's body language spells intensity. Hard-eyed, hard-mouthed, he leans forward, ready to spring, his gaze a dangerous warning."

There were fears that Malignaggi-Broner would be like Arturo Gatti versus Floyd Mayweather. "He's bringing pillows to this fight," Broner said. "I'm bringing bricks."

"A lot of people who care about me didn't want me to take the fight," Paulie acknowledged. "They're rooting for me, but they don't give me a chance."

It was left for writer David Greisman to pen words of caution.

"Broner's speed, power and overall ability have allowed him to be regarded as the proverbial cream of the crop," Greisman wrote. "However, he has yet to actually earn the recognition of being not just one of several titleholders but a true champion. His final five fights at 130 were a disputed decision over Daniel Ponce De Leon, a gimme knockout over Jason Litzau, a gimme knockout over Vicente Rodriguez that gave him a vacant world title at age 22, an impressive win over prospect Eloy Perez, and a stoppage of Vicente Escobedo in a bout that saw Broner come in more than three pounds over the weight limit. Broner has done well since at lightweight, dominating in Antonio DeMarco a fighter who was considered to be one of the best in the division, then dispatching Gavin Rees with an emphatic conclusion earlier this year. There are other claimants in these divisions, though. Broner could easily be the betting favorite in matches against each of them. Alas, fights are not resolved on paper. You cannot become king without pulling someone else off, or away from, the throne."

Meanwhile, Malignaggi wasn't just showing up for a payday against Broner. He believed in himself. All good fighters do. In the weeks leading up to the fight, he voiced the view that he would emerge victorious:

★ "Broner has talent. But at the end of the day, what have we seen from Adrien Broner? We've seen a lot of handpicked opponents. We could have all been 26-and-0 against that level of opposition. There are better opponents on ESPN."

★ "He's a good little fighter. He's got some skills. I just don't think he's big enough. He'll be giving up physical strength and get pushed around and muscled around by a bigger guy, which is me. His trainer said Adrien spars with middleweights so he can handle me. I don't care who he spars with. I spar in the gym. I don't spar on fight night. There are weight classes in boxing for a reason."

★ "People assume he's faster than me. One of the ignorant comments I've seen is that Amir Khan's speed bothered me, so Adrien Broner's speed is going to kill me. Amir Khan is faster than Adrien Broner and his speed is used in a different way. He throws punches in bunches. Adrien Broner is more of a pick-your-shots kind of guy. I like the fight. I like the fight a lot."

★ I'm not convinced of his power. He's going to see how overrated his power is. I'm not going to sit here and tell you that I'm going to knock him out with one punch, but he's going to feel a lot of punishment. He won't know what to do when he's in a tough fight. He may just tell himself it's not worth it and quit."

Malignaggi had more to gain from the fight than Broner. If Adrien won, the reaction would be "so what?" If Paulie won, it would constitute the big win that had eluded him against Miguel Cotto, Ricky Hatton, and Amir Khan. But before long, any attempt at intelligent analysis of the fight was drowned out by a wave of trash-talking.

This was the second Golden Boy promotion in a row at Barclays Center (the first being Danny Garcia vs. Zab Judah) that devolved into what writer Jimmy Tobin correctly labeled "a tasteless and offensive promotion." Trash-talking might energize a fighter's core supporters, but it turns off casual sports fans and potential corporate sponsors.

The ugliness began in mid-March before the fight was signed when Broner proclaimed, "I'll fight that motherfucker in the closet. Tell Paulette it's his time of the month and I understand he's going through some things. He's going to get fucked up. I don't care if it's at the Barclays

Center. I don't care if it's at the barbecue. Anybody that Adrien Broner fights is easy money. I don't care who it is. Paulette, pull your fucking skirt up."

That led Malignaggi to counter, "I don't know what kind of bedroom life Adrien Broner has. But with him calling me 'Paulette' and wanting to fight in closet; I don't go that way. Nothing against him if he does, but my personal preference is women. If he's going to start calling men 'Paulette' and starts talking about fighting in the closet with them, it's not my cup of tea. There won't be any role playing where he calls me 'Paulette' and we both go in the closet. He has to find another Paulette. I'm into role playing, but I role play with females in the bedroom and not with dudes in the closet. I don't know how Adrien and his boys get down in Cincinnati, but me and my boys in Brooklyn don't get down like that."

Thereafter, Malignaggi said that Broner looked like an ugly ninja turtle and called him a sissy, a punk, and retarded. Broner responded that Paulie was "like a female who wears his feelings on his sleeve."

If Golden Boy had donated a dollar to the Susan G. Komen for the Cure Foundation each time one of the fighters said "I'm gonna fuck you up and beat the shit out of you," breast cancer might soon be cured.

But there was worse. On May 4, Golden Boy held a kick-off press conference for Malignaggi-Broner at the MGM Grand in Las Vegas. Floyd Mayweather versus Robert Guerrero was to be contested at the hotel-casino that evening, so the media was there in full force.

"I'm going to bring a guest [to the Malignaggi fight] who is one of my closest friends now," Broner told the media. "Jessica, or 'Jess' as he used to call her. She's my sweetheart right now. And she told me some things. Last week, she came to my hotel room. She was depressed because [Team Malignaggi] sent threatening messages and stuff like that. They were threatening to do this and threatening to do that. She was crying and I told her to take a drink because that brings the truth out. I'm like, 'Just chill, calm down. I'm willing to talk you through this.' She says, 'Well, he hit me.' She said—and I don't know how true this is, I'm just repeating what I was told—she said [to Paulie] 'Why don't you knock anybody out?' And he got mad and said, 'I got five knockouts. Fuck you! What do you mean, I don't knock anybody out.' She said, 'Maybe you should do more push-ups.' She said, 'Maybe God didn't bless you with power.' That struck a match and he [hit her] right across the chin, flush. She said it was one of the best left hooks he ever threw. To make a long story short, they broke up. Paulie wasn't hitting it hard enough, and now she's with a heavy hitter."

In response, Paulie exploded.

"Here's the difference between me and Adrien," he told reporters. "We both got money, but I'm good looking. There are girls who are close to you and girls that we call weekend pussy. Jessica was weekend pussy. That means Jessica could fuck anybody she wants. And when I got time on the weekends, I could do whatever I wanted to do and she loved it. She loved getting hit [while role playing] when we slept together. As a matter of fact, Adrien, if you fucked her, you already know that. Weekend pussy is exactly that. The only weekend pussy Adrien gets is the kind he pays for. He doesn't understand what it's like to be good looking and get regular pussy and the weekend pussy and you don't pay for none of it. It just comes to you. That's my life. If I wasn't boxing, I would still be getting laid."

Jessica (who goes by the name "Jessica Corazon") surfaced through-out the promotion. In an interview with FightHype.com, she claimed to have had an intense seven-month relationship with Paulie and declared, "I'm not a slut. I'm not a whore. I'm a really girly girl. I'm far from a groupie. I modeled for *Maxim*. I have my own attention. This is not for attention. Adrien is an amazing person. I love Adrien. Anything that Adrien and his team has to do regarding this fight, I'm gonna make sure I'm there. There might be a fight before the fight. I'm not sure. I can't wait to sit there and watch Adrien kick his ass."

On June 20, Jessica appeared at the final pre-fight press conference at Barclays Center. Sensing trouble, Richard Schaefer made a plea for civility between the fighters.

"I want them to focus on the fight, not girlfriends or ex-girlfriends," the promoter said.

When it was Broner's turn to speak, he began by telling the media, "I didn't come here to talk trash."

Then he talked trash with an emphasis on Jessica, who told the media, "I'm just here to support Adrien."

Jessica, it should be noted, looked like a woman who wanted to be represented by Gloria Allred in a lawsuit for something against someone in the not-too-distant future. She also looked like a woman who would share a bed with Malignaggi and Broner (but not at the same time, one assumes). Perhaps she will be Adrien's next baby momma.

When it was Paulie's turn to speak, he told the media, "This is how the creation of Adrien Broner happened. They put everything that's wrong with boxing in one room, did everything that's wrong with boxing in that room, and gave birth to Adrien Broner. This guy is nothing, and on Saturday night I'm going to prove how nothing he is."

Paulie could out talk Broner. The question was, "Could he outfight him?"

★   ★   ★

After lunchtime, the crowd at Portobello's thins out. The restaurant is usually quiet from then until mid-afternoon, when students from nearby Stuyvesant High School come in. Paulie sat with his back to the front door. Patrons didn't recognize him as they passed by from behind. But if they sat facing in his direction, there was a connection for some of them.

A young man came over to say hello and wish Malignaggi well. A woman with a toddler in a stroller smiled in his direction. Paulie had a welcoming word for everyone who approached him.

Malignaggi-Broner was still on his mind.

"I know that trash-talking is part of boxing," Paulie said. "I can't criticize someone for talking trash because I do it myself. There are times when it motivates me, and promoters like it because it helps sell the fight. That says something about where boxing is today, that we need that sort of thing to sell tickets. But it is what it is."

"I didn't mind Broner's shtick about how great a fighter he says he is," Paulie continued. "If he wants to say that I'm a bum and tell people how he's going to beat the shit out of me, I have no problem with that. It comes with the territory. But when you bring my private personal life into it and tell lies about me, that's going too far. Maybe Broner is such a lowlife that he doesn't care what people think about him and his family. But I care."

"Let me set the record straight about Jessica. I met her in a nightclub and we had sex together. That part of her story is true. If I had it to do over again, knowing what I know now, would I go to bed with her? No way! But most guys at one time or another sleep with a woman they wouldn't bring home to their mother. As far as I was concerned, it was a good time with no strings attached. And I thought she felt the same way. Then she started putting pictures of her and me up on social media like it was a serious dating relationship, so I dropped her. After that, she starts texting me that she has morning sickness and she's pregnant. That was a horrible time for me. Jessica was sending me sonogram pictures of the baby that turned out to be phony. I asked her for the name and phone number of her doctor, and she wouldn't give it to me. I knew by then that I didn't like this woman. But I also knew that, if a child was born, that child was blameless and I had a responsibility to see that the child was provided for financially and had the opportunity to grow up happy."

"Then, toward the end of March, three months after Jessica supposedly got pregnant, a friend of hers called and told me, 'Jessica has decided to have an abortion. We need you to send her some money for it.' I said, 'I won't send you money. But I'll take Jessica to the abortion clinic myself to make sure that she's okay and I'll pay for everything on the spot.' That was a no-go, at which point I knew the whole thing was a hustle. After that, I cut her off."

Paulie took a smart phone out of his pocket and scrolled through a series of text messages. The last one, dated April 12, 2013, was from Jessica and read, "All I want to do is have sex with you. I really need you."

"She tried to keep the relationship going," Paulie said as he resumed his recounting of events. "But I wanted nothing to do with her. Finally, this woman was out of my life. You have no idea how much pain her supposed pregnancy caused me. And then Broner brings her back into my life again."

"I shouldn't have called her weekend pussy. I got mad. What I should have said was that this is a woman who's a very bad representative of what women can be. But after everything I'd gone through, it ticked me off when Broner and this woman made my private personal life public and did it in such a dishonest way."

Anthony Catanzaro came over to join Paulie at the table. The conversation turned to the fight.

"Broner is a good fighter," Paulie said. "He has speed. He's hard to hit clean in the head, but he's open for body shots. He throws sharp punches, but he doesn't hit that hard. His punching power is way overrated. After the fight, I heard people saying, 'Oh, Broner was hitting Paulie much harder than Paulie was hitting Broner.' That's not true. I'm not a big puncher, but I've been hit by big punchers. Trust me. I know when a guy can punch. But people had this preconception that Broner is a big puncher and they viewed the fight that way. I've been in the ring with much better fighters than Broner. Fighters who hit harder, fighters who are faster and technically better. The problem I had here was that my legs don't last now the way they used to. That was the difference between the first half of the fight and the second half."

"And the referee was incompetent," Catanzaro interjected. "I've never criticized a referee for one of Paulie's fights before. But Benji Esteves had a very bad night. This isn't MMA. Kidney punches are illegal. Stuffing a forearm into your opponent's throat is illegal. Hitting on the break is illegal. Trying to knee an opponent in the face and groin is illegal. When a fighter deliberately knees his opponent, the referee should take a point away. What is it that Benji Esteves doesn't understand about that?"

"It's one thing if the referee is not cognizant of a foul," Catanzaro continued. "If he doesn't see it, he doesn't see it. It's a whole different thing when the referee sees foul after foul and doesn't enforce the rules. You can say that one point wouldn't have made a difference in who won on the judges' scorecards. But if the referee had taken a point away, it would have forced Broner to fight a clean fight or risk disqualification. And if Broner has to fight within the rules, maybe it ends differently."

As for the decision—

"Scoring is subjective," Paulie acknowledged. "It was a close fight. When Jimmy Lennon said it was a split decision, I knew the first two scores he read were going different ways. And as he's reading, things are going through my mind. The New York judge is the one who's left. I'm from New York. I'm the champion. Then I hear 117-111. I knew the fight was closer than that, so I knew there was something wrong with Schreck's score. And I figured, Broner is the one with connections. If there's something wrong with Schreck's score, I'm the one who's getting screwed."

Then Broner proclaimed, "I beat Paulie. I lifted his belt and his girl."

That set Malignaggi (who moments before had told Showtime interviewer Jim Gray that the decision could have gone either way) off on a diatribe about Schreck's scorecard.

"There's always a little animosity between the fighters before a fight," Paulie said, sitting in Portobello's. "You're getting ready to punch each other in the face. But for the most part, things are respectful. And after the fight is over, you're cool with each other. I thought it would be that way with Broner. After the final bell, I went over to tell him it had been a good fight. And you know what happened after that."

"The thing that eats away at me the most is that, if you change one round on one judge's scorecard, I keep my title on a draw. Glenn Feldman had it 115-113 for Broner. If I do a little more in one round and Feldman gives me that round, I'm still the champion. Then Broner wants a rematch and I'm in line to make a million-and-a-half, maybe two million dollars."

Paulie shrugged.

"It's hard to beat someone that the people who control the sport are calling the next face of boxing."

But Broner's coronation might never come. Before the fight, he was being hailed as "the next Floyd Mayweather." Now comparisons with Zab Judah are in the air. That's not bad, but it isn't great either.

Don Turner knows a thing or two about boxing. Fifty-three years ago, he was a sparring partner for Sugar Ray Robinson. Later, he trained Larry Holmes and Evander Holyfield, earning recognition from the Boxing Writers Association of America as the 1996 "Trainer of the Year."

"I told you before the fight that Broner was overrated," Turner reminded this writer the day after Broner-Malignaggi. "He has the potential to be a great fighter, but he'll never live up to his potential because he's an out-of-control asshole. You have all these people around him, who do what he wants them to do and tell him what he wants to hear instead of telling him the truth. That's one of the biggest problems now with boxing. When there's money involved, nobody wants to tell the truth to anybody about anything."

Before fighting Malignaggi, Broner talked the talk. But when it came time to walk the walk, he stumbled a bit. Adrien isn't Superman. The odds are that he'll be carefully protected in the choice of an opponent for his next fight.

Malignaggi won't have that luxury, nor does he want it. Sitting in Portobello's, he ruminated, "I'd love a rematch, but I know Broner won't give it to me. Other offers will come my way. I'll look them over. But to be honest with you; I was sick of the boxing business before this fight. The way boxing is today, talent is secondary to connections in the fights you get, the purses you're paid, the officiating of your fights. That's been thrown in my face for years."

"I'm not as good as I used to be," Paulie continued. "I was at my best four to eight years ago. I'm a smarter fighter now than I was then and maybe a little stronger. But I was sharper when I was young and my legs were better. The young Paulie Malignaggi would have beaten the fighter I am today by, let's say, 116-112."

Three years ago, after Malignaggi lost to Amir Khan, it was suggested that he retire from boxing. There were a lot of reasons for his decision to keep fighting. One of them, voiced at the time, was, "Boxing is my getaway from stress. The stress of life, all the personal bullshit. I let it all out in boxing. For that reason alone, if nothing else, I've got to keep boxing."

Does he still feel that way?

"It's a mixed bag," Paulie says. "I still let a lot of things out in boxing. But in some ways, boxing is now the main stress. I never had any love for the business. Now I'm losing my love for the training and, to a degree, even for the competition. It might just be that I needed this kick in the ass to get out."

Paulie Malignaggi will never be the superstar that he so desperately wanted to be. But he's a professional fighter who has honored the craft of prizefighting.

Bart Barry has written, "No Floyd Mayweather fight is a victory for anyone but Mayweather." That said; Mayweather has become central to the contemporary boxing scene.

The Event: A Look Back at Mayweather-Alvarez

Now that the dust has settled and there has been time for reflection, it's worth taking a look back at the boxing event of 2013: the much-hyped, enormously successful promotion known as "The One."

Budd Schulberg once wrote, "I've always thought of boxing, not as a mirror but as a magnifying glass of our society."

That certainly was true of the September 14, 2013, fight between Floyd Mayweather and Saul "Canelo" Alvarez at the MGM Grand in Las Vegas.

Boxing's first million-dollar gate was $1,789,238 for the fight between Jack Dempsey and Georges Carpentier on July 2, 1921, at Boyle's 30 Acres in New Jersey. Adjusted for inflation, that number, according to Bureau of Labor Statistics, is equivalent to $23,377,744 in today's dollars.

Mayweather-Alvarez came close. The official gate was $20,003,150, which exceeded the previous mark of $18,419,200 set by the May 5, 2007, encounter between Mayweather and Oscar De La Hoya.

The best guess at present is that Mayweather-Alvarez generated 2,200,000 pay-per-view buys in the United States. That would place it second behind De La Hoya vs. Mayweather, which generated 2.45 million buys for a total of $136,000,000 ($153,400,000 in today's dollars). When all the numbers are in, that $153,400,000 figure is likely to be exceeded by Mayweather-Alvarez.

Mayweather was guaranteed a minimum purse of $41,500,000 to fight Alvarez. That's more than the entire 2013 player payroll for either the Miami Marlins ($36,341,900) or Houston Astros ($22,062,600). And Floyd's take is expected to rise significantly once all the pay-per-view buys and other revenue streams are counted.

So let's take a look at the good and the bad, the fantasy and the reality of Floyd "Money" Mayweather.

It's starts with Mayweather's skill as a fighter.

Mayweather seeks to control every aspect of his life. Thus, it's ironic that his chosen sport is boxing. In baseball, everyone waits for the pitcher. A golfer does what he can do with the laws of physics as his only adversary. Boxing is the hardest sport in the world for an athlete to control.

Over the course of twelve rounds, Mayweather controls the confines of a boxing ring as few men ever have.

The most admirable thing about Floyd is his work ethic and dedication to his craft.

Years ago, Luis Cortes wrote, "A majority of upsets occur when the more naturally talented fighter forgets that boxing is not just about talent."

Mayweather doesn't forget. He gives one hundred percent in preparing for a fight every time out.

"I'm a perfectionist," Floyd says. "No one works harder than I do. I worked my ass off to get to where I am now. Nobody is perfect, but I strive to be perfect."

Heywood Broun once wrote of Benny Leonard, "No performer in any art has ever been more correct. His jab could stand without revision in any textbook. The manner in which he feints, ducks, sidesteps, and hooks is unimpeachable. He is always ready to hit with either hand."

The same can be said of Mayweather. He and Bernard Hopkins have two of the highest "boxing IQs" in the business. Like Hopkins, Floyd shuts down his opponent, taking away what the opponent does best.

"Floyd has man strength and he knows how to use it," Hopkins says.

When Mayweather is stunned (the last time it happened was in round two against Shane Mosley three years ago), he holds on like the seasoned pro that he is. What's more instructive is what Floyd does when he's hit solidly but is fully compos mentis. His instinct is to fire back hard rather than let an opponent build confidence.

"Floyd does all things necessary to win a fight," Mosley notes.

That includes fighting rough and pushing the rules up to, and sometimes beyond, their boundary if the referee allows him to do so.

Against Mosley, Mayweather pushed down hard on the back of Shane's head and neck as an offensive maneuver seventeen times and used a forearm-elbow to the neck aggressively twenty-three times.

"Winning is the key to everything," says Leonard Ellerbe (CEO of Mayweather Promotions). "As long as Floyd keeps winning, there's no limit to the things he can accomplish."

Mayweather keeps winning. His split-decision victory over Oscar De La Hoya is the only time that a fight went to the scorecards and a judge had Floyd behind. Tom Kaczmarek scored that bout 115-113 for Oscar.

Floyd walks through life with a swagger. He flaunts his lifestyle and wealth. First HBO, and now Showtime, have put tens of millions of dollars worth of time and money into cultivating the Mayweather image. Floyd, for his part, has created and nurtured the "Money Mayweather" persona. "You can't be a thirty-five-year-old man calling yourself 'Pretty Boy'," he said last year, explaining the change in his sobriquet.

When Mayweather speaks of his "loved ones," one gets the feeling that Floyd holds down the top three or four spots on the list. He lives in ostentatious luxury (a 22,500-square-foot primary residence in Las Vegas and a 12,000-square-foot home in Miami) surrounded by beautiful women and devoted followers who adore him. The money that he puts in their pockets, we're told, has no bearing on their affection.

Tim Keown has tracked Floyd on two occasions for *ESPN: The Magazine* and reported, "This is a man who wears his boxer shorts once before throwing them out. This is a man who keeps his head shaved, yet travels on a private jet with his personal barber; who has two sets of nearly identical ultra-luxury cars color-coded by mansion—white in Las Vegas, black in Miami ["roughly two dozen" Rolls Royces, Lamborghinis, Bentleys, Ferraris, Bugattis, and Mercedes].

"Along with gaudy possessions and unlimited subservience comes something far more vital," Keown continues. "Self-justification. It's wealth as affirmation. A case filled with more than $5,000,000 in watches is not a mere collection. It is a statement."

Keown further reported that, on a recent shopping trip to New York, Mayweather spent "close a quarter of a million dollars on earrings and a necklace for his thirteen-year-old daughter, Iyanna."

One might question how a gift of that magnitude affects a young adolescent's values.

Meanwhile, tweets regarding Mayweather's gambling winnings (he regularly wagers six figures on a single basketball or football game) read like reports of Korean dictator Kim Jong-il's maiden golf outing, when the Korean state media reported eleven holes-in-one en route to a final score of 38 under par.

Sports Illustrated reported in its March 12, 2012, issue that Mayweather had lost a $990,000 wager on the March 3 basketball game between Duke and North Carolina. Floyd didn't tweet that.

Working for Mayweather means being available twenty-four-seven. When Floyd says "jump," his employees ask "how high?"

"They have to be ready to get up and go at four o'clock in the morning," Floyd says. "If I call and say 'I need you now,' I don't mean in an hour. I mean now."

Keown confirms that notion, writing, "His security crew routinely receives calls at two or three a.m. to accompany the nocturnal Mayweather to a local athletic club for weights and basketball. On this day, his regular workout finished, the champ tells one of his helpers to beckon two women from his entourage into his locker room. As he showers, he calls for one of them, a tall, dark-haired woman named Jamie, to soap his back while he continues to carry on an animated conversation with five or six men in the room."

That leads to another issue. The subservience of women in Mayweather's world and his treatment of them.

Floyd likes pretty women. No harm in that. He's on shakier ground when he says, "Beauty is only skin deep. An ugly motherfucker made that up." In late-September 2012, it was reported that Floyd spent $50,000 at a strip club called Diamonds in Atlanta. That's a lot of money.

More seriously, over the years, Mayweather has had significant issues with women and the criminal justice system. In 2002, he pled guilty to two counts of domestic violence. In 2004, he was found guilty on two counts of misdemeanor battery for assaulting two women in a Las Vegas nightclub. Other incidents were disposed of more quietly.

Then, on December 21, 2011, a Las Vegas judge sentenced Mayweather to ninety days in jail after he pleaded guilty to a reduced battery domestic violence charge and no contest to two harassment charges in conjunction with an assault against Josie Harris (the mother of three of his children). Floyd was also ordered to attend a one-year domestic-violence counseling program and perform one hundred hours of community service.

Was Mayweather chastened by that experience? Did he become more aware of his obligations as a member of society and the responsibilities that come with fame?

Apparently not.

"Martin Luther King went to jail," Mayweather told Michael Eric Dyson on an HBO program entitled *Floyd Mayweather: Speaking Out.* "Malcolm X went to jail. Am I guilty? Absolutely not. I took a plea. Sometimes they put us in a no-win situation to where you don't have no choice but to take a plea. I didn't want to bring my children to court."

That theme was echoed by Leonard Ellerbe, who declared on an episode of *24/7*, "All you can do is respect the man for not wanting to put his kids through a difficult process. Things are not always what they seem. I have the advantage of actually knowing what the facts are in this particular case. The public doesn't have this information. I know that he stepped up and did what was needed to do to protect his family."

Did Mayweather go to jail to protect his children from having to testify at trial? Or did he go to jail to avoid a longer prison term and protect himself from the public spectacle of his children telling the world what they saw?

Either way, Floyd did his children no favors by claiming on national television that they were the reason he went to jail. The children know what they saw on the night that Floyd had an altercation with their mother. If he was taking a bullet for his kids, he should have done so quietly without exposing them to further public spectacle and the taunts of other children telling them in the playground, "You're the reason your father went to jail."

One might also ask why Dyson (a professor of sociology at Georgetown University) didn't confront Mayweather with the fact that Floyd's confrontation with Josie Harris wasn't an isolated incident; that there were two previous convictions on his record for physically abusing women.

As for Josie Harris; she was so troubled by Floyd's denials after his plea of "no contest" to physically assaulting her in front of their children that, in April of this year, she broke a self-imposed silence and told Martin Harris of Yahoo Sports, "Did he beat me to a pulp? No. But I had bruises on my body and contusions and [a] concussion because the hits were to the back of my head."

Somewhere in the United States tonight, a young man who thinks that Floyd Mayweather is a role model will beat up a woman. Maybe she'll walk away with nothing more than bruises and emotional scars. Maybe he'll kill her.

That's the downside to uncritical glorification of Floyd Mayweather.

Also, as great a fighter as Mayweather is, there's one flaw on his résumé. He has consistently avoided the best available opposition.

A fighter doesn't have to be bloodied and knocked down and come off the canvas to prove his greatness. A fighter can also prove that he has the heart of a legendary champion by testing himself against the best available competition.

Mayweather has done neither.

Floyd said earlier this month, "I push myself to the limit by fighting the best."

That has all the sincerity of posturing by a political candidate.

Mayweather has some outstanding victories on his ring record. But his career has been marked by the avoidance of tough opponents in their prime.

There always seems to be someone who Mayweather is ducking. The most notable example was his several-year avoidance of Manny Pacquiao. Bob Arum (Pacquiao's promoter) might not have wanted the fight. But Manny clearly did. And it appeared as though Floyd didn't.

Mayweather also steered clear of Paul Williams, Antonio Margarito, and Miguel Cotto in their prime. He waited to fight Cotto until Miguel (like Shane Mosley) was a shell of his former self. Then Floyd made a show of saying that he'd fight Cotto at 154 pounds so Miguel would be at his best. But when Sergio Martinez offered to come down to 154, Floyd said that he'd only fight Martinez at 150 (an impossible weight for Sergio to make).

Thus, Frank Lotierzo writes, "Mayweather has picked his spots in one way or another throughout his career. Floyd got over big time on Juan Manuel Marquez with his weigh-in trickery at the last moment. He fought Oscar De La Hoya and barely won when Oscar was a corpse. Shane Mosley was an empty package when he finally fought him seven years after the fight truly meant anything. As terrific as Mayweather is, he's not the Bible of boxing the way he projects himself as being. He came along when there were some other outstanding fighters at or near his weight. Yet, aside from the late Diego Corrales, he has never met any of them when the fight would have confirmed his greatness. It would be great to write about Mayweather and laud all that he has accomplished as a fighter without bringing up these inconvenient facts. But it can't be done if you're being intellectually honest."

"Mayweather, "Lotierzo continues, "wouldn't be the face of boxing today if there was an Ali, Leonard, De La Hoya, or Tyson around. But they're long gone. Give him credit for being able to make a safety-first counter-puncher who avoided the only fight fans wanted him to deliver into the face of what once was the greatest sport in the world."

Three days prior to Mayweather-Alvarez, Floyd responded to those who have criticized his choice of ring adversaries: "If they say Mayweather has handpicked his opponents; well, then my team has done a fucking good job."

Mayweather has a following; those who like him and those who don't. But whatever side of the fence one is on, it's clear that Floyd has tapped into something.

"This is a business," Mayweather says of boxing.

Team Mayweather has played the business game brilliantly. Give manager Al Haymon and the rest of The Money Team credit for maximizing Floyd's income; making the pie bigger; and getting him a larger percentage of it. Through their efforts, Mayweather has become the epitome of what modern fighters strive to be. He has the ability to attract any opponent, determine when they fight, and enjoys the upper hand in any negotiation.

"His ability not only to understand but to capitalize on his value is unrivaled in the sport," Tim Keown writes. Then Keown references Mayweather's "singular brand of narcissism, ego and greed," and notes, "It helps to exhibit an unapologetic brazenness that incites allegiance and disgust in equal measure. Indifference, as any promoter will attest, is hell on sales."

"Love him or hate him," Leonard Ellerbe adds, "he's the bank vault. Love him or hate him, he's going to make the bank drop."

Mayweather's box-office appeal is consistent with other trends in contemporary American culture.

Charles Jay has mused, "There is a constituency that is very attracted to the Mayweather persona. Maybe there is an overlap between that constituency and the one that enjoys the antics of Charlie Sheen."

Carlos Acevedo opines that Floyd has led "a charmed life inside the ring if a rather charmless one outside it," and posits, "Being nasty in public under the guise of entertainment is now as American as baseball and serial killers."

More tellingly, Acevedo argued last year, "Mayweather generates a disproportionate amount of media coverage. Never mind the fact that probably somewhere around six million people in the U.S. saw Mayweather bushwhack Victor Ortiz [and roughly ten million saw him defeat Miguel Cotto]. Compare that, say, to the night Ken Norton faced Duane Bobick on NBC in 1977. That fight, aired on a Wednesday evening in prime-time, earned a 42% audience share, and was estimated to have been viewed by 48 million people. If we want to pretend that more than a few million people care about 'Money,' we have to keep listening to penny-click addicts and websites obsessed with celebrity cellulite and tanorexia."

According to Nevada State Athletic Commission records, all five of Mayweather's fights between the start of 2009 and mid-2013 (against Juan Manuel Marquez, Shane Mosley, Victor Ortiz, Miguel Cotto, and Robert Guerrero) were contested in front of empty seats. Even with 1,459 complimentary tickets being given away, there were 139 empty seats for Mayweather-Guerrero. More troubling were credible reports that Mayweather-Guerrero registered only 850,000 pay-per-view buys. That's a healthy number for most fights. But not for a Mayweather fight. And not for Showtime, which had spirited Mayweather away from HBO and entered into a six-fight contract with the fighter that guaranteed him $32,000,000 per fight against the revenue from domestic pay-per-view buys.

Showtime had heavily promoted Mayweather-Guerrero with documentaries, a reality TV series, an appearance by Floyd at the NCAA men's basketball Final Four, and numerous promotional spots on CBS Sports television and CBS Sports Radio. Factoring in the cost of production and other outlays, there were estimates that the network had lost between five and ten million dollars on Mayweather-Guerrero. That might have been justified as a "loss leader" to bring Mayweather into the Showtime fold.

But it couldn't be repeated in Floyd's next fight without speculation that corporate heads would roll.

Mayweather's fights have been promoted in recent years by Golden Boy, which now has a strategic alliance with Showtime and Al Haymon. The idea that Golden Boy Promotions would crumble once Oscar De La Hoya stopped fighting is now an outdated fantasy. CEO Richard Schaefer has played the promotional game masterfully.

But Golden Boy has little control over Mayweather. According to Leonard Ellerbe, Mayweather Promotions pays Golden Boy to handle logistics on a per-fight basis. "If you run a construction company," Ellerbe says, "you have to hire someone to pour the cement."

Schaefer confirms that Golden Boy presents The Money Team with a budget for each fight that includes projected revenue streams and costs (for example, fighter purses, marketing, travel, arena set-up, and its promotional fee).

Showtime could have been forgiven for thinking that guaranteeing Mayweather $32,000,000 a fight for six fights would have entitled it to the most marketable Mayweather fights possible. But there was no such assurance.

After Mayweather beat Guerrero, word spread that the frontrunner in the sweepstakes to become Floyd's next opponent was Devon Alexander. That raised the likelihood of another sub-one-million-buy Mayweather outing and the loss to the network of another five to ten million dollars.

There was little point in Showtime appealing to Mayweather to upgrade the commercial viability of his opponent on grounds that Floyd is a team player. Floyd is a team player as long as it's Team Mayweather. Thus, Showtime rolled the dice and increased Mayweather's contractual guarantee to $41,500,000 to entice him to fight Saul "Canelo" Alvarez.

If boxing fans in America have a love-hate relationship with Mayweather, Mexican fans have a love-love relationship with Alvarez. Canelo's résumé is a bit thin. But Mayweather vs. Alvarez on Mexican Independence Day weekend was sure to sell out the MGM Grand Garden Arena and generate a massive number of pay-per-view buys.

Alvarez agreed to a financial guarantee believed to be in the neighborhood of $12,500,000. His purse as reported to the Nevada State Athletic Commission was $5,000,000. But that didn't include the grant of Mexican television rights and other financial incentives.

The thorniest issue in negotiating the fight contracts was the issue of weight. Mayweather has filled out over the years. He's now a full-fledged welterweight. But Alvarez fights at 154 pounds.

On May 29, it was announced that the two men had signed to fight at a catchweight of 152 pounds. Schaefer said that there was a seven-figure penalty should either fighter fail to make weight.

Thereafter, Ellerbe stated publicly that the Alvarez camp had begun the negotiations with an offer to fight at a catchweight and declared, "His management is inept. We take advantage of those kinds of things. They suggested it. Why would we say no and do something different. They put him at a disadvantage, his management did. It wasn't that Floyd asked for a catchweight because, absolutely, that did not happen. Floyd would have fought him regardless. His management put that out there. So if you have an idiot manager, that's what it is."

The Alvarez camp responded by saying that Ellerbe was lying.

"Why would I give up weight?" Canelo asked rhetorically. "I'm the 154-pound champion. When the negotiations started, they wanted me to go down to 147, then 150, then 151, finally 152. I said I'd do it to make the fight. But it's not right that they're lying about it. I don't want to fight two pounds below the weight class, but it was the only way I could get the fight."

"Being the A-side is about having leverage," Ellerbe fired back. "We're always going to put every opponent at a disadvantage if we can."

Once the fight was signed, the marketing began with an eleven-city, nine-day kick-off media tour. Schaefer proclaimed that the tour was "like Beatlemania." Independent media reports noted that the crowds at many of the tour stops were smaller than the numbers inserted in press releases and later repeated by trusting writers.

Tickets were priced at $2,000, $1,500, $1,000, $600, and $350. Golden Boy announced that they had sold out within hours of going on sale. Left unsaid was the fact that, pursuant to contract, virtually all of the tickets had been presold to casinos, Team Mayweather, and Golden Boy itself. Only a handful of seats were available at list price to the general public.

That created a blue-chip market for ticket scalping. David Greisman subsequently reported, "Five days after tickets went on sale and four days after they supposedly sold out, Ticketmaster's resale website had 378 seats

available that ranged from $995 for the farthest row up in the MGM
Grand Garden Arena to $26,156 for a seat three rows back at ringside. Of
course, if you wanted to settle for the row behind that one, that's just
$18,310. StubHub had 915 tickets available as of early Sunday evening,
ranging from $1,098 for the final row of the arena to $29,999 for six rows
back at ringside."

Those numbers were an opening gambit, a concerted effort to set and
maintain high ticket-resale prices for the thousands of tickets that would
later enter the resale market. But as time went by, it became clear
Mayweather-Alvarez was catching on. More resources were being poured
into marketing "The One" (as the promotion was styled) than had been
poured into any fight ever.

"Mayweather-Alvarez is being pushed like a blockbuster movie," Tim
Smith wrote. "The only thing missing is the action figures that come with
a Happy Meal."

"The purpose of the spectacle is saturation," Bart Barry added.
"Flashing images that say nothing so profoundly as, 'This is important
because everyone is watching it because it is important enough for everyone to watch.'"

The build-up had many of the characteristics of the lead-in to a
national political convention. The fact that Mayweather was listed as one
of the "executive producers" for Showtime's *All Access* promotional series
was a pretty good clue as to the objectivity of its editorial content. But as
in politics, the powers that be in boxing can't always get out the vote on
the day that matters most. The unanswered marketing question was how
many people would buy the pay-per-view on fight night at a price of
$64.95 ($74.95 for HDTV).

Fight week began with an unexpected twist. Oscar De La Hoya
(president of Golden Boy Promotions) announced that he would not be
attending the bout because he had voluntarily admitted himself to a treatment facility after suffering a relapse in his ongoing battle with substance-
abuse problems.

De La Hoya's difficulties were common knowledge in boxing.
Indeed, in September 2011, after Oscar had called for a rematch between
Mayweather and Victor Ortiz, Leonard Ellerbe told FightHype.com,
"Oscar must be having a relapse, and Victor must still be sloppy drunk

from when I saw him last Sunday night in the lobby of the MGM Grand. They sound stupid, and it's embarrassing to boxing that they would hold a conference call and look like a bunch of morons. It's no secret that Oscar is insanely jealous of Floyd's success. Floyd don't have no drinking problem. Floyd don't have no drug problem. Floyd don't wear fishnets. And Floyd don't have a number of kids out there that he doesn't claim."

Oscar's decision to go into rehab for the second time in twenty-eight months was a sound one. But there was a school of thought that it had been timed to avoid his having to be in Las Vegas to witness Mayweather's week of glory.

There was a time when people hung on De La Hoya's every word. No more. His eyes are sad these days. It seems to tear at his gut that he was the most important building block in catapulting Floyd to superstardom. He dislikes Mayweather; has talked openly about wanting him to lose; and more often than not, predicts that Floyd's opponent will beat him.

Insofar as Mayweather-Alvarez was concerned, Oscar had been largely reduced to a promotional prop. Mayweather was openly disdainful toward him.

"You might as well call me the Golden Boy," Floyd said during the kick-off press tour for Mayweather-Alvarez. At the last tour stop, with Schaefer and De La Hoya sitting with him on the dais, Mayweather turned toward Richard and declared, "I've been working hand-in-hand with this man. I can't really speak about Oscar. But one thing I can tell you; Richard Schaefer is Golden Boy."

De La Hoya was hardly missed during fight week. That in itself was sad. Explaining Oscar's absence on Tuesday, Schaefer told the media, "He called me on Monday afternoon and sounded terrible. He told me he needed help, that he can't go on. I put him in touch with the proper people, and they helped him get into a rehab facility for substance abuse. Obviously, the timing isn't good. But when you have an illness, it's not like you can choose the timing and say, 'I'm not going to go today; I'm going to go next Monday.' When you need help, you need help. And, of course, I'm support-ive of that because health and life and family come before everything else."

Had Schaefer known previously of Oscar's relapse?

"I'm very busy," Richard answered. "I'm nobody's babysitter. It took me by surprise."

There was a buzz in Las Vegas during fight week. The Money Team logo (TMT) was much in evidence.

Mayweather was forty minutes late for the final pre-fight press conference on Wednesday. One day later, he would blow off the Showtime fighter meeting without notice.

Alvarez is twenty-three years old and has been fighting professionally for eight years. At first glance, he gives the impression of someone who has not yet physically matured. He has red hair (hence the nickname, Canelo, which is Spanish for cinnamon) and a soft high-pitched voice. Walking through the casino during fight week, but for the entourage around him, he might have been mistaken for a bellhop or restaurant busboy.

Introducing Alvarez at the final pre-fight press conference, Schaefer declared, "Many can fight but few can inspire. Canelo inspires hope in millions of people."

"I've visualized this fight for years," Alvarez told the media. "I have my fans. I am their gamecock. Floyd has his fans. He is their gamecock."

Among the thoughts that Mayweather offered were:

★ "I'm the main man in boxing now. There's only one man that counts and that's Mayweather."

★ "Canelo is a main event fighter. I'm a pay-per-view fighter."

★ "He's just another opponent to me; that's all. He's 42 and 0. He hasn't faced forty-two Floyd Mayweathers or he'd be 0 and 42."

★ "This is not a fight. This is an event."

Bottom line . . . Mayweather-Alvarez was catching on. The hype was translating into genuine excitement and financial reality. Events this big are rare in boxing.

In the six years since De La Hoya vs. Mayweather was contested, the number of homes in the United States addressable for pay-per-view has increased from sixty to ninety million. That meant the 2.45 million buy-mark set by Oscar and Floyd was not necessarily out of reach. By mid-week, the projections were that Mayweather-Alvarez would generate in excess of two million pay-per-view buys. Schaefer was predicting a gross of $200 million: $140 to 160 million in domestic pay-per-view sales, a $20 million live gate, $5 to 10 million in closed-circuit sales, $5 to 8 million in foreign sales, $5 million from sponsors, and low seven figures for merchandise.

Friday brought more evidence that Mayweather-Alvarez had become a special promotion.

Even for the biggest fights, a lot of what happens in Las Vegas during fight week is cookie-cutter stuff. The press luncheon and final pre-fight press conference on Wednesday . . . Satellite-tour interviews and the undercard press conference on Thursday . . . The weigh-in on Friday. Very little is spontaneous or left to chance.

Normally, the MGM Grand Garden Arena is configured to accommodate six thousand fans for a big-fight weigh-in. A platform is erected near one end of the arena facing the stands, and the rest of the venue is blocked off by a black curtain.

The weigh-in for Mayweather-Alvarez was spectacularly different.

A huge stage with a giant backdrop was erected at one end of the arena, blocking off four thousand seats. The other twelve thousand seats were open to the public. That meant the promotion would, in effect, be setting up twice. After the weigh-in, the stage would be taken down and the arena reconfigured for the fight. There would be overtime costs for clean-up and reconstruction, not to mention audio-visual and other production expenses.

Schaefer estimated that the promotion spent close to $250,000 on the weigh-in.

"If you think big, big things will happen," Richard said. "If you think little, little things will happen."

The weigh-in was scheduled for 2:30 PM. By noon, all available seats were filled and the doors had been closed to the public. At the appointed hour, one Golden Boy fighter after another was announced to the crowd and brought to the stage.

Bernard Hopkins, Adrien Broner, Austin Trout, Abner Mares, Keith Thurman, Shane Mosley, Paulie Malignaggi, Leo Santa Cruz, Omar Figueroa, Alfredo Angulo, Peter Quillin, Devon Alexander, Amir Khan, Marcos Maidana, Cornelius Bundrage, Seth Mitchell, Danny Jacobs, and more.

It was an impressive display of promotional might, not unlike the parading of ships in a military exercise. Despite the fact that Mayweather-Alvarez was a Showtime event, Andre Ward (who commentates for and fights on HBO) also appeared on the stage. That raised eyebrows, particularly since Ward isn't promoted by Golden Boy.

"I was waiting for Mike Tyson to walk out next," Schaefer joked. Then he added, "The weigh-in was about energizing the fans and promoting the pay-per-view. But it was also about sending a message. It was for the fighters to say 'I am part of this group' and for other fighters to say 'I want to be part of this group.'"

Alvarez weighed in at the contract weight of 152 pounds; Mayweather at 150.5.

Meanwhile, the odds (which had opened at 5 to 2 in Mayweather's favor) had remained constant throughout the build-up to the fight.

If Alvarez won, it would vault him to iconic status in Mexico. But that seemed unlikely. The case for a Canelo victory was based on speculation and hope. The case for a Mayweather triumph was based on past performances and cold hard facts.

Jimmy Tobin wrote, "Recognizing the danger Alvarez represents is easier than blueprinting how that danger produces a Mayweather loss. If Mayweather chooses you as an opponent, then he has determined you cannot beat him. He could be wrong, and the possibility of a misstep increases as he ages. But when Alvarez's prospects are largely dependent on Mayweather turning in a career-worst performance, it is hard to anticipate a cliff-hanger. We are getting exactly what we asked for. But what we asked for doesn't appear particularly competitive."

Having an adoring fan base is different from having the skills necessary to win a particular fight. Indeed, it was not unreasonable to suggest that Mayweather had chosen to confront Alvarez now, not because he wanted to fight the 23-year-old challenger before Canelo peaked, but because he wanted to fight him before someone else removed the "0" from Canelo's record. A loss would mean that Mayweather-Alvarez was no longer a mega-fight.

EPSN has a ten-man panel that ranks fighters periodically on a pound-for-pound basis. Each panelist lists his top ten P4P choices. Mayweather has been a runaway choice for the top slot for some time now. Alvarez has yet to receive a single top-ten vote.

Mayweather has better skills than Alvarez. He's also more physically

THOMAS HAUSER ON BOXING

gifted. Contrasting their records three days before the fight, Floyd proclaimed, "I fought Ricky Hatton. I didn't fight Hatton's brother. I fought Miguel Cotto. I didn't fight Cotto's brother."

Floyd Mayweather Sr was happy to be back in his son's camp as head trainer for the second fight in a row after what he calls "my exile from my son."

"Saturday is going to be a sad night in Mexicali," Floyd Sr said.

That thought was echoed by Bernard Hopkins.

"To have any chance against Floyd," Bernard explained one day before the fight, "you have to forget circling, moving, and counterpunching, and fight with him. In any fight, you want to take away from your opponent what the opponent does best. The first thing you have to take away from Floyd is his confidence. Whatever it costs, you have to find a way to hit him hard early and then do it again."

"Every fighter has a shot to win," Hopkins continued. "But some fighters' shots are more realistic than others. Canelo's shot isn't very good. When you're as good as Floyd is right now and you're in that zone and you believe in yourself and you train as hard as you can, it's hard to beat you. It's Floyd's fight to win or lose."

On Saturday afternoon, the MGM Grand was a mob scene. People without tickets or the money to buy them were there simply to feel the action and perhaps catch a glimpse of a celebrity. It was hard to navigate through the hotel lobby, where the crush of humanity included more than a hundred people standing on line to get into a makeshift concession stand to buy T-shirts and other memorabilia.

The arena filled up earlier than it usually does for a big pay-per-view fight. Fans wanted to see the semi-final bout between Danny Garcia and Lucas Matthysse.

Mayweather makes his home in Las Vegas. This was his tenth fight in a row in Sin City. But when it was time for the main event, the crowd was overwhelmingly pro-Alvarez. They cheered wildly as Canelo entered the ring; then booed vociferously as Floyd was escorted through the ropes by Justin Bieber (who looked like a lapdog) and rapper Lil Wayne (shirtless with gray pants that fell below his lavender underwear). The operative words of Lil Wayne's entrance music were difficult to discern but sounded like "Money Team" and "motherfucker."

Shortly after 9:30 PM, the millions of dollars in publicity, the eleven-city media tour, the endless promotional spots on multiple media platforms, and the stream of visitors to Las Vegas who would drop tens of millions of dollars at the gaming tables came together on a small square of powder-blue canvas that had been stretched taut across a platform of metal beams and wood boards.

Mayweather makes a show of his sports betting habit. But in the ring, he gambles as little as possible. One can, and should, appreciate the masterful nature of his performance against Alvarez. That said; Canelo looked ordinary and the bout was one-sided to the point where it lacked drama.

My notes from ringside read as follows:

Round 1: Tactical fight with little action . . . Works to Mayweather's advantage.

Round 2: Canelo can't hit Floyd and he's applying zero pressure . . . Floyd is too quick and fast for him.

Round 3: Canelo can't get off. He's a workman. Floyd is a craftsman . . . This is target practice for Mayweather.

Round 4: More exchanges than before, but Floyd getting the better of them . . . This fight is over. Floyd has won the first four rounds. No way Canelo is winning six of the next eight or knocking Floyd out.

Round 5: Floyd doing exactly what he wants to do. Deciding when they will and won't engage . . . Canelo looks befuddled and discouraged . . . Give Floyd credit. He's a great fighter.

Round 6: Floyd in total control. His punches are coming in harder now . . . Canelo has the crowd on his side but not much else going for him.

Round 7: Total domination by Floyd . . . The crowd has been reduced to cheering when Canelo throws a big punch that comes within six inches of landing.

Round 8: Canelo's best round so far. Doing some good body work. Floyd comes back harder up top, but at least Canelo hit him.

Round 9: Floyd running the table. He's not a big puncher, but he's a sharp puncher. Canelo totally ineffective.

Round 10: More of the same. Canelo has a mouse under his left eye and some other swelling on his face . . . This fight could have been at 160 pounds and it wouldn't have made a difference.

Round 11: Floyd landing some nasty rights. If ever he were to go for a knockout to burnish his image, this would be the time.

Round 12: Floyd taking the round off. Playing total defense . . . This has been less sport than spectacle.

I scored the last round even. Floyd could have won it if he'd made an effort to. That made my score 120-109. Then Jimmy Lennon stunned the crowd with the announcement, "We have a majority decision."

C. J. Ross's scorecard was read first. 114-114, a draw. Suffice it to say that Ms. Ross should never judge again. Three days after the fight, she informed the Nevada State Athletic Commission that she was "taking some time off from boxing" and would not be available to judge fights in the near future. One hopes that she will be unavailable to judge fights in the long-term future as well.

Judges Dave Moretti (116-112) and Craig Metcalfe (117-111) restored some semblance of sanity to the proceedings by giving the nod to Mayweather. But their scorecards were closer than circumstances warranted.

Bobby Hunter of Fight Score Collector polled eighty-six members of the media after the fight. All eighty-six scored the bout for Mayweather with the average score being 119-109. That was consistent with the final CompuBox numbers that had Mayweather outlanding Alvarez in eleven of the twelve rounds with one round even for a 232-to-117 margin.

So what does it all mean for boxing?

For starters, let's agree that a sport that generates $200 million from a single fight-card is not a dying sport. But let's also agree that trickle-down economics won't make boxing healthy again anymore than it will support a robust national economy. Not enough money trickles down.

Showtime rolled the dice on Mayweather-Alvarez and won. But just as it was wrong to deride the economics of Showtime's deal with Mayweather based on the first fight in the package (Mayweather-Guerrero), it would be wrong to say that the six-fight contract will be an unqualified success for the network.

Mayweather says that he plans to fight twice in 2014, with his next bout in May. Amir Khan has been prominently mentioned as an opponent. The assumption has been that Golden Boy would love it if Khan beat Devon Alexander in their tentatively scheduled December 7 match-up at

Barclays Center in Brooklyn. The problem with that thinking is that Khan has looked vulnerable in recent outings and might not make it past Alexander. It wouldn't be surprising if Khan-Alexander were cancelled and Golden Boy goes right to Mayweather-Khan at Wembley Stadium. The Brits won't travel to Las Vegas in large numbers for Khan the way they did for Ricky Hatton. But they will travel to London.

Danny Garcia is another possible opponent. Now that Sergio Martinez's body is failing him, Floyd might finally accept that challenge. If Manny Pacquiao looks exciting but vulnerable in his November 23 outing against Brandon Rios, it's not beyond the realm of possibility that we'll see Mayweather-Pacquiao.

But boxing fans can be certain that Floyd won't fight Gennady Golovkin at 154 pounds. Not even if HBO releases Golovkin from his obligation to the network in order to facilitate the fight.

"Boxing, unlike saner, better organized sports," Hamilton Nolan notes, "is prone to leaving its fans wishing for matchups that never take place."

Thus, the words of Richard Schaefer: "Floyd Mayweather is never going to run out of options and alternatives because, frankly, he can fight Joe Schmo and it's going to be a big event."

The "0" on Mayweather's record is important to Floyd. If he retires undefeated, he can join Sven Ottke, Joe Calzaghe, and Rocky Marciano; none of whom are on history's short list of boxing's greatest fighters. Floyd would have been competitive with the best in any era. Whether he would have beaten the best is open to question.

Danny Garcia vs. Lucas Matthysse didn't have the fireworks that most fans expected. That was to Garcia's advantage.

Daniel in the Lions' Den

Fights don't always follow the script in boxing. They have a story of their own to tell. Such was the case when Danny Garcia squared off against Argentinean Lucas Matthysse on September 14, 2013, in a much-anticipated semifinal bout prior to Floyd Mayweather vs. Canelo Alvarez at the MGM Grand in Las Vegas.

Garcia-Matthysse didn't come cheaply. The official bout contracts filed with the Nevada State Athletic Commission listed Garcia's purse at $1,500,000 and Matthysse's at $800,000. There was a school of thought that the real numbers were higher and had been adjusted for tax purposes.

That said; matching Garcia against Matthysse energized boxing fans and helped build momentum for the pay-per-view promotion. It also freed up the license fees that Showtime would otherwise have been called upon to spend had Garcia and Matthysse fought on *Showtime Championship Boxing* this autumn. And Garcia-Matthysse increased the value of the thousands of tickets that those involved with the promotion had retained for resale on the secondary market.

Garcia, age twenty-five, is soft spoken and likable with little bravado about him. "I work hard and I believe in myself," is as far as he goes in extolling his own virtues as a fighter.

He came into fight week with a 26-and-0 record and 16 knockouts. But most of his fights had been against has-beens and never-weres. The most notable names on his ledger (Zab Judah, Erik Morales, Kendall Holt, and Nate Campbell) were past their prime when he fought them. The exception was Amir Khan, who Garcia knocked out in four rounds in July 2012. But Khan had been putting a beating on Garcia before a single left hook changed the course of the action.

Matthysse sported a 34-and-2 record with 32 knockouts. His two losses were to Judah and Devon Alexander. In each instance, the Argentinean knocked his opponent down but came out on the short end of a razor-thin split decision. His most impressive victory was a third-round devastation of Lamont Peterson earlier this year.

Under normal circumstances, Garcia (as the unified WBA-WBC 140-pound champion) would have been the center of attention during fight week. But this particular week was hardly normal. Danny was the odd man out; overshadowed by Mayweather, Alvarez, and Matthysse.

Golden Boy was grooming Matthysse for the role of a future Floyd Mayweather mega-fight opponent. Garcia, the undefeated champion, was a 5-to-2 underdog.

"On closer inspection and perhaps with a jaundiced eye," Jimmy Tobin wrote, "Garcia-Matthysse looks like a sanctioned [mob] hit."

Zab Judah, who'd fought both men, was reluctant to pick a winner. But he did note, "I hit Danny Garcia with my best punch and hurt him. I hit Matthysse with my best punch and he smiled."

Garcia's biggest booster in the build-up to the fight was his father, Angel, who also trains him. When Danny was a boy, Angel served two years in prison for cocaine distribution.

Angel has a confrontational, conspiratorial, us-against-them view of the world and the habit of speaking his mind in a way that often leads to the threat of violence. In a combustible situation, he's likely to light a match.

"I let him be him," Danny says of his father. "And I'm me."

Angel has Danny's back. That's his number one priority. It's also numbers two and three.

"He's the star," Angel says. "I'm just a bum. But I'm his father."

Angel knows a thing or two about boxing. He was aware that Matthysse has a much better chin than Khan or Judah and hits harder. But he also knew that Lucas wasn't as fast as Amir or Zab.

"Underdogs that win are the true champions," Angel said two days before the fight. "Danny will win."

One gets the feeling that Danny has saved his father's life. Without the mission of caring for his son, where would Angel be?

There were heightened expectations for Garcia-Matthysse. If Mayweather-Alvarez was The Event that people wanted to be seen at, Garcia-Matthysse was the fight that people wanted to see. Some members of the media jokingly referred to Mayweather-Alvarez as the evening's walk-out bout.

Garcia-Matthysse began with Lucas as the aggressor, trying to work his way inside and engage. His punching power had been advertised in pre-fight publicity to the extent that, each time he landed a blow, the crowd "oohed" whether he was doing damage or not.

Mostly, he was not.

Garcia was wary of his foe's power and, in the early going, circled out of harm's way. But he understood that he couldn't keep Matthysse off or score points by playing defense only. So he looked to counter with left hooks and launched some go-for-broke righthand leads that kept Lucas honest. Danny also went low often enough that it seemed just a matter of time before referee Tony Weeks deducted a point for the infractions.

Matthysse was ahead four-rounds-to-two at the midway point. Then, as expected, the fight turned on one punch. But it was a fluke punch rather than a concussive one.

Garcia caught a break. And Matthysse caught a bad one.

"I hit him with a jab [in round seven]," Danny said at the post-fight press conference. "I saw him blinking his eye. And forty-five seconds later, the eye was closed."

Matthysse knew then, if he hadn't known before, that he was in for a hard night. He was now a one-eyed fighter. A closed eye affects a fighter's depth perception, balance, and field of vision. Lucas could no longer see Danny's money punch (the left hook) coming.

From that point on, Garcia was able to potshot Matthysse with regularity. Lucas landed some good right hands at the start of round eleven. But a hook to the body (Danny's best punch of the night) drove the Argentinean to the ropes, after which a hook up top deposited him on the canvas.

In round twelve, the referee finally deducted a point from the champion for repeated low lows. But it was too little too late. Garcia prevailed on the judges' scorecards by a 114-112, 114-112, 115-111 margin.

Garcia has accomplished a lot in the ring for a twenty-five-year-old and is developing nicely as a fighter. As an undefeated unified champion with victories over Lucas Matthysse, Amir Khan, and Zab Judah, he's also an increasingly marketable commodity.

The lead-in to Tim Bradley vs. Juan Manuel Marquez touched on some issues that are crucial to boxing.

Why Bradley-Marquez Matters

On October 12, 2013, Tim Bradley and Juan Manuel Marquez will meet in the ring at the Thomas & Mack Center in Las Vegas. The fight (which is being promoted by Top Rank and televised by HBO-PPV) falls midway between two more heavily hyped pay-per-view match-ups involving Floyd Mayweather and Manny Pacquiao. That said; if Bradley wins, it will force the boxing establishment and boxing fans to give him his due. That would be good for Bradley and good for boxing.

Bradley comes across as a man you'd let babysit for your children.

"I try to be the best person I can be," Tim says. "I focus on my family and my job, which is boxing. I stay out of trouble. I always try to do the right thing. I don't like a lot of drama in my personal life."

In nine years as a pro, Bradley has fashioned a 30-and-0 record and beaten opponents like Junior Witter, Lamont Peterson, Luis Abregu, and Devon Alexander. On June 9, 2012, he won a twelve-round split-decision over Manny Pacquiao.

"First round of the Pacquiao fight," Tim recalls, "I was like, 'Wow; this is it?' This is the best fighter in the world? I can deal with him.' Second round, something in my foot popped. I'm like, 'Damn! I think I broke my foot. I can't believe this is happening.' I'd spent years trying to get to that place. It was the biggest fight of my life. So I told myself, 'Forget about the pain. Do what you gotta do.'"

"Over the years, I've learned how to block out pain," Bradley continues. "So I bit down hard on my mouthpiece and kept fighting. Then, trying to protect my left foot, I sprained my right ankle. So now I had pain wherever I put my weight. But I fought every minute of every round. It was a close fight. I thought I'd done enough to win, and the judges agreed with me. They announced the decision. I was on top of the world. And then the roof caved in."

HBO's commentating team thought that Pacquiao won and had called the fight accordingly. Most on-site members of the media agreed with them. Brian Kenny (who handled the blow-by-blow commentary for Top Rank's international feed) scored the bout for Bradley. But his voice was drowned out in the tumult that followed.

In the media center immediately after the fight, Bob Arum (who promoted both fighters) declared, "I have never been as ashamed to be associated with the sport of boxing as I am tonight. To hear scores like we heard tonight; it's unfathomable. This isn't arguing about a close decision. This is an absurdity."

Much of the dialogue in the days that followed focused on round seven, which was labeled "the smoking gun." The CompuBox "punchstats" had Pacquiao outlanding Bradley in round seven by a 27-to-11 margin. Yet all three judges scored the round for Bradley.

A smoking gun?

This writer watched a video of round seven in its entirety from multiple camera angles . . . Several times . . . In slow motion . . . I think that Bradley outlanded Pacquiao 16 to 12 in round seven. I won't quarrel with those who say that Pacquiao deserved the decision. But it was a close fight, and I've been at ringside for many decisions that were worse.

I also think that Bradley deserved better treatment than he got from fans and the boxing establishment after Pacquiao-Bradley.

"This should have been the biggest moment of my life," Tim says. "And it was ruined. They dragged my name through the mud and everybody piled on. People were saying, 'You're a fake champion. Give the belt back.' I got hate mail like you wouldn't believe. The ridicule got so bad that there were times when I didn't know if I wanted to fight anymore."

"I watched the tape of the fight again and again," Bradley continues. "I can be obsessive. I watched the tape maybe fifty times. It was a close fight, but I think I won. Part of the problem, I believe, was that the HBO announcers had Pacquiao on a pedestal. It was like they were calling *The Manny Pacquiao Show*. Don't get me wrong. I like HBO. But their call was way off that night. A lot of the punches the announcers said were landing didn't land. And everything they said was going into viewers' minds. I was shattered. It was a dark time for me. I was walking around angry, bitter. Finally, my wife asked me, 'Aren't you tired of this?' I said, 'You're right.

Enough is enough. This isn't me. I'm not going to let these people change who I am. The fight is over. It's in the past."

"God sure kept me humble after that fight," Bradley adds.

There are times when it seems that, outside the ring, Bradley can't win. He dominates Devon Alexander, and the media focuses on the abysmal nature of the co-promotion by Don King and Gary Shaw. He decisions Manny Pacquiao, and the decision is trashed.

In his one fight after beating Pacquiao, Bradley was rendered semiconscious by Ruslan Provodnikov in round one and fought the next eleven rounds with a concussion. He was knocked down twice, dug as deep as a fighter possibly can, and went places inside himself that few people ever go en route to winning a razor-thin twelve-round decision. It was, Bart Barry later wrote, "as valorous a display as an athlete can make."

Now the boxing world is readying for Bradley-Marquez; a confrontation between the two fighters who beat Manny Pacquiao in the Filipino icon's last two fights.

Bradley, irrespective of his aggravation over Arum's comments regarding Pacquiao-Bradley, has made good money with Top Rank. He received a $5,000,000 purse to fight Manny and seven-figure paydays for outings against Joel Casamayor and Provodnikov. A $4,000,000 guarantee to Team Bradley is in place for the Marquez fight.

Bradley is ten years younger than Marquez; thirty versus forty. But Juan Manuel has a style that will be difficult for Tim. He's an excellent counterpuncher and fights well going backward, which could blunt Tim's natural aggression. Also, Marquez has a good uppercut, which Bradley is open to when he leans in. And Tim might not have the power (only twelve knockouts in thirty fights) to make Juan Manuel pay for his mistakes.

"I work with what I have," Bradley says. "This isn't my first fight. I'm not undefeated because everything went right in all of my fights. I'm undefeated because I did what I had to do to win every time."

Then Tim offers the reminder, "People talk about how I was out on my feet in the Provodnikov fight. They talk about the heart I showed and how exciting it was. They forget how beat up the other guy was when it was over."

But the Provodnikov fight is cause for concern to Bradley partisans on several levels.

"After the first round," Tim recalls, "I lost track of what round it was. I was just fighting from one round to the next. I had trouble following my corner's instructions. I felt buzzed and unbalanced the whole fight. It was like I was falling down but I didn't fall down. The lights were going on and off and then I'd reboot. My condition and training got me through the fight. I was in great shape. And I'd done things again and again in the gym so many times that I did them without thinking during the fight."

But there were problems afterward.

"After the fight," Bradley acknowledges, "for two-and-a-half months, I had symptoms. My speech was slurred. I felt like I was leaning to one side. I felt weak. I flew to New York and saw some specialists for evaluation and therapy. Then I saw another neuro-specialist in California. My health comes before anything. That's the most important thing. It's not about the money all the time. I want to grow old with my children and grandchildren and be healthy enough that we all have a good time together. Eventually, my condition got better. Some of that was from therapy and some of it was healing through time. My balance and speech got back to where they were. My strength came back. But I still wasn't sure how I'd react when I got hit. You see guys who get knocked out once and, all of a sudden, they're getting knocked out all the time. So I decided to spar with Lucas Matthysse [in late-August]. He can punch. I didn't let him hit me on purpose. But if you spar, you know you're gonna get hit. He hit me solid a few times, and I was fine. I'm back to normal now."

But what's normal?

Bradley appeared to have been concussed in the ring at least twice prior to fighting Provodnikov. In 2009, he was knocked down and hurt badly in the first round by Kendall Holt. He survived and won a twelve-round decision. Three years before that, he suffered a concussion against Eli Addison.

"In the second round [of the Addison fight]," Tim remembers, "we both threw right hands and missed and our heads collided. I got whacked on the right side of my temple and didn't know where I was at. I lost control of my body. I thought I was walking fine, but I was staggering around like Zab Judah did against Kostya Tszyu. People were laughing. They thought I was kidding around. Then the referee said 'box' and

Addison came at me. I was on autopilot. The next thing I remember, it was the seventh round."

Bradley's extraordinary will enables him to fight through pain. Fighting through a brain disconnect is another matter. Unlike Addison and Provodnikov, Marquez is skilled enough to finish off a fighter who's concussed and in front of him.

Here, the thoughts of neurologist Margaret Goodman (former chief ringside physician for the Nevada State Athletic Commission and a foremost proponent of fighter safety) are instructive.

"There's so much we don't know about the brain," Dr. Goodman states. "A concussion can clear up within a few days or it can take eighteen months. Sometimes the brain never fully heals. A fighter can be more susceptible to further damage after a concussion or not. We do know that he won't be less susceptible. Someone who has suffered a concussion should not place himself at risk of another concussion until those post-concussive symptoms have completely resolved. Seven months have passed since Tim's last fight, which has given him a chance to recuperate. That's a good start. All that can be done now is to ensure that he gets the best pre-fight testing possible."

Because of the concussions that he has suffered in the past, Bradley will go into the ring against Marquez with an aura of vulnerability about him. And there's another factor that might put him at further risk.

If any sport should test thoroughly for PEDs, it's boxing. The sweet science isn't about running faster or hitting a baseball further. Fighters are getting hit in the head hard by men trained in the art of hurting.

For years, Juan Manuel Marquez has honored the craft of prizefighting. But there's now a cloud hanging over him in the suspicion that, sometime before his fourth fight against Manny Pacquiao, Marquez stopped drinking his own urine in preparing for fights and began using performance-enhancing drugs under the supervision of conditioning coach Angel "Memo" Heredia.

That suspicion was echoed by Jim Lampley in a December 15, 2012, telecast of *The Fight Game* in which Lampley referenced "the presence in Juan Manuel Marquez's training camp of a man who once admitted under oath to being a world-renowned purveyor of performance enhancing drugs" and "Marquez's stunning appearance on the scale [prior to Pacquiao-Marquez IV] followed by his stunning power in the fight."

Whatever the cause, Marquez (who several years ago looked old in the ring), appears with the assistance of Heredia to have found the fountain of youth that Ponce De Leon sought. With that in mind, Bradley wanted the most comprehensive drug-testing possible for Bradley-Marquez.

"Before I ever talked money with Top Rank," Tim says, "we talked drug testing. It's in my contract. I don't know what Marquez's contract says, but my contract says that VADA testing was supposed to be done on both fighters starting July 13. And someone reneged."

Marquez refused to be tested by VADA (the Voluntary Anti-Doping Association), which is widely regarded as having the most comprehensive PED testing program currently available in boxing.

Initially, Bradley threatened to pull out of the fight.

"I'm not going to fight someone at this level and risk everything if they cheated," Tim told Boxing Scene Radio. "My contract says VADA [with the possible addition of USADA, the U.S. Anti-Doping Agency] is going to be involved, so that's what I'm going with. If they are not going to be involved, there is not going to be a fight."

Then Top Rank announced that it had resolved the issue by agreeing to underwrite the cost of a special PED-testing program for Bradley-Marquez to be overseen by the Nevada State Athletic Commission.

"The whole State of Nevada is getting involved and doing their drug testing," Bradley responded. "That's fine. But in my contract, it still says VADA-USADA is going to be involved. At the end of the day, if that doesn't happen, it's a breach of my contract."

Eventually, Bradley backed down on the issue. He has submitted to VADA testing for himself at his own expense as a demonstration of his integrity. Both Marquez and Bradley will be tested by the Nevada State Athletic Commission. But Marquez will not be tested by VADA or USADA.

It's unclear what tests will be conducted by the NSAC, which drugs will be tested for, how a positive test will be reported, when, and to whom.

Moreover, the NSAC tests began so late (August 6) that a fighter, hypothetically, would have been able to use PEDs and then, after benefiting from their use, stop "juicing" in time to get the illegal drugs out of his system before testing began.

One might also note that the NSAC is using a collection agency whose first-stated mission is paternity testing (see www.jagexam.com). One assumes that neither Marquez nor Bradley is pregnant.

"Let's put it this way," Bradley says. "Marquez and I are two of the guys at the top in boxing. When you're at the top, you want the best of everything. But Marquez isn't willing to do the best drug testing in the world, which is VADA. No offense to the Nevada commission; but their drug testing is like an old cell phone. VADA is like the iPhone 5. I said, 'If you don't trust VADA, we'll do VADA and USADA and Nevada. I'll test with anyone you want as long as VADA is included. Even Pacquiao and Rios are doing VADA now. But it didn't happen. Even the timing on what they're doing is wrong. I wanted testing three months out. As soon as we got into July, testing should have started. But Marquez kept stalling, stalling, buying time until we got into August."

"If you're clean," Bradley continues, "why not do the best testing out there? It doesn't add up unless you're playing games. Marquez is getting his way on testing, but I don't think it's the right way. It looks shady to me. PEDs are a real problem now in boxing. More fighters have to step up and insist that testing be done right or we're all going to pay a price."

Meanwhile, let it be noted that Bradley is (1) articulate, (2) good-looking, (3) inherently likable, (4) charismatic, and (5) a good family man. He (6) treats people with respect, (7) is undefeated, (8) is willing to go in tough, and (9) gives everything he has in training and during each fight. He's also (10) an American. He has never been criminally convicted for beating up a woman (think Floyd Mayweather). Nor has he been seen on YouTube giving oral sex to a stripper or sitting on a toilet in Popeye's in the manner of Adrien Broner.

Bradley-Marquez matters because Bradley matters.

Tim Bradley joined boxing's elite with his victory over Juan Manuel Marquez

Tim Bradley: R-E-S-P-E-C-T

On October 12, 2013, Tim Bradley fought Juan Manuel Marquez at the Thomas & Mack Center in Las Vegas. The belts were irrelevant. Most fight fans had no idea which sanctioning body strap (WBO welterweight) was on the line. This was a bout between two elite fighters, period. And it was particularly significant for Bradley.

"Beating Marquez will make me one of the top pound-for-pound fighters in the world," Tim said days before the fight. "I don't do this just to make money. The money is important, but I want to fight the best to be the best. That's what motivates me. After I beat Marquez, there's no way that people will be able to deny me what I'm due."

Bradley stands just under 5-feet-6-inches tall and wears size twelve shoes. "Big heart too, baby," he's quick to note. He's a volume puncher without knockout power (unbeaten but with only 12 knockouts in his pro career). Roy Jones calls him "a 147-pound Evander Holyfield without the punch."

Like most fighters, Bradley dreams big dreams. But he pushes himself harder than most to accomplish them.

"I can be stubborn at times," Tim says. "I never doubt myself. Doubt me; tell me I can't do something. I love it. I admire people who push themselves beyond what anyone thinks they can do. Diana Nyad; sixty-four years old, swimming in the ocean with sharks, jellyfish; keeps swimming for more than fifty hours. That's me. I'll go into the devil's mouth, dive into the deepest part of the ocean, do whatever I have to do to win."

Bradley knew that he'd have a hard road to travel against Marquez.

Mexican pride has taken a beating in the boxing ring lately. Earlier this year, Canelo Alvarez was whitewashed by Floyd Mayweather; Julio Cesar Chavez Jr embarrassed himself against Brian Vera; Alfredo Angulo quit against Erislandy Lara; and Rafael Marquez was stopped by Efrain Esquivias. In 2012, Erik Morales lost twice to Danny Garcia; Jorge Arce was demolished by Nonito Donaire; and Chavez Jr lost eleven of twelve rounds against Sergio Martinez. Prior to that, Antonio Margarito was bludgeoned by Shane Mosley and Manny Pacquiao and out-finessed by Miguel Cotto. Marco Antonio Barrera disappeared from the spotlight after being terminated by Amir Khan four years ago. ·

That left Marquez, whose most recent outing was a one-punch high-light-reel knockout of Pacquiao last December.

"I've seen every one of his fights," Bradley said during a media conference call in early October. "I've always been a fan of Marquez. I always thought he was a great fighter and I still think he's a great fighter. He's one of the best counterpunchers in the game. People struggle when they fight him. He never ducked anybody. He has been in there with Mayweather. He fought Pacquiao four times. There's nothing he hasn't seen. Marquez isn't easy for anyone."

Two issues were troubling to Tim's fans where Bradley-Marquez was concerned. The first was PED testing.

In other sports, the great athletes are getting younger. In boxing, they're getting older. Age thirty-five used to be washed up and over-the-hill in the sweet science. Marquez is forty and as formidable as he has ever been. Indeed, it recent years, Juan Manuel seems to have gotten bigger, faster, and stronger. Sort of like Barry Bonds.

Bradley is an awesome physical specimen. "I've got the six-pack, the back-pack, and the ninja turtle shell," Tim says. But he's within three pounds of the weight that he turned pro at nine years ago. And the fact that he has made a commitment to VADA testing (all of his VADA tests came back negative prior to Bradley-Marquez) entitles him the presumption that he's clean.

Marquez, by contrast, has elevated through six weight divisions during the course of his career. And after joining forces with conditioning coach Angel "Memo" Heredia (who previously admitted under oath to being a purveyor of performance-enhancing drugs), Juan Manuel has come into the ring with a significantly more muscular physique and added punching power.

Marquez refused to submit to VADA testing prior to fighting Bradley.

Also, in Bradley's most recent fight—a narrow decision win over Ruslan Provodnikov on March 16—he was seriously concussed and suffered from slurred speech and dizziness for ten weeks afterward.

Most fighters don't talk about their vulnerabilities. Bradley does. In fact, he talked more openly about his concussion and its after-effects than any active fighter in recent memory.

"One of the reasons I've been so open about this," Tim explained several days before Bradley-Marquez, "is so other fighters will get the help they need when they've been concussed. Every fighter knows that, when he enters the ring, he might not come out the same. But a lot of times, there are things you can do to get better. Testing, therapy. And you've got to do them."

Marquez was a 6-to-5 betting favorite. Bradley dismissed those numbers, saying, "The odds are about the last punch in Marquez's last fight. And then you look at my last fight, when I was concussed. But I was trying to prove something against Provodnikov that I shouldn't have tried to prove. And Pacquiao was beating Marquez until he got sloppy-overconfident. I'm fine now, Everything is back to normal. I am not worried about getting punched or can I take a punch."

Still, many of those who predicted a Bradley victory over Marquez did so with a caveat: "If Tim is okay."

Both fighters made the 147-pound limit with room to spare. Bradley weighed in at 146 pounds; Marquez at 144-1/2. An announced crowd of 13,011 was on-hand when the main event began.

It's hard to outbox Marquez. But for much of the night, Bradley did it.

"Concentration will be very important in this fight," Tim had said earlier in the week. "Never taking a second off physically or mentally, but especially mentally."

Bradley stayed true to that creed, making adjustments throughout the night in a tactical fight fought at a high skill level with neither man able to establish control.

"The game plan was to move and keep moving," Tim said afterward. "I felt his power in the first round. He caught me with an uppercut that hurt . . . My speed and footwork were the key. I got in a rhythm early . . . You have to be careful when you fight him. He's really dangerous when he backs up. You follow him in and BOOM . . . He knocked Pacquiao out with that big right hand. I knew he'd be going for that . . . I had a good tight defense. I was blocking a lot of his shots and making him miss . . . He changed gears in the second half of the fight, kept making adjustments, started closing the gap. After a while, he started timing my jab and I said to myself, 'It's time to do something else' . . . A lot of times when we had big exchanges, I wanted to fight with him. But he was throwing heavy shots and I told myself, 'Stay disciplined; stay smart' . . . Marquez is a smart smart fighter and very dangerous."

It was a hard fight to score. According to CompuBox, neither fighter outlanded the other by more than six punches in any round. In six of the twelve rounds, the differential was two punches or less. There were only five rounds in which the judges were in agreement.

Glenn Feldman scored the bout 115-113 for Marquez. But he was overruled by Robert Hoyle (115-113) and Patricia Morse Jarman (116-112), each of whom gave the nod to Bradley.

Marquez and Nacho Beristain (his trainer) were notably ungracious at the post-fight press conference.

"The judges did it again," Juan Manuel said, alluding to his previous losses by decision to Pacquiao in Sin City. "To win in Las Vegas, I need to knock my opponent out."

"Bradley is a good fighter and he's also very lucky," Beristain added. "He's the only undefeated fighter with two losses [the other "loss" being Tim's controversial decision victory over Pacquiao in 2012]."

But in truth, there's no judging controversy here. Bradley-Marquez was a close competitive fight that could have gone either way. Two of the three judges thought that Bradley won. It's as simple as that.

One might also note that Juan Manuel's face was bruised and swollen after the fight, particularly around his left eye, while Bradley was largely unmarked.

How good is Bradley?

Tim doesn't talk constantly about the "0" on his record. But it's there. After decisioning Marquez, he has a 31-and-0 record. In addition to beating Juan Manuel, he has victories over Manny Pacquiao, Devon Alexander, Lamont Peterson, Junior Witter, Ruslan Provodnikov, Luis Abregu, Joel Casamayor, and Nate Campbell to his credit,

Floyd Mayweather, at the same age, had a 36-and-0 record with wins over Genero Hernandez, Diego Corrales, Jose Luis Castillo, Arturo Gatti, Zab Judah, Carlos Baldomir, Angel Manfredy, and Jesus Chavez.

"Fighting Mayweather is a huge goal for me," Bradley says. "I'm not Manny Pacquiao. I'm not Juan Manuel Marquez. I'm not Floyd Mayweather. But you can put my name in the conversation. I'm Tim Bradley and I know how to fight. If you think you can beat me, come on and try."

Tim Bradley has arrived. Enjoy the show.

As 2013 drew to a close, Gennady Golovkin gave fans a reason to feel optimistic about the future of boxing.

Is GGG P4P?

Times Square in New York City is often referred to as "the crossroads of the world." On November 2, 2013, the crossroads moved nine blocks south to Madison Square Garden where Brooklyn and Kazakhstan converged for the middleweight title fight between Curtis Stevens and Gennady Gennadyevich Golovkin.

Golovkin was born in Kazakhstan in 1982. He won a World Amateur Boxing Championship in 2003 and a silver medal at the Athens Olympics a year later. The most reliable accounting of his amateur record is 345 wins against 5 losses. He has never been knocked down as an amateur or professional and is undefeated in 28 pro fights with 25 knockouts. He currently holds the WBA and IBO titles.

Outside the ring, Golovkin smiles a lot and has a gentle demeanor. On the street, he could pass for a computer geek. His first language is Russian, but he speaks fluent Kazakh and some German. In interviews with the American media, he sometimes waits for a question to be translated into Russian but answers in English.

Too many fighters want to live like rock stars when they reach the top. Golovkin's life is focused on boxing, not partying or other distractions. His wife and four-year-old son live in Germany.

"I see them between my fights," Gennady says. "I am lonely sometimes without them because I train in California. But my work is here. I like California. California is perfect for me and, I hope, someday for my family. Life for me is good now. I am happy."

Golovkin doesn't look like a world-class fighter, but he fights like one. His trainer, Abel Sanchez (who Gennady calls "coach") likens his pupil's relentless attack to that of Julio Cesar Chavez in his prime.

"Gennady is a joy to work with," Sanchez says. "His mentality is about improving every day. My biggest problem is, I can't get complacent. I have to make sure that I don't become a fan."

Golovkin in the ring is like a threshing machine cutting through a wheat field. Or a tank that's firing live ammunition. Choose your metaphor. He's exciting to watch, methodically destroys opponents, and has the highest knockout percentage of any current beltholder in boxing.

"I can throw ten punches very fast," Gennady says, mimicking shoe shining. "Br-r-r-r-r-r-r-r . . . But why throw ten punches when you can knock a man out with two?"

Some fighters keep the "0" on their record by avoiding other top fighters. To date, Golovkin hasn't turned down a single opponent. He has always been willing to fight the best available opposition. But other fighters with belts and fighters who are in line to fight one of the other middleweight beltholders have distanced themselves from Gennady.

Also, Golovkin is under the promotional umbrella of K2 promotions. And while K2 managing director Tom Loeffler has worked hard to advance Gennady's career, one can make the argument that Vitali and Wladimir Klitschko could and should be more supportive. Indeed, in the "About Us" section on the K2 website, Golovkin is listed after Johnathon Banks and Ola Afolabi.

Golovkin introduced himself to the American public with a fifth-round knockout of Grzezorz Proksa on HBO in September 2012. Knockouts of Gabriel Rosado and Matthew Macklin followed. The network then slated a November 2 date for Gennady and needed an opponent. Curtis Stevens stepped into the void.

Stevens, age twenty-eight, has lived his entire life in Brooklyn. He turned pro in 2004 and came into the fight against Golovkin with a 25-and-3 record. Most his bouts were at light-heavyweight. He was undefeated with three first-round knockouts in four fights after going down to 160 pounds.

There was a modest amount of trash talk prior to Golovkin-Stevens; most of it from Curtis, who called Golovkin "an overrated hype job" and promised to "knock him the fuck out."

That earned a rejoinder from Gennady, who observed, "Dangerous atmosphere, different style. I am sportsman. He has big mouth."

"Gennady doesn't get angry," Abel Sanchez noted. "He gets focused." Then Sanchez said of Stevens, "He's going to get destroyed. He doesn't belong in the ring with Triple-G. You've seen what Gennady has done so far. He can do that to anybody."

That led Curtis to respond, "Abel saying I'm gonna get knocked out in three rounds; Abel saying I'm gonna get knocked out in six. Abel is stupid."

Meanwhile, in a calmer moment, Stevens told writer Tom Gerbasi, "This is something that I dreamed about since I was eight years old and stepped in the ring for the first time. And to be here and to have it in my grasp, it's amazing. I think about it every night. Some nights, there's anxiety from thinking about it too much and I don't get good. So in my mind, I'm saying, 'You've just got to grab it. You're either gonna give it up or go in there and take it right out of his hands.' Come November 2nd, I'm gonna be great."

Golovkin was a heavy favorite. Stevens is a puncher. But Gennady, who was coming into the fight riding a wave of fourteen consecutive knockouts, is a bigger puncher. Also, Golovkin had proven himself to be the more technically proficient fighter of the two. And while no one has ever questioned Curtis's courage, his chin was suspect.

Legendary cornerman Al Gavin once opined, "If you're making a list of all the attributes a fighter needs, start with a chin. If you don't have a chin, forget about being a fighter."

Golovkin's chin is the stuff of legends.

Still, Stevens was coming to win. And during fight week, he projected a calm confidence.

"Golovkin is a fighter," Curtis acknowledged of his opponent. "He might not look like one outside the ring, but I know he's good. With his knockout ratio and my knockout ratio, the way it's supposed to go is, it won't go twelve rounds. But I'm ready to go twelve if I have to. And he's not used to fighting someone who hits as hard as me. All he's fought is blown-up junior-middleweights. Now he's fighting a bigger man who's coming down in weight. People are saying he's the best middleweight in the world. After I beat him, what does that make me?"

★   ★   ★

Golovkin arrived at his dressing room on the second floor of The Theater at Madison Square Garden on fight night at 8:05 PM. His brother (Max Golovkin) and two other team members were with him.

The room was small, roughly twelve feet square with cream-colored cinderblock walls and a speckled-gray tile floor. A large blue-and-gold Kazakhstani flag hung from the wall above a rectangular plastic table. Seven folding metal chairs with black cushions and television cables taped to the floor made the space seem smaller than it was.

Gennady began doing stretching exercises. At 8:20 PM, Abel Sanchez entered. The trainer had three fighters on the undercard including heavyweight Mike Perez who would be in HBO's first televised fight of the evening. Sanchez would move back and forth between dressing rooms for much of the night.

Other members of Team Golovkin came and went. Gennady checked his cell phone for text messages. Music at a low decibel level sounded in the background; an eclectic mix ranging from a woman's soft voice over a gentle rock beat to gangsta rap.

There was little conversation. Almost always, Gennady was on his feet, pacing, stretching. At one point, he sat down and massaged his own fingers, hands, and wrists. At nine o'clock, he took a milk chocolate Hershey bar out of his gym bag and peeled off the wrapper.

"Is that for energy?" a state athletic commission inspector asked.

"No. I'm hungry, and it tastes good."

All fighters are aware of the stakes involved when they fight; financially and in terms of their physical well-being. But in the hours before a fight, they process it in different ways. At a time when many fighters' nerves are gyrating on the edge, Golovkin seemed calm and emotionally self-sufficient, almost serene.

Referee Harvey Dock came in and gave the fighter his pre-fight instructions.

"The three-knockdown rule is waived . . . The Unified Rules of Boxing are in effect . . . If your mouthpiece comes out, keep fighting until I call a lull in the action. You have two mouthpieces, correct?"

"Three," Sanchez answered.

The referee left.

Abel wrapped Gennady's hands.

There was more moving and stretching. But the stretching was becoming more vigorous. Golovkin lay down on a towel and contorted his body into positions that most people would find troubling. Then he rose, took a jar of Vaseline, and greased down his own face.

Sanchez gloved Gennady up. Max massaged his brother's legs, back, and shoulders.

Golovkin's eyes hardened. A transformation had begun. The gentle smile was gone. Now he was stomping around the room, growling, flexing his muscles.

Round one of Mike Perez vs. Magomed Abdusalamov came into view on a small television monitor. Sanchez had opted to remain with Golovkin. Ben Lira was the head man in Perez's corner.

Gennady hit the pads with Abel for thirty seconds. Each punch was thrown with technical precision and thudding power. Then he paced and stretched some more before hitting the pads for another thirty seconds. Finally, he slapped himself on the temple with closed gloves. Left, right, left, right. More than a tap.

He was ready.

Sanchez applied more Vaseline to Golovkin's face.

Perez vs. Abdusalamov dragged on.

"What round is it?" Abel asked

"Six."

Twenty minutes lay ahead before Gennady would leave for the ring. He paced, shadow-boxed, and paced some more.

Sanchez gave him a sip of water.

Perez-Abdusalamov ended with Perez winning a unanimous decision. No one knew it at the time. But hours later, Abdusalamov would be in a coma in critical condition after emergency surgery to relieve bleeding and swelling in his brain.

Golovkin sat on a chair in a corner of the dressing room and bowed his head in concentration.

"It was for focus," Gennady said later. "This is a serious business. I understand my situation. It was for concentration in the fight. To concentrate on speed, power, and distance. To concentrate on what I must do to win for myself and my family."

★ ★ ★

A casual observer who saw Golovkin and Stevens at the opening bell and knew nothing about either man might have thought that Gennady was a sacrificial lamb. Curtis was shorter but more visibly muscled with a menacing glare and heavily tattooed torso and arms. He can beat a lot of middleweights, but Golovkin isn't one of them.

Gennady began by working off of, and controlling the fight with, his jab. Curtis cranked up left hooks from time to time but couldn't connect solidly. With thirty seconds left in round two, Golovkin fired a short compact textbook left hook that landed flush on Stevens's jaw and deposited him on the canvas.

Curtis struggled to his feet, dazed, and survived till the bell. Thereafter, he tried valiantly to work his way back into the fight. There was no quit in him. Late in round four, he flurried off the ropes and landed some good shots. Midway through round five, he scored with a solid hook and right hand up top followed by a hook to the body. But Gennady took the punches well and was soon stalking his man again.

It was the kind of fight that keeps fans on the edge of their seats. Both fighters were throwing bombs and both fighters were dangerous. It seemed as though—BOOM—at any moment, something might happen. But most of the "booms" were coming from Golovkin.

Gennady showed once again that he's a complete fighter. His footwork is such that he all but glides around the ring. He's always looking to attack and do damage. He's relentless but not reckless and cuts off the ring well. His jab, straight right, hook to the head and body, and uppercut are all potent. Every punch in his arsenal has the potential to debilitate an opponent.

Stevens started round six aggressively. Then Gennady unloaded on him. Boxing demands courage of fighters, and Curtis showed it. But from that point on, Golovkin-Stevens was a one-sided display of brutal artistry.

"Compassion," Jimmy Cannon wrote decades ago, "is a defect in a fighter."

A minute and fifteen seconds into round eight, Golovkin landed two thudding hooks to the body that hurt Stevens. Curtis backed into the ropes, and Gennady battered him around the ring with sledgehammer blows to the head and body. Stevens refused to submit, but his cause was helpless.

At the end of the round, referee Harvey Dock followed Curtis to his corner and told trainer Andre Rozier, "That's it."

"Okay," Rozier responded.

The final "punch-stats" showed Golovkin outlanding Stevens by a 293-to-97 margin. And a lot of those 293 blows were particularly damaging.

So . . . How good is Golovkin?

The more people get to know him, the more they like him as a person and as a fighter. Most athletes, not just fighters, need some meanness in them to be great. Despite Gennady's gracious persona, the assumption is that there's some meanness there.

Golovkin has yet to fight an elite opponent. One can also make the argument that he doesn't move his head enough and gets hit more than he should. And as Sugar Ray Leonard noted years ago, "There's a way to beat everybody." Invincible warriors only exist in movies and novels.

That said; Gennady is a special fighter. One hopes that, in the not-too-distant future, he'll be in the ring with an inquisitor who has the ability to test him in a megafight commensurate with his talents.

Golovkin's best weight is 160 pounds.

"Right now," he says, "I am a middleweight. But this is boxing. For money, I would go to super-middleweight to fight Andre Ward. For money, I would fight Mayweather at 154 pounds."

But would Ward or Mayweather fight him?

Mayweather? No way.

Ward? We'll find out.

That, of course, leaves the lineal middleweight champion of the world, Sergio Martinez.

There are numerous similarities between Martinez and Golovkin. Both are dedicated professionals and superb fighters who honor boxing with their presence. They're gracious men who treat people with dignity and respect. Even their personal mannerisms are similar. The ready smile; the nod of the head when in agreement with something that someone else has said. One can imagine that, under different circumstances, they'd be friends.

Martinez is on the downside of his career. In recent years, his body has betrayed him. Sergio has earned the right to be called "middleweight champion of the world." But right now, Golovkin is the world's best middleweight and it's unlikely that Martinez will fight him.

Meanwhile, Golovkin is a reminder of the nobility of boxing at its best as contrasted with the duplicity and pettiness of so many of the people who connive and preen around fighters. That nobility was on display in the ring at Madison Square Garden on November 2. And it was evident again in Gennady's dressing room an hour after the fight when the door opened and a short stocky man wearing a navy-blue hoodie and dark glasses to obscure the bruises around his eyes walked in.

Curtis Stevens extended his hand to Gennady Golovkin and spoke his next words with sincerity and respect: "Champ; you're a great fighter. Congratulations."

In and out of the ring, boxing is a hurting sport.

Malignaggi-Judah
and the Subway Ride Home

Paulie Malignaggi would have been more appreciated in an era other than his own. He wouldn't have beaten Henry Armstrong. But in an earlier era, he would have been honored by media and fans alike for the pride he takes in his craft, his willingness to go in tough, and doing the best he can with the tools he has.

I met Paulie several days before his pro debut in 2001. Since then, I've written tens of thousands of words about him. I've been in his dressing room in the hours before and after some of his biggest fights, wins and losses. We've talked and shared meals together away from the spotlight. I've always gotten an honest answer from him. There's no slipping and sliding and avoiding the truth. We don't agree on everything, but we listen to each other's opinions with respect.

Several years ago, I wrote an article about Paulie meeting my then-eighty-five-year-old mother. The article quoted her as saying, "Paulie is adorable; a little cocky, but as cute as can be."

The next time I saw Paulie, he told me, "Tell your mother I think she's cute but a little cocky."

On December 7, 2013, Paulie fought Zab Judah at Barclays Center in a bout that was marketed as a fight to determine which man deserved to be called "the King of Brooklyn."

Judah has been fighting professionally for half of his thirty-six years. Like Paulie, he has shown a willingness to go in tough en route to a 42-and-8 record with 29 knockouts. Paulie entered the bout with a 32-and-4 ledger.

Zab's history suggests that he's more effective and dangerous in the ring when he feels that his opponent can't punch. Paulie has two knockouts in the past ten years.

I didn't want to be at ringside for the fight.

I had no quarrel with Golden Boy Promotions for making the bout. It was a competitive match-up between two world-class boxers. I had no quarrel with either fighter. They treated each other with respect during the build-up to the fight rather than acting like confrontational idiots (which we see too often in boxing these days). I just didn't want to be there.

In 2006, Paulie fought a prime Miguel Cotto at Madison Square Garden on the eve of the Puerto Rican Day Parade. He was cut from a head butt in round one, knocked down in round two, suffered a fractured orbital bone, and still won four or five rounds depending on which judge's scorecard one looked at. Paulie has permanent nerve damage in his face as a consequence of that fight.

I've been at ringside when two fighters were beaten to death. I won't be overly dramatic and say that I had similar concerns for Paulie. I don't go to fights expecting a tragedy. But I knew that Zab would hit Paulie in the head with the same certainty that I know a person who walks in the rain without an umbrella will get wet.

"Blood is not the scary part of boxing," Hamilton Nolan has written. "Blood is an annoyance, a split lip, a split eyebrow, lending a vivid bit of color to a fight, but taking little physical toll. Far more scary is the thought of the unseen damage being inflicted inside one's skull. Blood is cleaned up with a rag and some Vaseline and adrenaline and stitches and a scar. Brain damage is not cleaned up, ever."

"How old is Paulie?" my mother asked me the day before Malignaggi-Judah.

"Thirty-three."

"He's smart; he's good-looking. Isn't there something else he can do to support himself?"

"He's a commentator for Showtime and Fox Sports 1,"

"Then why is he risking his health like this?"

"For the money," I answered.

"And what if he ends up like Muhammad?"

Professional obligation brought me to Barclays Center on December 7. The annual meeting of the Boxing Writers Association of America and the kick-off press conference for the January 30, 2014, fight between Victor Ortiz and Luis Collazo were scheduled on-site for late that afternoon.

Ortiz's last fight was a loss to Josesito Lopez that ended with Victor choosing not to continue after nine rounds despite the fact that he was ahead on all three of the judges' scorecards. That choice seemed eminently sensible given the fact that his jaw was dangerously and painfully broken.

At Barclays, several members of the media asked Victor if that made him a quitter. He handled the questions with grace. When the press conference ended, I went over and told him, "Anyone who says you're a quitter, fuck 'em. You were the only one with enough sense to stop the fight that night."

Paulie arrived at Barclays Center at 6:45 PM. I wished him well. Then I left the arena and went home.

It's a half-hour subway ride from Barclays to my apartment on the upper west side of Manhattan. The train was half-empty when I got on. I took a seat and was alone with my thoughts.

I met Paulie at the final pre-fight press conference for a July 7, 2001, HBO doubleheader. Paulie was slated for the non-televised undercard. He sat through the entire press conference and hardly said a word. He seemed shy.

The subway moved through Brooklyn toward Manhattan. A drunk got on at the Borough Hall stop, bottle in hand. When the train reached Clark Street, he started spewing racial epithets. Other passengers moved away from him toward safer areas of the car.

"Very few people in the media challenge you face-to-face," Paulie told me once. "Most of them do it from behind the protection of their computer screen. It used to bother me when people in the media wrote negative things about me. I'd say to myself, 'These guys are experts. Some of them have been writing about boxing since before I was born.' Then I realized that a lot of the writers and even some of the network TV guys don't know shit about boxing. All they do is criticize and shoot their mouth off."

The drunk got off the subway at 14th Street.

"A fighter can always talk himself into fighting one more fight," Paulie told me over pizza several days after his split-decision loss to Adrien Broner this past June. "I'm not stupid. I know that."

I arrived home at 7:30 PM and turned on the television. Auburn was leading Missouri 59-42 in the closing minutes of the SEC championship game.

At eight o'clock, I switched to Showtime. There would be seven fights on Showtime and HBO over the next five hours. Sakio Bika vs. Anthony Dirrell was up first; then Erislandy Lara vs. Austin Trout. At 9:45 PM, with Lara and Trout in snooze mode, I turned to HBO. Matthew Macklin looked like a fighter who has seen better days in outpointing an overmatched Lamar Russ. James Kirkland vs. Glenn Tapia was a great fight for two rounds and a brutal beatdown for four more. After Kirkland disposed of Tapia, I switched back to Showtime.

Malignaggi and Judah were in the ring.

The fight began.

Paulie controlled round one with his jab. He was the faster busier fighter. In round two, he tripped over Zab's leg while spinning away from a punch and his glove touched the canvas. Referee Mike Ortega mistakenly called it a knockdown. That error registered as a three-point swing on the judges' scorecards (from a 10-9 round in Malignaggi's favor to 10-8 for Judah).

In round three, an accidental clash of heads opened a small cut above Zab's left eye and a more serious cut on Paulie's left eyelid. Now I could envision the fight being stopped because of the cut, going to the judges' scorecards after an abbreviated number of rounds, and Judah coming out on top because of the incorrectly called knockdown.

But Paulie controlled the rest of the bout, working behind a stiff jab, straight right hands, and occasional hooks to the body. He put everything on the line and initiated the action throughout, while Zab fought with the purpose of a man in a sparring session.

Paulie was faster than Zab had thought he'd be. He outlanded Judah by a 220-to-121 margin. And another factor was at work. Zab has a good "boxing IQ." It's an edge that he brings into most of his fights. This was one of the few times that he'd been in the ring with a fighter who could outthink him.

Malignaggi gave Judah a boxing lesson. One could argue that he won every minute of every round. Certainly, he showed that he can still fight competitively at the elite level. The judges rewarded him with a unanimous decision.

I'd prefer it if Paulie stopped boxing and concentrated on his commentating career. But I know that he won't. Now that he has beaten Judah, another big-money fight awaits him. It will be big-money because the opponent, whoever it is, will be a top-echelon fighter skilled at inflicting pain and physical damage.

I'm glad that Paulie won on December 7. And I'm at peace with myself for choosing to not be at ringside to see it. Television cosmetizes the violence of boxing. And watching at home, one doesn't feel the blood lust of the crowd.

For many people in boxing, Adrien Broner versus Marcos Maidana defined "schadenfreude."

A Note on Adrien Broner
vs. Marcos Maidana

Gordon Marino has written, "You can't get into boxing without an ego. But you have to keep an eye on it."

Self-control has never been twenty-four-year-old Adrien Broner's strong point. Much of his life has been a study in excess.

This summer, Broner sat for a video that showed him half-dressed while purportedly defecating into a toilet in Popeye's and then wiping himself with United States currency. The video was posted on YouTube with the title "Adrien Broner takes a shit in Popeye's." Four days later, it had close to fifty-thousand hits. The posted comments were not favorable: "Lowlife scum ... What a fucking idiot ... Retarded ... Cancer to society ... Disgusting asshole ... His kids are doomed ... Keep up the good role modeling, Broner."

Undeterred, Broner posted a sex video in October. This one showed him having intercourse with two women and no condom. On-line comments from viewers indicated that Adrien has more of a future as a fighter than as an X-rated film star.

The circus is fun. But sooner or later, most kids outgrow it. There's a line between being your own man and doing things that are self-destructive.

"I was young once too," trainer Don Turner (who has worked with fighters like Larry Holmes and Evander Holyfield) says. "That's no excuse. Everybody was young once. You make choices."

Earlier this year, Broner was being hyped as "the future of boxing." And he'd come to believe the hype that was accompanying his ring success.

"Boxing is hit and don't get hit," Adrien told the media. "It's not, hit, okay, now you hit me. I don't care if I come out my whole career without getting touched. I'm not in it to go in there and let someone beat up my face. That's not how you do it. Stay slick."

But Broner was hitting and not getting hit against lesser fighters. And as Don Turner notes, "You have to be on the receiving end sometimes to know what this game is about. You have to be tested, so you learn how to pass the tests."

Then, in June, Broner challenged Paulie Malignaggi for the WBA 147-pound title and emerged with a split-decision triumph. But the bloom was off the rose. Malignaggi exposed some of Adrien's limitations: the wide spread of his feet that inhibits movement, his vulnerability to attack, the inability to transition seamlessly from defense to offense.

But Paulie didn't have the firepower to finish the job. Adrien upped his record to 27-and-0. That set the stage for the December 14, 2013, match-up between Broner and Marcos Maidana.

Maidana is a volume puncher who gives one hundred percent every time out. His record was 34 and 3 with 30 knockouts. But he'd barely survived a shopworn Erik Morales and struggled in victories over Victor Ortiz, Jesus Soto-Karrass, and Josesito Lopez. His idea of defense is sitting on his stool between rounds.

Broner was a 3-to-1 betting favorite. However, in most of Adrien's previous fights, in addition to his skills, he'd enjoyed a size and strength advantage over his opponent. That wouldn't be the case against Maidana.

Thus, Jimmy Tobin wrote, "Maidana has the power to put Broner's lights out and the toughness to take second and third helpings of whatever leather he is served. Maidana also boasts the puncher's resolve, that stubborn arrogance that concedes damage to reciprocate it exponentially. He will not temper his aggression simply because he is punished for it and he has crawled off the deck to practically invade two other prematurely anointed superstars [Victor Ortiz and Amir Khan]. He is never an easy out."

Boxer versus puncher is one type of classic match-up in boxing. Another is fighters who quit (e.g., Mike Tyson and Andrew Golota) versus fighters who don't (e.g., Arturo Gatti). Everyone knew that Maidana wouldn't quit. The jury was out on Broner.

It was an exciting action fight.

Adrien views himself as a master craftsman. Marcos is a simple brick maker, but he makes a lot of bricks and was in attack mode all night.

Ten seconds into round one, Maidana tagged Broner with a left hook that propelled Adrien into the ropes. Suddenly Broner had a bad case of the wobbles, and Marcos was all over him. Later in the round, Adrien spun out of the corner and thrust his hips against Maidana's rear end, simulating anal intercourse. Showtime (the network that prides itself on the miniseries *Masters of Sex*) chose not to replay the moment in the sixty seconds between rounds. More significantly, referee Laurence Cole let it pass, which was a prelude to his losing control of the fight. Broner led with his head, raked his gloves across Maidana's face, and used his forearms and elbows as offensive weapons throughout the bout. Marcos went low often enough that it was also an issue.

Meanwhile, twenty-five seconds into round two, Broner was floored by a left hook, the first time in his pro career that he'd been on the canvas. He rose on shaky legs and took a pounding.

That set the pattern for bout. Maidana was relentless, winging punches from all angles with both hands and keeping the pressure on all night. Broner is accustomed to pot-shotting opponents who can't hurt him. Here, Maidana exchanged because he wanted to, and Broner traded blows when he had no choice. Often, Adrien held on like he and Marcos were slow dancing.

Simon and Garfunkel sang, "I'd rather be a hammer than a nail,"

Broner was the nail to Maidana's hammer. Marcos beat the confidence out of him and exposed one more flaw: Adrien's inability to make adjustments during a fight.

Midway through round eight, a left hook up top put Broner on the canvas for the second time. He rose; Maidana came in for the kill; Adrien clinched; and Marcos head butted him. Broner thought about the situation for a moment. Then, looking very much like a drowning man who has just seen a life preserver bobbing in the water, he gave a thespian performance that saw him sink to the canvas (carefully, so as to break his fall with his knee) and roll over onto his back while simulating agony. When finally he rose, he refused to answer the referee's query, "Are you all right?" Cole then deducted a point from Maidana for the head butt and, to Adrien's apparent dismay, decreed that the fight should continue. Lost in the drama was the fact that Broner's performance had earned him an additional seventy seconds to recover from the knockdown.

When it was over, Broner had been outlanded by a 269-to-149 margin that included a 231-to-122 disadvantage in power punches. Adrien's best punch of the night was a cheap-shot left hook to the jaw after the bell ending round eleven. The judges scored the fight 117-109, 116-109, and 115-110 for Maidana.

In some ways, the most disheartening aspect of the evening for Broner was how limited his ring skills (as opposed to his natural physical gifts) looked. Maidana has limitations. Last year, Devon Alexander won ten out of ten rounds against him and made Marcos look like an amateur by simply moving and jabbing.

Broner left the ring immediately after the bout and refused to give an on-air interview. Later that evening, he told Barry Tompkins, "I'm still young, fly, and flashy. We're going to live tomorrow like we won the fight. I'm still going to party. My first party is going to be on Tuesday in Cincinnati. If you want me in your club. I will be in your club. We're gonna have fun."

That's part of the problem.

Broner is a good fighter with potential that has not yet been fully developed. The question is, where does he go from here? Does he work to get better, or does he go back to fighting less challenging opponents and leave it at that?

Non-Combatants

Michael Buffer is quick to say, "I've had a lot of good luck." He's also very good at what he does. Better than anyone ever.

Michael Buffer: "Let's Get Ready to Rumble"

WBO welterweight champion Tim Bradley and Juan Manuel Marquez had just fought twelve hard competitive rounds at the Thomas & Mack Center in Las Vegas. Both fighters were on edge. The outcome of their fight was very much in doubt. The winner would be ranked among the top pound-for-pound boxers in the world.

As the fighters paced nervously in their respective corners, a tall slender man wearing a tuxedo stood in the center of the ring, microphone in hand. He was meticulously groomed with perfectly manicured nails, every hair in place.

The man knew something that virtually no one else knew. The judges' scores were on a piece of paper in his hand. Millions of people around the world were waiting for his next words. He was riding on the back of a tiger that he had tamed.

Michael Buffer is boxing royalty, better known than all but a handful of fighters in the world today. He's the gold standard by which ring announcers are judged, having taken his craft to a whole new level. There's Buffer, and then there's everyone else. Before the start of each main event that he works, the crowd waits with anticipation as he builds to his trademark phrase.

Five words: "LET'S GET R-R-R-READY TO RUMBL-L-L-E . . ."

Those words have become part of the pageantry of boxing. It's hard to think of a parallel in any other sport. Buffer's presence confers legitimacy on a fight, making it seem bigger and more important than would otherwise be the case. No other ring announcer in history has done that.

Buffer was born in Philadelphia on November 2, 1944. He began ring announcing in the early 1980s to supplement his income as a model, having worked previously as what he calls "the worst car salesman in the world." He first used the phrase "Let's get ready to rumble" in 1984.

"I used to watch films of old fights on television," Buffer recalls. "In the old days, the ring announcer would introduce the important fighters who were in attendance. But that had evolved to announcing five commissioners, three sanctioning-body officials, two ring doctors. And it chilled the crowd. I wanted something comparable to 'Gentlemen, start your engines' at the Indy 500; a hook that would excite people and put some energy back into the arena. I tried 'man your battle stations' and 'batten down the hatches' and 'fasten your seat belts,' but none of them worked. Then I remembered Muhammad Ali saying, 'Float like a butterfly, sting like a bee; rumble, young man, rumble.' And when Sal Marchiano was the blow-by-blow commentator for ESPN, he'd say, 'We're ready to rumble.' So I took those ideas and fine-tuned them."

By 1990, ring announcing was a full-time job for Buffer. Today, he's a brand unto himself. Retail sales of products that have licensed the phrase "Let's get ready to rumble" are near the $500,000,000 mark.

Buffer estimates that, during the last three decades, he has been the ring announcer for roughly one thousand fight cards. He has plied his trade in North America, South America, Europe, Africa, Asia, and Oceania.

Does he hope that someday he'll be called upon for a fight card in Antarctica?

"No," he answers after a moment's thought. "I wouldn't trust the runway."

At present, he works thirty to thirty-five cards a year. By the time fight night arrives, most buyers have purchased their tickets. No one calls anyone at the last minute, saying, "You have to watch the pay-per-view tonight. Michael Buffer is going to be on." But he's good branding and he adds to the entertainment value of the show.

Buffer also works a dozen conventions and other special events annually, including past appearances at the World Series, Stanley Cup Finals, NBA Championships, and NFL playoff games.

"I enjoy the spotlight," he acknowledges. "It's exciting to be there. I was very nervous the first year. Then I got used to it. I'm comfortable and confident now, so I enjoy it more. Where boxing is concerned, I root for a good fight more often than I root for one fighter or the other. There are times when I like both fighters and feel bad for the one who loses more than I'm happy for the winner. But it's all very gratifying to me. There's a legacy there."

What makes Buffer so good?

Ring announcing is an underappreciated art. It looks easy. It isn't.

Buffer is consistent and technically sound. He has a smooth silky baritone voice that's a gift of nature. And the camera is kind to him.

In the old days, ring announcers shouted to the crowd through megaphones.

"I'm lucky," Michael notes. "I came along at the right time. Television and today's technology capture what I do and the overall scene very well. I'm a performer. And I'm never fully satisfied. After each fight, I go home and watch the introductions and my announcement of the winner to see what I could have done better."

"And most important," Buffer continues, "I always remember that the fighters are the stars. The cheers are for them, not me. I never forget that."

Buffer appreciates the irony of his celebrity status and also the financial rewards that have flowed from his success. He and his wife live comfortably in suburban Los Angeles in a fashionable home on one-and-a-half acres of land with the mandatory swimming pool, waterfall, and fountains. They have five dogs, three of which are rescue animals. The garage holds a Mercedes S500 sedan, Mercedes SL55AMG, Cadillac Escalade, and Bentley convertible.

Friends appreciate Buffer for his loyalty and also his sense of humor. He has a talent for celebrity impersonations, the best of which is Johnny Mathis singing the national anthem while the public address system keeps cutting out.

He also has strong feelings on a wide range of issues from politics to the less savory aspects of boxing, but keeps them private.

"I'm troubled by the way things have changed for middle-class families in America," Michael says. "It bothers me that people are finding it harder and harder to get by, and too many parents are no longer optimistic that their children will enjoy a better life than they've had. But I've made a conscious decision to not speak out publicly on political issues because I think that my job requires neutrality."

There are hassles that come with being Michael Buffer. The evolution from occasional fans with Kodak Instamatics to everyone having a cell phone and wanting a photo equates to nuisance.

"And they give their cell phone to someone who doesn't know how to use it to take the picture," Buffer notes. "So they have to take the picture three times."

"I get recognized in New York more than anyplace else," he continues. "Or at least, New Yorkers are more open about. They'll come up to me and say, 'Hey, you're Michael Buffer.' About three times a week, someone asks me to say 'Let's get ready to rumble' for them. If I'm in New York or a fight environment like a casino, it's more like a half-dozen times a day."

How does Buffer respond to the request?

"Sometimes, I'll do it for children. Or if it's red carpet stuff like the season premiere of *Boardwalk Empire*, I'll do it for a video camera. Usually, I ask, 'Do you have your checkbook with you?' and that ends it."

But not always.

"Every now and then, there's some tension. One time, I was having dinner in a restaurant. A guy came over, leaned on the table, and said, 'Hey; you're that guy, right?' Then it became, 'Say it for me! Say it for me!' And he's getting more and more aggravated because I'm not going start shouting 'Let's get ready to rumble' in a restaurant. After a while, his girlfriend came over. She's telling him, 'Come on, Vinny. He's eating dinner. Leave him alone.' So then Vinnie gets pissed off at her."

In many respects, Buffer has lived a charmed life. But there was one period of crisis.

"In February 2008," Michael recounts, "I took the dogs out for a walk. I got home, looked in the mirror—I can't walk by a mirror without looking; that's the image; right? And I noticed a tiny protrusion on the side of my neck. I went to the doctor and it was misdiagnosed as a blockage in my salivary gland. 'Suck on some lemon sours and it should go away.' But it didn't go away. So I went to another doctor. He dropped a light in and said to me, 'I want you to get an MRI today.'"

"They did the MRI," Buffer continues. "They took a biopsy. I was in New York to emcee a press conference for the Klitschko-Ibragimov fight at Madison Square Garden when I got the call. Cancer. I emceed the press conference, worked the fight [on February 23, 2008], and went home to face the unknown. This was my life, And even if I survived the cancer. I didn't know if I'd be able to talk again. It wasn't just my livelihood. I didn't know if I'd be able to talk. We're talking about my throat. I was a smoker when I was young. I told myself, 'Well, if this is it, I'm going to do one of those antismoking commercials before I go. It's not the way I want people to remember me, but maybe it will save some lives.'"

On March 15, 2008, Buffer worked the second fight between Manny Pacquiao and Juan Manuel Marquez at Mandalay Bay in Las Vegas. Then he went under the knife.

"I got the right doctor. There was one surgery. They opened me up and took out three small tumors—squamous cells—that were attached to my tonsils along with some lymph nodes and part of my tonsils."

One month later, Michael was in the ring for Joe Calzaghe vs. Bernard Hopkins. In 2013, he passed the five-year mark, which means that, from now on, he'll undergo a PET-scan once a year instead of once every six months.

"I don't know how long I'll keep announcing," Buffer says. "I definitely don't want to stay too long at the dance. A while back, I thought that sixty-five would be it. But I'll be sixty-nine in November. Things are still going well and I still enjoy it."

On the afternoon of October 12, 2013, Buffer was at the Wynn Hotel and Casino in Las Vegas readying for Bradley vs. Marquez. Earlier in the day, he'd gotten bout sheets for the evening's pay-per-view fights from the HBO production team. After reviewing the sheets, he went online to Boxrec.com to supplement the information. Next, he wrote the data necessary to introduce to each fight in red and blue ink on four-by-six-inch cards.

Then he dressed.

Buffer owns eight tuxedos. Once, he had twenty. The tuxedos share closet space in his home with two dozen suits, a half-dozen sport jackets, and fifty dress shirts.

He doesn't own many shoes.

"I have a wide foot, so it's hard to find a good fit."

And he loves watches. Buffer's collection of fifteen high-end time-pieces includes Rolex, Cartier, and the like

In his hotel room at the Wynn, Buffer re-ironed his shirt.

"I'm fussy about my shirts. I usually wash and iron them myself. If I do send them to the cleaner, I touch them up when they come back. Sometimes, when I buy a new shirt, the collar button doesn't line up perfectly. I'll take it off and sew it back on myself so it fits just right."

Then there's the matter of Buffer's ties.

"People who are righthanded tie their knot so that the bottom of the knot goes to the right," he explains. "If you're lefthanded, it's the reverse. But a lefthanded knot has a better fit because it's snug against the top button so you get a cleaner look. I'm righthanded, but I reverse my hands and tie my knot lefthanded. It takes forever, but it looks better when I'm done."

Michael smiles.

"I know. I sound like Tony Randall playing Felix Ungar in *The Odd Couple.*"

Buffer also cuts his own hair with a three-way mirror once every three weeks and trims his sideburns weekly.

"I grew a moustache when I was twenty-three years old and in the Army," he admits. "But it was so sparse that I had to fill it out with an eyebrow pencil."

At 4:30 PM, Buffer was standing at the Wynn's south valet station, waiting for his car and driver. Michael was close to trainer Emanuel Steward, who died of cancer in October 2012. Now, every time he works a fight, he pins a campaign-type button with Steward's image on it inside his tuxedo jacket over his heart. The button was in place.

The car was fifteen minutes late. A half-dozen fans stopped and asked for cell phone pictures.

Buffer's gold-and-diamond Tiffany cufflinks and tuxedo studs glittered in the sunlight, as did his rose-gold Rolex Presidential watch with diamond dial and diamond bezel. The diamonds were small, not gaudy. His style is elegance, not bling.

At 5:10 PM, Buffer arrived at the Thomas & Mack Center and made his way to his seat in the technical zone within arm's reach of the ring apron. The fights that he was scheduled to work on the card would begin at six o'clock.

Bill Brady (chairman of the Nevada State Athletic Commission) came over and asked if he could introduce Buffer to a friend that he and his wife had brought to the fight. Referees Robert Byrd (who would work the main event) and Tony Weeks approached to say hello. Four roundcard girls seated to Michael's left smiled enticingly at him.

At six o'clock, Buffer walked up the steps in the neutral corner nearest to him and entered the ring. During the course of the evening, he would make that journey eight times (before and after each of four fights).

The first three fights ended in knockouts, which meant there was little suspense in announcing the result.

Then it was time for the main event. Marquez entered the ring to the thunderous cheers of his supporters. Bradley followed, greeted by boos.

"I get anxious like a fan gets anxious before a fight," Buffer says. "It's anticipation. not nerves."

At 8:12 PM, Buffer took the microphone.

"Ladies and gentlemen. This is the moment we've all been waiting for."

There were the mandatory introductions of state athletic commission officials and sanctioning body personnel, the referee and judges.

"And now, the officials are ready. The fighters are ready. Ladies and gentlemen, are you ready? For the thousands in attendance and for the millions watching around the world; ladies and gentlemen, "LET'S GET R-R-R-READY TO RUMBL-L-L-L-E . . ."

The crowd roared.

Buffer introduced Marquez first, then Bradley.

The fight began. Michael watched intently throughout, commenting on the flow of the action.

"Bradley is boxing nicely . . . Now he's getting countered . . . Marquez is controlling the distance between them . . . Good shot by Marquez, but Bradley rolled with it . . . There's not much body-punching by either guy . . . The swelling around Marquez's eye is starting to cause him problems . . . Bradley is telegraphing his righthand every time he throws it."

It was a close fight between two highly skilled boxers. At the final bell, Buffer rose from his chair and entered the ring. Nevada State Athletic Commission executive director Keith Kizer handed him a sheet of paper with the judges' scores on it. Bradley had won a split decision.

Announcing a knockout is fairly straightforward. Decisions, particularly after a close fight, are another matter.

Buffer read the commission sheet carefully to himself and organized his thoughts. Whenever there's a split decision, the first two scores that he reads are one for each fighter. Then comes the deciding tally.

"I try to read the first two scores the same," he says. "Then, on number three, I give it a big pause. I knew there would be a bad reaction from the crowd on this one because it was a pro-Marquez crowd and the decision could have gone either way."

"Ladies and gentlemen; we go to the scorecards. Glenn Feldman scores the contest 115 to 113. He scores it for Marquez . . . Robert Hoyle scores it 115 to 113, and he has it for Bradley."

A pause for drama.

"Patricia Morse Jarman scores the contest 116 to 112 for the winner by split decision . . .

There was dead silence. Buffer was holding history in the palm of his hand.

"And still WBO welterweight champion of the wor-r-r-ld, from Palm Springs, California, Timothy 'Desert Stor-r-r-m' Bradle-e-e-e-y."

There was a post-fight press conference. Members of the boxing community would congregate and discuss the fight into the wee small hours of the morning. But Buffer was not among them.

Minutes after the fight ended and he'd announced the winner, he slipped out of the Thomas & Mack Center and returned to the Wynn. One could imagine Buffer as James Bond, walking into the casino and sitting down at a high-stakes baccarat game, every hair still in place. Beautiful women would stare. A casino host would bring him a martini; stirred, not shaken. Across the table, perhaps, Auric Goldfinger would be cheating.

But it was not to be. Buffer went directly to his room, ate a granola bar, drank some hot tea with honey, and went to sleep.

The public-at-large doesn't know Marc Payton. That's a shame.

Marc Payton: The Director

For three decades, Marc Payton has been one of the cornerstones of HBO Sports.

Payton directed his first boxing telecast for HBO on January 17, 1981 (Marvin Hagler vs. Fulgencio Obelmajias). Since then, he has personified the best of what viewers expect from the network.

Seth Abraham (the original architect of HBO's boxing program) states, "There are certain directors whose names are associated with greatness in a particular sport. Chet Forte with football; Frank Chirkanian with golf; Harry Coyle with baseball. That's how I think of Marc Payton and boxing. Marc has set the standard that people who direct boxing aspire to."

Payton plans to retire at the end of this year. This is a good time to explore the legacy that he'll leave behind.

Marc Payton was born in Kansas City on January 19, 1948. His father was an engineer for Phillips Petroleum. By the time Marc was twelve, the family had moved ten times. Then they settled in Borger, an oil town in the Texas panhandle.

Payton graduated from Borger High School as class salutatorian in 1966 and enrolled at the University of Texas. On August 1, 1966, his second day at college, he walked out of the building after an orientation session and heard a boom.

"There's shooting," someone told him. "Go back inside."

Marc returned to the building, went up to the second floor, and looked out a window. Four bodies were lying on the ground below. A former United States Marine named Charles Whitman had shot and killed his wife and mother that morning. Then he'd gone to the Tower at the University of Texas, climbed to the observation deck, and opened fire with multiple weapons on passers-by below. By the time Whitman was shot to death by an Austin police officer, he'd killed seventeen people and wounded thirty-two more.

During his senior year of college, Payton took a job at night operating the switchboard for the NBC affiliate in Austin. When he graduated in 1971, the station hired him as a studio cameraman. Then his boss moved to an ABC affiliate in Baton Rouge, and Marc went with him to direct public-service announcements and work on the evening news; his first taste of live television.

Growing up, Payton had been a self-described "sports junkie." To this day, he carries a heavy anchor around his neck. He has been a Houston Astros fan since the team came into existence in 1962 as the Colt .45s. And he'd always wanted to be involved with sports television. In 1973, he moved back to Texas to work for an independent television station in Houston that needed a director for commercials and local sports.

"There was another company in Houston at the time called Mobile Color," Marc recalls. "They furnished trucks and crews for local sports events. After I'd been in Houston a while, I applied for a job with Mobile Color. Someone else got it. I was heartbroken and left town to work for a CBS affiliate in Shreveport. Then, in 1975, I got a call from Mobile Color. They'd just signed a contract to provide video services and crew for events at the Summit [a multipurpose sports arena that was home to the Houston Rockets, Houston Aeros, and an arena football team]. They offered me a job as a technical director and I moved back to Houston. I was the guy who came with the truck when directors like Chet Forte, Sandy Grossman, Joe Aceti, Tony Verna, and Andy Sidaris came to town. I got to observe them and see how they handled things technically and also in terms of how they worked with their crews. Later on, I tried to incorporate some of the things they did well into my own work."

In 1979, Payton added ESPN to his résumé. The network was in its infancy, and he directed more slow-pitch softball than he might have liked. But over the next two decades, he worked his way into an ESPN director's chair for prime-time college football and Major League baseball.

Meanwhile, in 1980, he began working for HBO.

"Tim Braine was the executive producer," Marc recounts. "But it was Ross Greenburg who hired me. I came to New York with a contract to direct two weeks of *Inside the NFL*. After the first show, Ross came into the studio, said 'I just tore up your contract,' and hired me for the full twenty-six week season."

On January 17, 1981, Payton journeyed to Boston to direct his first fight. For the next three decades, he directed virtually all of HBO's boxing telecasts. In recent years, first Mike Sheehan and then Doug Getts have directed *Boxing After Dark*.

"I love boxing," Marc says. But ironically, he has attended only one fight live inside an arena; a *Boxing After Dark* event in Houston.

"I had great seats," Payton recalls. "But I missed being able to see the tight shots in the corner."

So . . . Marc Payton directs HBO's boxing telecasts. What does a director do?

In brief, the director is responsible for almost all of the visual images and background sounds from the arena that go on the air. The producer is responsible for the rest of the audio editorial content and also for selecting between-rounds video replays.

HBO has between nine and fifteen cameras in the arena depending on the magnitude of a given fight. Payton decides which images people will see on their television screens at home. That involves instructing multiple camera operators on split-second notice as to what to shoot and then selecting the best image at a particular moment from a wall of monitors in front of him.

"My job," Marc says, "is to make sure that the viewer at home has the best look possible at what's going on. That means the best picture at the right time without missing anything. I hope my telecasts are easy to watch, that we don't miss too much, and that they're not repetitive."

Directors must deal with cameras malfunctioning during a telecast. There's also the bizarre; everything from a riot at Madison Square Garden in the aftermath of Riddick Bowe vs. Andrew Golota to an idiot thrill-seeker known as "Fan-Man" parachuting into the ring during a heavyweight championship fight.

Payton is alert every moment. Things are happening live in front of him and there's no "erase" button.

Executive producer Rick Bernstein, who began working with Marc at HBO in 1980, notes, "On fight night, the director is the captain of the ship. If he guides the telecast in the wrong direction, we sink."

Or to use a different analogy, one might liken the executive producer of a sports telecast to the owner of a restaurant. The onsite producer is the restaurant manager. The director is the chef in the chaos of the kitchen. Without a good chef, the food is mediocre.

A director can't turn John Ruiz vs. Hasim Rahman into Marvin Hagler vs. Thomas Hearns. But he can make any fight a more entertaining viewing experience.

"There are two types of directors for televised sports," HBO blow-by-blow commentator Jim Lampley says. "Most directors follow the game pursuant to a well-established formula and choose their images accordingly. Cut-from-the-pattern directors can last in the business for thirty or forty years but they'll never be great. A handful of directors resist the formula. Every selection they make is an individual choice. If they choose badly, it's a disaster. But when those directors do their job well, they give viewers a much fuller picture of the event. These are the great directors. Marc Payton is a great director."

What makes a director great?

It starts with preparation.

When HBO is televising a fight from a new venue, Payton conducts an onsite survey several months in advance to learn what has to be done. He scouts for camera locations, cable runs, where lights need to be placed, and the like.

"Yankee Stadium [where Miguel Cotto vs. Yuri Foreman was contested] was tough because of the long cable runs and camera locations," Marc says. "We had to build huge camera towers for that one. Cowboys Stadium [where Manny Pacquiao fought twice] is so big that, no matter what we did, it was a bit impersonal. The MGM Grand and Mandalay Bay are easy. They're like well-oiled machines. And I love Madison Square Garden."

During fight week, Payton arrives on Wednesday for pay-per-view events and on Thursday for *World Championship Boxing* telecasts. The rest of the week features meetings, meetings, and more meetings. He prepares and rehearses his crew again and again for fight night and, if one is scheduled, for the pay-per-view weigh-in show.

"I like things organized," Payton says. "I like order. I like to uncomplicate things and keep them simple."

"Marc reminds me of Dwight Eisenhower preparing for D-Day," Seth Abraham observes. "Eisenhower thought of everything and every contingency that might happen and then went over it again and again so he was prepared for any eventuality. That's Marc."

Then there's raw talent.

The selection of images is an art form. Payton has an excellent eye for choosing and framing shots. Telecasts mix tightly scripted segments with the unpredictable flow of a prizefight. Marc delivers the images that best capture the drama of the moment. He makes a fight feel big and, at the same time, sees intimate details that make a telecast special.

It was Payton who instructed the camera to come in close on the horrific cuts that Vitali Klitschko suffered against Lennox Lewis and left an image that's as indelibly scarred in the memory of viewers as Joe Theisman's broken ankle is for those who were watching *Monday Night Football* twenty-eight years ago.

Marty Corwin is director of television production for Top Rank and has interacted with Payton on numerous HBO telecasts where Top Rank had its own international feed.

"You can teach someone to be a director," Corwin says. "You can't teach someone to be a great director. What sets Marc apart is his wonderful ability to tell the story of a fight and everything that goes with it better than any director I've ever known. Any director can get the flow of the action right. Marc, through his camera selection, shows viewers the fighters' physical condition and state of mind. He's objective. He doesn't impose himself on the event or get locked into a predetermined storyline. He follows the story of the fight as it happens and lets things unfold without missing a bit of drama. He gives you a clean show every time."

Great symphony conductors have a sense of pacing. But they also know what their musicians are capable of doing and bring out the best in them. That leads to Payton's third great asset: his temperament.

The members of HBO's production team are effusive in praising Payton.

"Marc is completely reliable and honest . . . He's forceful when he has to be, but he never steps out of his lane and he's never unkind . . . He never complains . . . I've never seen Marc panic or lose his composure . . . He's loyal to everyone and engenders loyalty in return . . . It's wonderful when a director with his talent is also such a great guy."

Payton teaches by instruction and also by example. He never just goes through the motions. He enters rooms quietly and says hello to everyone. He's as happy hanging out with the crew as he is spending time with high-priced talent and corporate executives. He always makes new crew members feel welcome. And he doesn't just show up during fight week. He keeps in touch with his crew between telecasts.

When Marc talks—not just in the truck, but also in production meetings and planning sessions—people listen. Everyone on the team trusts him.

"Marc is the human glue that bonds the HBO production team together," Jim Lampley states. "He has a kind word for everyone and treats all people as equals. Equal with each other and equal with himself. It's not an affectation. It's how he is. It's never about Marc. His focus is always on what's presented to viewers and the crew that's helping deliver it to them. The crew doesn't feel that the telecast is his. He makes them feel that it's shared by all of them. He makes everyone around him better. And on top of everything else, he's a magnet for great cameramen, great engineers, people with creativity and talent. They all want to work with him."

"Marc taught me a lot," HBO boxing analyst Roy Jones says. "He helped me way beyond what it was his job to do."

As television technology has gotten more sophisticated over the years, Payton has mastered it at every turn. But he has never let the technology overwhelm the hardcore human drama of what's happening in the ring.

The nerve center of HBO's fight-night telecasts is an onsite production truck with equipment valued at eight to ten million dollars inside. Payton is joined in the truck on fight night by a crew that usually includes the executive producer (Rick Bernstein), a producer (Dave Harmon, Jon Crystal, or Tom Odelfelt), a technical director, two graphics operators, a clock operator, two ORAD coordinators (who provide virtual elements), and a technical manager. There's an audio booth and video-tape area in the back of the truck. A second unit used primarily for storage and small editing is nearby.

The truck has basic camera monitors, replay monitors, graphics monitors, and the like; close to thirty monitors in all. In some ways, it feels as though everyone has come together in quarters as tight as a submarine to play a giant video game.

Payton sits in the middle of the front row with a wall of monitors in front of him. Throughout the telecast, he scans the monitors and tells the technical director which images he wants viewers to see on their home screens. At the same time, he's communicating with the camera operators, telling them what to shoot. It's essential that he be aware of his crew's tendencies and everything that's going on around him.

In a way, Marc is like a racecar driver making split-second judgments at 150 miles per hour as he navigates through a crowded field. Or one might analogize him to a quarterback going through his reads before hitting the receiver who's his third or fourth option.

"People think that directing a boxing match might not be challenging," Rick Bernstein says. "You're not talking about twenty-two men on a football field or a baseball game where important action is taking place away from the ball. It's two fighters in a twenty-by-twenty-foot ring. But on premium cable, there are no commercials. We can be on the air for three hours or more without a break. We don't send things back to the studio for a halftime show. There are times when it feels like a runaway train."

In the truck, Payton is a reassuring presence; calm and collected but very much in control. Some directors impose their will by the decibel level of their commands. Marc is not a screamer, but everyone knows that he's in charge. Because of the culture that he has created, everyone is pulling in the same direction. There might be problems behind the scenes, but viewers watching at home don't know it. Everything is designed to make the telecast look seamless.

"Fight night can be crazy," former HBO commentator Larry Merchant says. "You never know what's going to happen. You might think you do, but you don't. It's live and it's instant, and you have to react in a hurry. You can go in with a script, but things don't always work out the way you think they will."

"In all the years I worked with Marc," Merchant continues, "things always seemed under control at his end. I never found myself asking, 'Why are we doing this?' or saying, "Uh oh. I'm talking about one thing and the camera is showing another.' He's a craftsman. He knows what he's doing. And on top of all that, he's one of the nicest people I've ever known. No one asks for Marc's autograph or to have their picture taken with him. But I probably should have a long time ago."

Ross Greenburg oversaw Payton's work at HBO for decades; first as a producer, then as executive producer, and finally as president of HBO Sports.

"Marc was a genius at the helm of a telecast," Greenburg says, summing up for everyone who has worked with Payton over the years. "He had an eye for a shot and was a cinematic storyteller. When Hearns succumbed to Hagler after those brutal seven minutes and fifty-two seconds, it was Marc who cut to the overhead camera and had it zoom into Hearns flat on his back. As Angelo Dundee was telling Ray Leonard, 'You're blowing it son, you're blowing it' between the twelfth and thirteenth rounds, it was Marc who cut to the corner hand-held and told his cameraman to zoom into Ray's swollen left eye as he readied to desperately launch himself at Hearns to knock him down in the thirteenth and out in the fourteenth. It was Marc who cut to the hand-held camera after Buster Douglas's uppercut and lefthand knocked down Tyson as Tyson reached in vain for his fallen mouthpiece. It was Marc who kept his cool and followed the story as 'Fan-Man' flew into the ring disrupting the Holyfield-Bowe fight. Marc covered the sport with all of its artistry and brutality rolled into one. More than all of that, he treated his staff with love and respect. He rarely raised his voice. But he demanded perfection and was determined to get the very best out of his cameramen, audio personnel, replay operators, and entire hand-picked crew. He stayed loyal to everyone on the staff, and his team followed him everywhere. He made every one of those men and women feel like their job was a part of recording boxing history. But he was the conductor. He called the shots. And like every great artist, his life's work will live for the ages."

Curiosities

This essay is a change of pace. It's about Frank Sinatra and a sweeter science than boxing. Sinatra and boxing are explored in the article that follows this one.

Frank Sinatra and His Music

Frank Sinatra sang with an attitude. At its best, his music radiated energy, vulnerability, and joy. He was gracious, charming, and generous when he wanted to be. Also coarse, bullying, and occasionally violent. His life was marked by acts of personal kindness and cruelty. He was a drinker and not always a good family man.

Sinatra's better angels were reflected in his music. He was a great singer and a great performer. His voice was instantly recognizable. Nobody else sang like Sinatra. During his career as an entertainer, he excelled onstage and in the recording studio, on the radio and television and in films.

Always, it came back to his music.

Sinatra sang within the framework of what had come before. He just did it better than anyone else. He could take a three-minute song and make it part of his listeners' lives.

Francis Albert Sinatra was born in Hoboken, New Jersey, on December 12, 1915. His parents were Italian immigrants who were familiar with ward politics. Antonino Sinatra rose to the rank of captain with the Hoboken Fire Department. Dolly Sinatra was convicted twice for performing illegal abortions. Frank, their only child, dropped out of high school after forty-seven days and worked at a series of menial jobs while trying to build a singing career.

When Sinatra began his climb in the 1930s, the emphasis in popular music was on big bands. The public knew who the bandleaders were: Tommy Dorsey, Benny Goodman, Glenn Miller, Artie Shaw. The singer was an add-on.

In June 1939, Sinatra signed a one-year contract at a salary of $75 a week to sing with the Harry James Band. Six months later, James released Sinatra from the contract so he could join Tommy Dorsey.

It was a time when song lyricists were America's poets and wonderful music was being written. Extraordinary sounds were flowing from the imagination of Cole Porter, Jerome Kern, Richard Rodgers, Oscar Hammerstein II, Lorenz Hart, Harold Arlen, Johnny Mercer, and Irving Berlin.

Sinatra was Italian-American and dark-complexioned. "Just a skinny kid with big ears," Dorsey called him. Hardly the All-American boy. The big bands lent him an aura of elegance.

And there was something about him.

"You could almost feel the excitement coming up out of the crowd when that kid stood up to sing," Dorsey reminisced years later.

Sinatra recorded several dozen songs with the Tommy Dorsey band. He had his first solo studio session in January 1942 and left Dorsey eight months later to go out on his own.

Before that time, there had been two transformative popular singers in America. Rudy Vallee emerged in the 1920s, capitalizing on the burgeoning medium of radio. A decade later, Bing Crosby had become the first massively popular "microphone" singer.

Sinatra, like Crosby, was a "microphone" singer. The new technology magnified even the softest sounds and captured nuances in singing that previously would have gone unheard. Sinatra later spoke to that advance, saying, "One thing that was tremendously important [to me] was learning the use of the microphone. Many singers never learned to use one. They never understood, and still don't, that a microphone is their instrument."

"To Sinatra," E. B. White wrote, "a microphone is as real as a girl waiting to be kissed."

On December 30, 1942, Sinatra opened at the Paramount Theatre in New York. Despite having left Dorsey, he was continuing to appear with big bands. Here, he was billed as an "extra added attraction," singing between a feature film and the Benny Goodman orchestra.

Popular music in the early 1940s was aimed primarily at an adult market. Indeed, teenagers weren't regarded as a separate market segment for much of anything. That was about to change.

Sinatra had begun his career singing to adults. Then teenage girls started showing up. For his engagement at the Paramount, the bobby-soxers gathered in full force. They swooned, they screamed.

"The booming frenzy," John Lahr later wrote, "was the start of the Sinatra era."

He had become America's first teen idol.

The mid-1940s were a heady time for Sinatra. In 1939, he and Harry James had recorded "All or Nothing at All." The record sold eight thousand copies. Rereleased in 1943, it topped the one-million mark in sales. Also in 1943, Sinatra signed a recording contract with Columbia. During the next few years, he starred in three films with Gene Kelly. His piercing blue eyes had captured the imagination of a generation. He was the voice of make-out music in America.

Then things soured.

In the late-1940s, the big bands dwindled in popularity and the musical standards that Sinatra sang were overrun by a wave of new songs.

Young men returned from war. Sinatra had risen to stardom while soldiers his age were fighting and dying overseas. The public had been told that he was exempt from military service because of a perforated eardrum. But there were rumors of bribery and reports that Sinatra had been classified 4-F because of psychiatric concerns.

New singers became popular.

And Sinatra was wearing his fame poorly. In 1939, he'd married his childhood sweetheart, Nancy Barbato. Now his profligate womanizing was well chronicled. There were whispers about violent outbursts and socializing with mob figures. His record sales declined. By the end of the decade, his career had stalled.

On November 7, 1951 (ten days after his divorce from Nancy became final), Sinatra married Ava Gardner. They separated less than two years later. Meanwhile, in 1952, Columbia terminated his record contract. No one at that time would have considered Sinatra a candidate to be known someday as "Chairman of the Board." From autumn 1951 through early 1954, he was absent from the *Billboard* chart of best-selling recording artists.

In 1952—begging, pleading, and using every resource at his command—Sinatra landed the role of Angelo Maggio in the film *From Here to Eternity*. The movie, released in 1953, won eight Academy Awards. Sinatra, who had been paid the meager sum of $8,000 to appear in the film, was honored as Best Supporting Actor.

It was a time when movies were central to American culture. Wilfrid Sheed later wrote, "It is quaint to think of our greatest singer being saved by a movie in which he doesn't sing."

Accepting the honor, Sinatra told the Academy of Motion Picture Arts and Sciences, "Uh . . . That's a very clever opening . . . Ladies and gentlemen, I'm deeply thrilled and very moved. And I really don't know what to say because this is a whole new kind of thing, you know, from song-and-dance-man type stuff. I'm terribly pleased. And if I start thanking everybody, I'll do a one-reeler up here, so I better not. I'd just like to say, however, that they're doing a lot of songs here tonight, but nobody asked me [to sing]."

From Here To Eternity put Sinatra back in the spotlight and was the fulcrum on which his career turned yet again.

Long-playing records had been introduced in 1948 and, by the early 1950s, were generating large amounts of revenue for record companies. LPs were an ideal format for Sinatra. They enabled him to create and sustain whatever mood he wanted.

In 1953, Sinatra signed a recording contract with Capitol and began to further reinvent himself. In the past, he'd worked in the studio with arranger Axel Stordahl and been a crooner singing as a vulnerable young man. Now, recording with Nelson Riddle, Gordon Jenkins, and Billy May, he reinvented himself as the epitome of elegance and cool.

Songs for Swinging Lovers, recorded with Riddle in October 1955 and January 1956, was the perfect representation of the new Sinatra. There were no layered recordings, no tracks over tracks. That would come later in the world of music. The album, with its overtones of swing-era jazz, was simple straightforward musical genius. Sinatra's voice blended perfectly with the orchestra. And what a voice it was.

Sinatra made his singing look effortless. It wasn't.

"The amazing thing about his technique," Stephen Holden noted, "was how barely noticeable it was. The beautifully formed notes, perfect diction, astonishing consistency of tone, and long flowing phrases seem so natural that they almost sound tossed off."

A listener never had to strain to make out the words of a lyric that Sinatra was singing. His voice had character. There was a bit of an edge in it when he wanted it there. Also vulnerability, joy, a whole range of emotions.

Sinatra created a mood and sense of intimacy when he sang. There was authenticity to his music. He sang as though each song meant something special to him; that whatever he was singing about, he had been there himself. Listeners felt that, when Sinatra was singing, he was flaunting his spirit and baring his soul.

Jonathan Schwartz referred to Sinatra's recordings as "a collection of short stories."

John Lahr opined, "Sinatra's best acting was not on film but in song."

"You use the lyrics of a song as a script, as a scene," Sinatra explained. "I always believed that the written word was first. The word dictates to you in a song."

With that philosophy as his guide, Sinatra deepened the meaning of the lyrics he sang. Virtually every lyricist who wrote a song wanted him to sing it. Nobody could work a song like Sinatra.

Sinatra live onstage was as great as Sinatra in the recording studio. He was a commanding presence, a showman without need of flashing lights, smoke machines, or other props. When Sinatra performed, the atmosphere was charged. He was magnetic. The audience couldn't take its collective eyes off him. His smile was dazzling. He owned the stage. Every woman within the sound of his voice thought that he was singing to her.

Sinatra could change the phrasing of a lyric from performance to performance and make it sound right every time. He always seemed confident and in total command.

"You've got to be on the ball from the minute you step out into that spotlight," he elaborated. "You've got to know exactly what you're doing every second on that stage. I think I get an audience involved, personally involved in a song, because I'm involved myself."

Walter Cronkite summed up, saying, "He could make any audience feel he was their kind of guy."

In 1960, Sinatra formed his own record company (Reprise Records) so that he would have total artistic control over his music. He knew which arrangers and musicians he wanted to work with and which songs he wanted to sing.

What he didn't want to sing—and couldn't sing well—was rock and roll.

In the 1950s and '60s, a tidal wave of new music washed over American culture. Sinatra railed against rock and roll from its advent. Unlike

Elvis Presley and the Beatles (who succeeded him as teen idols), Sinatra as a teen idol had "acted like an adult." Unlike the art of Presley and the Beatles, his music had represented the prevailing order and hadn't challenged the status quo.

Sinatra belittled Presley as "utterly lacking in talent" and labeled the Beatles "unfit to sing in public." While rock and roll was changing the culture, he sought to fortify it. In the preceding decades, Sinatra had moved from outsider to a symbol of the establishment. Now that he had it made, he hated the thought of a cultural shift that might threaten his entertainment primacy. Once he'd reached the top of the mountain, he didn't want rivals there.

"In a grown-up's world [the 1940's]," Walter Cronkite observed in 1965, "Sinatra was a teenager's idol. Today, in a teenager's world, he's a grown-up's idol."

From 1957 through 1966, Sinatra failed to record a top-ten hit in the youth-oriented "singles" market. But he was credited with twenty-seven top-ten albums on the more adult-friendly LP charts.

Meanwhile, as John Lahr observed, "As Sinatra's power grew over the years, he became a kind of law unto himself."

There were times when Sinatra was exceedingly generous with his time and money. He was a principled advocate for minority rights. But as Wilfrid Sheed wrote, "His hide seemed to thicken before our eyes. The women who once fainted over him were now likely to be called 'broads' or 'bimbos.' His companions of the night were no longer sweet Nancy or even sexy Ava, but a bunch of perennial bachelors and assorted roués on their second wind."

"The Rat Pack" (as the bachelors and roués were known) were entertainers and others who reveled in their ties to Sinatra and accepted his "my way or the highway" mentality.

Peter Lawford (an early member of the Rat Pack) was dropped after Sinatra took offense at what he felt was a snub by Lawford's brother-in-law (John F. Kennedy, the president of the United States). In his autobiography, Lawford later wrote of Sinatra, "Just because he punched a few defenseless girls, broke a few cameras of news photographers, instigated the roughing up of a couple of parking lot attendants who were guilty of the unpardonable faux pas that his car wasn't first in line, or by having one of his blindly loyal goons bury a six-inch glass ashtray in the head of a man sitting next to him in the Polo Lounge of the Beverly Hills Hotel whom he happened to overhear make a mildly derogatory remark about him; he's not all bad."

Sammy Davis Jr (another member of the Rat Pack) was temporarily banished after a giving an interview in which he said, "I love Frank. But there are many things he does that there's no excuse for. I don't care if you're the most talented man in the world. It does not give you the right to step on people and treat them rotten."

Sinatra's ties to organized crime figures were more problematic. Lauren Bacall (who was briefly engaged to the singer after the death of her husband, Humphrey Bogart) later recalled Sinatra's fascination with mobsters and acknowledged, "He was in awe of them. He thought they were fabulous. He always had one of those guys with him. Suddenly, you realize, 'Hey, wait a minute. This guy, I think, maybe has killed someone.'"

Yet through it all, any place that Sinatra went was "in." People from all walks of life wanted to be in his presence. They laughed at jokes they wouldn't have laughed at had they been told by anyone but Sinatra. He projected an aura of empowerment, a man who could do anything he wanted to do.

He was, in effect, a one-of-a-kind American godfather.

There was an ill-fated two-year marriage to Mia Farrow that began in 1966 when Sinatra was fifty and she was twenty-one.

He became breathtakingly wealthy from a variety of business interests.

Then, in 1971 at age fifty-five, Sinatra announced that he was retiring from show business. He knew that he could no longer perform at the level he once had.

Two years later, the retirement was over. Thereafter, Sinatra's outsized personality kept him in the public consciousness after he might otherwise have faded from view.

He was "Old Blue Eyes" . . . "The Chairman of the Board . . ."

There's a lasting image of the young Sinatra with his jacket off, casually holding it over his shoulder with one finger.

Sinatra performing in his sixties and seventies was impeccably dressed. It was all but impossible to imagine him with his jacket off. He looked as comfortable in a tuxedo as someone else might have looked wearing jeans. To many women, he was more attractive as he aged and his face filled out.

In 1976, Sinatra married for the fourth and final time. Barbara Blakeley Marx, a former showgirl and the ex-wife of Zeppo Marx, was his new bride.

Entertainers get old. They keep singing.

"There's a good chance that I should have gotten out by now," Sinatra said in 1988. "But I enjoy it."

His voice grew raspy. The high notes no longer floated in the air as they once had. The "skinny kid with big ears" got portly. When he traveled, quite a few hairpieces traveled with him.

But he still had charisma and there was a heat about him. He still sang with feeling. And he was pretty good until near the end, when dementia eroded what was left of his gifts.

Sinatra kept his fans as he and they grew older. When he died in 1998, he was mourned.

In evaluating Sinatra, there's his singing and, secondarily, everything else. In his early years, he made crooning a dramatic and sometimes erotic art. Through the ensuing decades, his music evolved but seldom strayed from a male view of the world and how love works.

The titles of Sinatra's albums reflect his music: *Songs for Swinging Lovers, A Swinging Affair, Come Fly with Me, Only the Lonely.* The songs he sang became part of the collective consciousness of generations: *You Make Me Feel So Young, In the Wee Small Hours of the Morning, I've Got the World on a String, A Foggy Day, Witchcraft, My Way, One for My Baby (and One More for the Road).*

He took songs and made them his own. That's common for an artist who's the first to record a particular song. But Sinatra could do it with songs that belonged initially to someone else. "New York, New York" was written for and first recorded by Liza Minnelli. It's Sinatra's song now and will be forever.

"It is a cliché of the Sinatra biography," John Rockwell wrote, "that his music ultimately excuses his life."

Wilfred Sheed elaborated on that theme, saying, "Through all the ficknesses of life, he has been heroically faithful to at least one thing— his art—and made it as great as it was in him to make it. After that, I'd say what he does in his spare time is pretty much his own business. Each time he clears his pipes for business, he pays all his debts to society."

Sinatra appears to have concurred with that view. "Whatever else has been said about me personally is unimportant," he proclaimed. "When I sing, I believe, I'm honest."

Shortly after Sinatra's death, Adam Gopnik wrote, "He made forty sound sexier than twenty, and sixty sound more swinging than thirty."

Even today, women in their eighties say, "It makes me feel so young when I hear him sing 'You Make Me Feel So Young.'"

Other singers will come and go. Some of them will be great. But Sinatra will always be Sinatra.

Frank Sinatra's father was a professional fighter. "Marty O'Brien's" son shared his love of boxing.

The Sinatras and Boxing

Frank Sinatra was a boxing fan.

At various times, he was involved in the business end of the sport, owning a piece of heavyweight Tami Mauriello and participating in the promotion of the 1947 bout between Jersey Joe Walcott and Joey Maxim. He was a regular at ringside for big fights and gave generously to Joe Louis when Louis fell on hard times.

Like much of America, Sinatra initially castigated Muhammad Ali and later embraced him. More notably, he was in the press section for the March 8, 1971 "Fight of the Century" between Ali and Joe Frazier.

John Condon (director of publicity for Madison Square Garden Boxing) later recalled, "All day long, the Garden was a madhouse. During the afternoon, I heard one of our security guys saying Frank Sinatra was going to be in the first row of the press section. I said, 'Joe'—that was the guy's name—I said, 'There's no way in the world Sinatra is going to be in the working press tonight. Get it out of your mind now and please don't embarrass him or me, because if he's there, he's going to get thrown out.'"

"That night," Condon continued, "the Garden was like a combination of New Year's Eve and the Easter Parade. I don't think there's ever been a night like it. It was one of those evenings where everybody who was anybody was there. I look in the press section and I see Sinatra. I'd just finished kicking out Dustin Hoffman and Diana Ross. So I went over to throw Sinatra out. And just as I got to him, one of the ABC cameramen said, 'He's got one of our tickets.' That meant I couldn't do anything about it. As long as he had a press ticket, he was entitled to be there."

Not only was Sinatra there, he had a camera. One of his photos was on the cover of the next issue of *Life* magazine.

Sinatra often postured as a tough guy, but he wasn't much of a fighter. In 1967, Carl Cohen (an executive vice president at the Sands Hotel and Casino in Las Vegas) removed the caps from two of Old Blue Eyes' front teeth with his fist when Sinatra became too abusive for Cohen's taste. In a less-adoring world, the singer might have become known as "Old Black-and-Blue Eyes."

The real fighter in Sinatra's family was his father.

Antonino Martino Sinatra was born in Sicily on May 4, 1894. He came to the United States in 1903 and apprenticed as a shoemaker before deciding to try his hand at boxing. Because of a prevailing prejudice against Italian-American fighters, he fought under the name Marty O'Brien.

"O'Brien's" first pro fight was a fifth-round knockout loss on January 6, 1911, at the hands of an 0-and-1 fighter named Bull Anderson at the Bedford Athletic Club in Brooklyn. Six weeks later, he was stopped in the third round by Hugh Ross.

After a five-month lay-off, Sinatra (a/k/a O'Brien) returned to the ring on July 5, 1911, to face Mickey Cashman, who was making his pro debut. One day later, a headline in the *New York Times* blared, "Knockout at Longacre: Mickey Cashman Puts Marty O'Brien Away In Forty-five Seconds."

The article read as follows: "The principal attraction last night at the Longacre Athletic Association furnished one of the quickest knockouts ever seen at the club, when Mickey Cashman of the Hamilton Athletic Club put Marty O'Brien of Hoboken away with a right hander on the jaw after forty-five seconds of fighting, which had the New Jersey lad on 'Queer Street' for fully fifteen minutes. The boys had only shaped up when O'Brien rushed his opponent to the ropes, putting over a straight jab to the face. Cashman rebounded and walloped his man with a right on the jaw, which put him down for the count of nine. They had barely got into action again when, once more, Cashman made a feint with his left and shot his right across with force enough to drop him and open a gash in O'Brien's mouth with the result that he bled profusely."

Nine months later, Sinatra was in the ring again, losing a decision to Mike Rosen at St. Nicholas Arena in New York. That brought his record to 0 and 4. There was another layoff, this one lasting twenty months. Then, in January 1914, Sinatra fought Young Sieger twice within the span of two weeks at Brown's Gym in New York. He was knocked out in the first of those bouts, but won the second on an eighth-round dis-qualification.

That disqualification was the first and last victory of Sinatra's ring career. On Valentines Day 1914, he eloped with Natalie Garaventa. On December 15, 1915, their only child, Francis Albert Sinatra, was born.

In 1920, needing money, "Marty O'Brien" returned to the ring after a six-year absence. He lost twice more and retired for good in 1921 with a record of 1 win against 7 losses with 5 KOs by.

Writing about Don Elbaum is like eating comfort food.

Don Elbaum and the Great American Heavyweight Box-Off

When one thinks of Don Elbaum, other famous Dons come to mind. Don Juan, for example. Now that Paul Newman is gone, Elbaum is the primary object of desire for a generation of older women. Word is that Sophia Loren is dying to meet him.

The preceding paragraph is false.

Elbaum also draws comparisons with Don Quixote, since he's perpetually tilting at windmills. Thus it was that I went to the kitchen for a grain of salt when the following press release arrived in my email inbox on January 9, 2013.

"The Great American Heavyweight Box-Off: Veteran promoter-matchmaker Don Elbaum will host a press conference Wednesday, January 16, at the world famous Gleason's Gym in Brooklyn to make a major announcement regarding the creation of The Great American Heavyweight Box-Off (TGAHBO). The tournament will launch in early 2013. Elbaum will reveal details of the tournament purse structure as well as projected dates, venues, and other pertinent information. The eight participating American heavyweights plus one reserve in case of injury will be announced and most will be in attendance. Food and beverages will be served."

The food and beverages were supplied by Rafael Torres of Baked in Brooklyn. The sandwiches and salads were very good. The chocolate chip cookies were exquisite.

As for The Great American Heavyweight Box-Off (TGAHBO), here goes.

Decades ago, Elbaum promoted a heavyweight from Syracuse named Greg Sorrentino, who compiled a 19-and-9 record with 2 knockouts and 6 KOs by before retiring in 1983. Elbaum says that Sorrentino is "as sharp as they come. He's like a razor blade," Don notes. "That's a new razor blade, not a used one."

Sorrentino has some money now and says, "America should be ashamed of itself for not having a heavyweight champ."

Elbaum concurs, proclaiming, "This tournament is a patriotic venture to put American heavyweights back in the spotlight. It's what boxing needs to be great again."

Back to Sorrentino: "Any fighter who fights for the championship is just one punch away from winning it. Whoever wins this tournament is going after the Klitschkos."

Elbaum and Sorrentino are co-promoting TGAHBO. The tournament (according to Don) is slated to launch in April with eight fighters and will be spread out over three dates. The first date will have four ten-round fights with the winner of each fight getting $25,000 and the loser $15,000. The winner of each semifinal bout will receive $50,000 and the loser $25,000. The final fight will be twelve rounds with $250,000 to the winner and $50,000 for the loser. The winner will be required to give $25,000 of his purse to a legitimate charity. Elbaum and Sorrentino have long-term promotional options on each of the participants.

Six of the eight tournament fighters were at Gleason's for the kick-off press conference. The final two entrants have yet to be chosen.

Who are the first six?

The cream of the crop—and it's heavy cream—is thirty-two-year-old Jason Estrada. Estrada is a chronically overweight 2004 US Olympian who has fought at weights ranging from 237 to 257 pounds. His record is 20 wins (with 6 KOs) and 4 losses (1 KO by). Elbaum says, "Jason is like a 250-pound Willie Pep. There's incredible talent there. He doesn't always put out in the ring, but he can fight when he wants to."

Devin Vargas, age thirty-one, is another 2004 US Olympian. Vargas has been knocked out in two of his last three fights and sports a record of 18 wins (with 7 KOs) and 2 losses (2 KOs by). "Devin is the only Mexican-Polish fighter in the world," Elbaum advises. "On a given night, he can beat anyone."

Joey Abell, also thirty-one, has had three fights in the past thirty months and been knocked out in two of them. His sole victory during that time was a fourth-round stoppage of a gentleman named Emerson Chasing Bear at Williston College in North Dakota. Mr. Bear has one victory in his last six fights. Abell's record stands at 28 wins (with 27 KOs) and 6 losses (4 KOs by). "Look at his knockout percentage," Elbaum instructs. "Except for Earnie Shavers, Joey is the hardest punching heavyweight I've ever seen."

Alonzo Butler, age thirty-three, is from Tennessee and hasn't won a fight in more than three years. Fighting mostly at home in the past, he has 28 wins (with 21 KOs) and 2 losses. "Alonzo is one of the best heavyweights in the world," Elbaum says. "He rededicated himself to boxing recently, and now everyone is afraid to fight him."

Emmanuel Nwodo, age thirty-eight, has fought three times in the past five years. In one of those fights, he was knocked out in the fourth round. In the other two, he beat forty-three-year-old Lenzie Morgan (Morgan's fifteenth loss in a row) and Michael Shanks (now on a thirteen-fight losing streak that includes eleven knockout losses). Nwodo's own record stands at 24 wins (with 20 KOs) and 5 losses (4 KOs by). Nwodo is from Nigeria. But Elbaum says that he now lives in Baltimore, which "makes him an American."

As the fighters gathered at Gleason's, the man Elbaum calls "the tournament dark horse" and "one of the most exciting prospects I've seen in my life" stood off to the side wearing blue jeans, work boots, and a gold T-shirt with "Let's Go Mountaineers" emblazoned across his chest.

Daniel Martz is twenty-two years old, 6-feet-7-inches tall, and weighs 257 pounds. He's a likable young man, who lives in Clarksburg, West Virginia, and works as a server at Applebee's. He enjoys "hanging out with my buddies and having a good time; eating pizza and stuff like that."

The trip to New York marked the first time that Martz had been on a plane.

"It was two planes, actually," he noted. "The first was a real small plane from Clarksburg to Washington. That plane was too small. It made me nervous. The plane from Washington to New York was kind of fun. Then I had my first cab ride in New York. I'm used to the small towns, and New York is a big crazy place. The cab ride made me more nervous than the plane. I haven't ridden the subway yet, but I've heard some interesting stories about it."

Martz's amateur career consisted of nine fights in two tough-man tournaments. He won all nine and turned pro last year. Since then, he has fought seven times, scoring seven wins with six knockouts.

"I love fighting," Martz says. "I love everything about it. I love getting paid. I love traveling. I've fought in places like Pennsylvania and Indiana. I used to want to play football, but it turned out I was better at fighting. I know I have to improve before I make it big. I have a local trainer. We're working on the technical stuff. It's coming together pretty quick. My goal is to be heavyweight champion of the world. Someone has to win it. It might as well be me."

A quick look at Martz on YouTube shows a fighter who's still learning the basics. For starters, he brings his jab back very slowly and very low, which leaves him very vulnerable to a righthand over the top.

"That doesn't worry me," Elbaum says. "Anyone who hits Daniel on the chin will break his hand. His jaw is like concrete."

What about the fact that Martz has never gone past four rounds?

"No problem," Elbaum answers. "I don't think there's a fighter in the world who can last five rounds with him."

Elbaum says he has offers "from all over the world, including China" to host the tournament. But since this is a patriotic venture, he'd prefer a site in America.

He's also looking for "a few more angles to dress up the show."

"It would be great if I could get Mick Jagger to sing the national anthem," he muses. "I know that's a long shot. And I'd love it if I could get Sharon Stone as a roundcard girl or the ring announcer. I think Sharon Stone is hot. I don't suppose you have a telephone number for her."

"No," this writer answers. "But maybe you could put a hyphen in the tournament acronym. That way, it would read, 'TGA-HBO'".

"Jesus! You're a genius. Why didn't I think of that?"

So . . . What can boxing fans realistically hope for from The Great American Heavyweight Box-Off?

"There's no Mike Tysons in the tournament," Elbaum admits.

There might not even be a Frans Botha. But if the tournament actually happens and offers evenly matched heavyweights in entertaining club fights, it could be fun.

I revisited Portobello's in July 2013 for the following article.

David Diamante Makes Pizza

Boxing fans know David Diamante as the ring announcer with the long dreadlocks and stentorian voice. He's also the in-arena voice for the NBA Brooklyn Nets.

Journeying through life, Diamante has worked as a fry cook, dishwasher, stock boy, and bike messenger. Closer to the arts, he has been a drummer in several punk rock bands, put in time as a bouncer, and emceed for Scores East (an upscale adult club in New York).

David also spent part of his working life making pizza.

"I started making pizza when I was thirteen," Diamante reminisced earlier this month. "There was a place in suburban Washington, DC, that I worked at after school and on weekends. I did it for a couple of years. And in the early nineties when I was living in San Francisco, I did it again. I haven't made pizza in close to twenty years. But it's like riding a bike. You pick up certain tricks and movements, and the muscle memory is good. I take a lot of pride in my pizza."

Diamante can talk the talk. That's evident from his work behind the microphone. The question was, could he walk the walk. To find out, nine people gathered with him at Portobello's pizzeria in lower Manhattan on a hot muggy afternoon this summer. Present were: Harold Lederman (HBO's unofficial culinary judge), Steve Farhood and Paulie Malignaggi (both of whom stood ready to commentate on the action, as they do so ably for Showtime), HBO producer Jon Crystal, writers Tom Gerbasi and Michael Woods, inspector George Ward of the New York State Athletic Commission (to make sure everything was on the up and up), Anthony Catanzaro (part owner of Portobello's), and yours truly.

Here, it should be noted that the HBO and Showtime personnel coexisted peacefully at the pizza party. If Top Rank and Golden Boy are ever in the mood for peace talks, Portobello's might be an ideal neutral site.

We toyed with the idea of scoring Diamante's pizza on a ten-point must system with the criteria being crust, sauce, cheese, toppings, aroma, appearance, and overall taste. But in the end, we decided to be less judgmental.

"When you eat my pizza," David assured us, "I think you'll all be pleasantly surprised."

There was a Greek Chorus of doubters.

"Are you going to wash your hands first?" Woods queried.

"Hopefully, nobody gets poisoned," Catanzaro offered. "It would be bad for our reputation, even if it isn't a Portobello's pizza that makes someone sick."

At 1:56 PM, Diamante washed his hands and tied his trademark dreadlocks above his head. At 2:03 PM, wearing a white apron, he was behind the counter, making pizza.

"You need good dough, good cheese, good sauce, and good toppings for good pizza," he explained. "And once you have the ingredients, you have to know what to do with them."

To supplement Catanzaro's dough, tomato sauce, and mozzarella, David had brought his own fresh garden basil, fresh garden oregano, fresh garlic, and freshly grated Parmesan cheese.

"Are you sure that's oregano and not marijuana?" Diamante was asked.

George Ward examined the ingredients and found them to be in conformity with New York law.

David sprinkled a mix of cornmeal and flour onto the pizza spatula so the pie, when ready to be cooked, would slide easily into the oven.

"I love all kinds of pizza as long as it's done right," he said, beginning a running commentary. "As far as the shape of the pie is concerned, I like making round. I'll leave the Sicilian to Anthony. That's his specialty."

"The temperature of the dough is important," Diamante added as he put a slab of dough on the marble counter and began kneading it. "This temperature is good. You can make the crust thick or thin. I like it thin. Let me get the bubbles out of it."

"This is a perfectionist," Catanzaro observed. "Look at the way he caresses the dough."

"I'm impressed," Farhood noted.

"I'm hungry," Harold announced. "It's two o'clock. I'm not used to eating lunch this late."

"I know," Anthony said in as soothing a way as possible. "But you can't eat raw pizza. You have to wait until it's cooked."

Diamante ladled tomato sauce onto the center of the pie and spread it outward in a circular motion toward the lip of the dough before mixing oregano and garlic into the sauce and adding cheese.

"He has a nice touch," Paulie offered.

"One key is getting the pie off the spatula into the oven," Diamante explained. "It's one of the trickiest parts of the game. If you're not careful, the pie will scrunch up or the ingredients will slide to the side."

At 2:10 PM, the pie went in the oven and David began making a second pizza; this one a "white" pie with pesto and no tomato sauce.

"This guy is serious," Catanzaro informed the gathering. "He knows what he's doing."

At 2:15, Diamante turned the first pie. "You have to rotate the pizza at least once while it's in the oven," he explained.

At 2:20, the second pie went in the oven and the first one came out. David put pizza #1 on a circular metal tray, sprinkled some Parmesan over the top, and added snippets of fresh basil.

"What finesse," Gerbasi said admiringly.

David cut the pie into eight identically sized slices.

"I was born to make pizza," he informed the gathering. "It's a passion for me."

Catanzaro had prepared one of his famed "Grandma's" Sicilian pies (mozzarella, tomato sauce, and pesto) as a supplement to Diamante's pizza. The proof of the pizza is in the eating. All three pies were very good.

The verdict is in. David Diamante is a true Renaissance man.

"I can't match the salary that Barclays is paying you to do the Nets games," Catanzaro told him when lunch was done. "But if things don't work out behind the microphone, you've got a job waiting for you at Portobello's."

There's a light side to boxing.

Fistic Nuggets

I have a photo of my mother with Muhammad Ali. It was taken in my apartment in 1989, when they met for the first time.

"You're so much bigger than I thought," my mother said when they came face to face.

"Did you call me a nigger?" Muhammad demanded.

"No! I said, 'bigger.'"

"She called me a nigger," Muhammad growled.

And he advanced menacingly toward my mother, slamming a closed fist into the palm of his hand until he was almost on top of her. Then he flashed that wonderful Muhammad Ali smile and reached out to embrace her. Howard Bingham (Ali's longtime friend and personal photographer) caught the moment on film.

Seventeen years later, I brought my mother to a Don King press conference at Madison Square Garden. They spoke briefly, and I recounted the occasion in an article entitled "My Eighty-Year-Old Mother Meets Don King." Since then, whenever I see Don, he asks, "How's your momma?"

Flash forward to March 9, 2013, at Barclays Center in Brooklyn. Tavoris Cloud (King's fighter) was defending his IBF belt against Bernard Hopkins. Don said that I could shadow him from the moment he entered the arena until the end of the night for an article I was writing. That included several hours in Cloud's dressing room and also sitting next to Don during the fight (he always sits front row center facing the primary television camera).

I wanted to thank Don for allowing me into his world. So I had the photo of my mother and Ali made into a greeting card and wrote a message of appreciation inside. At the beginning of the evening, I gave the card to Don. He opened it, looked at the photo, and exclaimed, "That's two of my favorite people!"

The Don King charm lives on.

And a footnote to the evening.

Arthur Mercante Jr refereed two fights on the Hopkins-Cloud undercard. While I was waiting for Don to arrive at Barclays, Mercante shared a memory with me.

"The day after my father passed away," Arthur reminisced, "the phone rang. I picked it up and a voice said, 'This is Don King.' I thought it was a crank call. I told him, 'Look; my father just died. I'm not in the mood for jokes.' And the person on the phone said, 'No; it's really me. I'll prove it to you.'"

Mercante smiled as he continued his tale.

"My father had a chinning bar in the doorway to the kitchen of our home. If any of us did something wrong, or sometimes if we just went into the kitchen to eat, he'd tell us, 'Do ten chins.' So the voice on the phone says, 'I came to your parent's home one time and my hair hit the chinning bar in the kitchen and your father told me I had to do ten chins.'"

"Okay," Arthur told the caller. "I believe it's you."

"Your father was one crazy white man," King added.

★   ★   ★

"The Greatest" has signed a lot of autographs; first as Cassius Clay and, for the past half-century, as Muhammad Ali. If one estimates that he signed fifty signatures a day for much of his adult life, that would equal almost a million signatures.

But one signature is particularly rare.

Ali (then Cassius Clay) defeated Sonny Liston to claim the heavyweight championship on February 25, 1964. Two days later, he told the media that he had accepted the teachings of the Nation of Islam. Then, on March 6, Nation of Islam leader Elijah Muhammad announced in a radio broadcast from Chicago, "This Clay name has no divine meaning. I hope he will accept being called by a better name. Muhammad Ali is what I will give him for as long as he believes in Allah and follows me."

Meanwhile, after beating Liston, Clay had journeyed to New York. On March 2, he and Malcolm X toured the United Nations and were photographed with various African delegates. While at the UN, Clay was asked numerous times for his autograph and signed "Cassius X Clay," incorporating the "X" as symbolic of his lost African heritage.

So . . . What is a "Cassius X Clay" signature worth?

Craig Hamilton is the foremost boxing memorabilia dealer in the United States.

"There's an insatiable demand for Muhammad Ali items," Hamilton says. "And the market is flooded with phony signatures, so the first issue you always have is authentication."

"Let's assume for the moment that an Ali signature is authenticated," Hamilton continues. "And we're talking now about a simple signature on a piece of paper. A vintage 'Muhammad Ali' signature—that is, an Ali signature from 1964 through mid-1967—is worth $500 to $750 dollars depending on its condition and how it looks. Non-vintage Ali signatures are common and generally sell for $100 to $200. Some of them, particularly the later ones, are hard to read and not particularly attractive. A vintage 'Cassius Clay' generally goes for between $1,500 and $2,000. Ali sometimes signed 'Cassius Clay' as a favor to fans when he got older, but those signatures have far less value."

And "Cassius X Clay"?

"They're rare," Hamilton acknowledges. "We know they're out there. But to be honest with you, I've never seen one. If you could authenticate it and place it within that brief time period and it's in good condition, my guess would be $3,000 to $3,500."

★ ★ ★

FROM AND ABOUT FIGHTERS

Micky Ward: "When you're fighting, you really don't want to hurt the other guy. But some guys, you wouldn't mind hurting a little bit."

Lou Savarese: "My dad didn't want me to fight. My two brothers and my sister were all college graduates. I was the baby, and he just did not want me to fight. Now I know what he went through. I come home and my kid's got a mosquito bite, and I'm freaking out."

George Foreman: "At a certain point in a man's life, he looks ridiculous running down a road."

★　★　★

With the baseball season fast approaching, it seems appropriate to reference what Top Rank's director of public relations Lee Samuels describes as his greatest moment in sports outside of boxing.

"I played second base for the Kurland's Drug Store team in the Pennsville [New Jersey] Little League," Samuels recalls. "We wore white jerseys with blue trim. Across the front, it said 'Kurland's.' I was very proud to wear that jersey. I couldn't hit or field well, but I loved being on the team."

"My father was a rough guy," Lee continues. "He wasn't a people person. He'd been in the Army for seven years and fought in World War II. When I was growing up, he watched wrestling on television every Friday night and loved it. We played catch occasionally, but that was about all. We never went to a ballgame together or anything like that. And he'd never come to any of my games."

"This time, I rode my bike to the game. And there he was, standing on the first-base line. In my first at bat, I hit the hardest ball I'd ever hit. It bounced over the fence in left field for a ground-rule double. That was it as far as moments of glory are concerned. To be honest, I don't think I ever hit a home run. A few years later, I got to high school and saw my first curve ball. I just stood there and said to myself, 'Oh, my God. This isn't going to work.' That's when I stopped playing baseball and started writing."

★　★　★

As boxing readies for the mega-fight between Floyd Mayweather and Canelo Alvarez, former HBO Sports president Seth Abraham reminisced recently about another big Las Vegas fight; the first encounter between Evander Holyfield and Riddick Bowe.

"It was at the Thomas and Mack Center," Abraham recalled. "I was there with Tim McCarver, who I'd gotten to know when he worked for

HBO on a baseball series called *Race for the Pennant*. We were sitting in the second row. One by one, the celebrities filed in around us. After a while, we were surrounded by Jack Nicholson, Bruce Willis, Kevin Costner, Arnold Schwarzenegger, Michael Keaton, and Sylvester Stallone. Tim was loving every minute of it, and I was having a wonderful time."

"Two women who must have been in their seventies were snapping photos of the celebrities," Abraham continued. "One of the women came over to me and said, 'I don't know who you and your friend are.'"

Seth readied to identify himself. But before he could, the woman added, "Would you mind getting out of your seats. You're ruining our photo."

Abraham and McCarver rose. Then, at Seth's suggestion, the women sat, albeit briefly, in the choice HBO seats while Seth snapped a photo of them surrounded by Hollywood royalty.

★   ★   ★

How does a person know that he or she has crossed the line between anonymity and celebrity status?

"There was a moment in the late 1980s," Michael Buffer recalls. "I was in Atlantic City. They were having a big baseball memorabilia show and Ted Williams was at some of the fights that were held that night. As you get older, you don't have the same hero worship you had when you were a kid but you still have passion. And Ted Williams was; what can I say? Ted Williams was Ted Williams. I went over to introduce myself, and he said, 'Hello, Mike. I see you on television all the time.' I was like, 'Omigod! Ted Williams knows my name.' That was special for me."

★   ★   ★

THINGS YOU'LL NEVER READ ON A BOXING WEBSITE

Our regular baby-sitter isn't available, so we've asked Roger Mayweather to take care of the kids tonight.

★   ★   ★

SOME THOUGHTS ON BOXING

At one point in the early 1980s, Mike Tyson, Teddy Atlas, Kevin Rooney, and Cus D'Amato all lived in the same house. That must have been an interesting house.

At boxing press conferences, the people that the media don't want to hear always seem to talk the longest.

Most marriages in boxing don't come with "for better and for worse, richer and poorer" attached to them

One needs at least a touch of cynicism to be a good boxing writer.

★ ★ ★

In the 1970s, Ken Norton's good looks and chiseled physique led him to Hollywood, where he landed more than a dozen film roles. The most notable of these was in the 1975 movie, *Mandingo*, in which he played a slave who was trained by a plantation owner to be a fighter. As a footnote to history, a struggling young actor had a bit part in *Mandingo* as "young man in crowd." But his scene was deleted from the final cut. One year later, the young actor rocketed to stardom in a boxing movie of his own. His name was Sylvester Stallone.

★ ★ ★

There were 4,618 fans in The Theater at Madison Square Garden when Gennady Golovkin knocked out Curtis Stevens. Only one of them had beaten Mike Tyson.

Kevin McBride is a genial man, 6-feet-6-inches tall, who turned pro in 1992 and fought for the last time nineteen years later. His pro-debut weight was 217 pounds. For his last fight, he toppled the scales at 296. He liked to eat, he liked to drink, and he could fight a bit.

On June 11, 2005, McBride entered the ring at the MCI Center in Washington, DC, as the designated victim for a comebacking Mike Tyson.

Iron Mike had nothing left. He quit on his stool after six rounds and never fought again.

"It was the greatest night of my life," McBride reminisced before Golovkin-Stevens. At one point, Mike cracked me with a good shot. I hugged him, held on for dear life, and whispered in his ear, 'If that's all you have, you're in trouble.' That got him so mad that he bit my nipple and tried to break my arm off at the elbow. If he'd hit me again instead of doing that stuff, he might have knocked me out."

"What a night that was," McBride continued. "At the press conference afterward, someone came over and whispered in my ear, 'Muhammad Ali is here. He's leaving but he wants to meet you.' Ali had been there to watch his daughter fight. So I got up and went over to say hello to Ali. It was like meeting God. In one night, I beat a legend and met the greatest fighter of all time."

McBride wasn't able to capitalize financially on his victory over Tyson the way he wanted to. He lost six of his next eight fights and left the sweet science with a 26-and-10 record. But the glow from that magical evening remains, leaving him to say, "I smile whenever I think of that night. I shocked the world and I shocked myself."

Issues and Answers

In 2013, Watch International asked for some thoughts on Muhammad Ali. After more than a quarter-century of writing about The Greatest, I found that there were still new perspectives from which I could view him.

Muhammad Ali: A Classic Hero

Let us celebrate Muhammad Ali.

We live in an age when people pay homage to celebrities, superstars, and champions.

Ali is something more. He is a hero.

Our record of heroes begins with *The Iliad,* the oldest known work in Western literature.

The Iliad was fashioned by a series of storytellers represented by the Greek poet, Homer. The telling began around 800 BC and was codified over hundreds of years. In final form, it recounts a period of several weeks during the last year of the siege of Troy.

The ancient Greeks revered heroes as a class of men who occupied a position midway between common mortals and gods. Heroes were worshipped by communities as protecting spirits. The failure to pay homage to them was often seen as responsible for misfortune such as poor crops and pestilence.

Achilles is *The Iliad's* greatest hero warrior. Neither his death nor his heel are referenced in the epic poem. It wasn't until the first century AD that the Roman poet Statius advanced the idea that Achilles' mother, Thetis, sought to make her son invulnerable by dipping him in the River Styx as she held him by the heel. Indeed, Book 21 of *The Iliad* recounts Achilles being wounded by a spear thrown by Asteropaeus that draws blood from his elbow.

The Iliad also contains the first telling of a boxing match in Western literature: the confrontation between Epeios and Euryalos at the funeral games for Patroclus. The winner is to receive an unbroken horse; the loser, a two-handled goblet.

Prior to the contest, Epeios declares, "I say no other of the Achaeans will beat me at boxing. I will mash his skin apart and break his bones. Let those who care for him wait nearby to carry him out after my fists have beaten him under."

Thereafter, "The two men strode to the middle of the circle and faced each other and put up their huge hands at the same time. Great Epeios came in and hit Euryalos on the cheek as he peered out from his guard, and he could no longer keep his feet."

Victory was followed by compassion.

"Great-hearted Epeios took Euryalos in his arms and set him upright, and his true companions stood about him and led him out of the circle, feet dragging as he spat up thick blood and rolled his head over on one side."

When Homer's tales were first woven together, the world known to those who listened to them was very small. No one could have imagined Muhammad Ali.

Ali, once known as Cassius Marcellus Clay Jr, burst upon the scene as a gold-medal winner at the 1960 Rome Olympics. In the decades that followed, he brought unprecedented grace to boxing and changed forever what we expect a champion to be.

Ali's accomplishments in the ring were grist for the milling of legends. There were two fights against Sonny Liston, when he proclaimed himself "The Greatest" and proved that he was; three epic wars against Joe Frazier; and a stunning victory over George Foreman, when Ali traveled to Africa and reclaimed the crown that had been unfairly taken from him.

In ancient Greece, hundreds of people gathered around fires to hear of Achilles' battle against Hector. Three millennia later, hundreds of millions of people waited for word of Ali's exploits on battlefields as far-flung as Kinshasa and Manila.

Ali is a hero for modern times. His personal magnetism, good looks, and charisma made him ideal for the age of television. And certainly, he meets the criteria for contemporary heroism.

A hero must achieve something substantial. Heroes can be presidents, military leaders, sports champions, or someone quite average (such as a teenager who leaps into a rushing river to save a drowning child). But a hero must do something that most people can't do or haven't done.

A hero overcomes substantial odds.

There must be an element of risk that has been met head-on.

Heroes often "do it alone."

Ali's ring exploits are in line with the above. But true heroism requires something more. A hero places principles and loyalty above personal gain, a higher good ahead of self-interest.

Ali's devotion to principle inspired the world.

Initially, Ali stood as a beacon of hope for oppressed people around the globe. Every time he looked in the mirror and said, "I'm so pretty," he was saying "black is beautiful" before that became fashionable. He demanded equality for himself and others. Then he refused induction into the United States Army at the height of the war in Vietnam, was stripped of his championship, and threatened with imprisonment. He became a symbol of the belief that, unless there's a very good reason for killing people, war is wrong.

Sadly, Ali's ring career tracked the arc of a classic Greek tragedy.

In that genre, a hero is endowed with *arete*; excellence, the attributes that make him great.

Ali had preternatural physical gifts; strength, speed, stamina, and a seeming imperviousness to pain.

Then the hero gives in to *hubris*; a mixture of overconfidence and pride leading to the belief that he's invincible and immune to the pitfalls that destroy other men.

Hear Ali's words: "I'm young, I'm handsome, I'm fast. I can't possibly be beat. I am The Greatest."

A *nemesis* is sent by the gods to threaten the hero's destruction.

Achilles versus Hector . . . Ali versus Joe Frazier.

Even if the hero triumphs over his nemesis, the seeds of his destruction have been sown.

Finally, there is *ate*; the demise, the inability to see one's own fate until it is too late.

In 1996 at the 26th Summer Olympiad in Atlanta, the world watched as Muhammad Ali lit a cauldron with a torch carrying the Olympic flame. Ali was in less than good health by then. It was a difficult physical task. More than one billion people around the world were watching.

The people who witnessed Ali's struggle that night were united in love and caring for one man. More than a billion people, if only for a moment, had all the hate and prejudice removed from their hearts.

Ali prevailed. The flame moved from torch to cauldron. It was the perfect benediction for a hero's life.

Too often, boxing suffers from self-inflicted wounds.

Billy Smith and the Case against Boxing

British boxer Billy Smith committed suicide on July 23, 2013.

Smith was born on June 10, 1976, and turned pro on March 28, 2000. According to Boxrec.com, he lost his first 24 fights, never knocked out an opponent, and had a final ring record of 13 wins, 145 losses, and 2 draws. Most of his 160 fights were scheduled for four rounds. He went ten rounds on two occasions and eight rounds six times.

Billy's younger brother, Ernie, was also a fighter and compiled a record of 13 wins, 142 losses, and 5 draws. Ernie Smith scored one knockout in his ring career and was knocked out nineteen times. On January 29, 2010, as his brother would do three years later, Ernie Smith committed suicide.

In the wake of Billy Smith's death, boxing websites have called him "a true and valued servant . . . a solid value-for-money journeyman . . . a key rung on the ladder for aspiring fighters to climb."

A Yahoo-Eurosport article proclaimed, "Smith played a huge role in British boxing. The journeyman was seen as an almost inevitable step for boxers making their way through the ranks, with everyone from Gavin Rees to Ricky Burns taking him on."

As for the dismal nature of Smith's record, the people who put him in the ring and their apologists maintain, "He had skills. He knew how to clinch and hold to survive . . . He fought mostly four-round fights . . . He was knocked out only eight times . . . This is boxing. Let them do what they want."

What happened to Billy Smith in the ring happens to thousands of club fighters around the world each month. But it happened to Smith more often.

A professional boxing match is supposed to be a competitive athletic event. Based on Smith's record, it's fair to say that, when he came to fight, he was expected to lose.

Smith won two of his last 88 fights. The final losing streak of his career began on December 10, 2011, when he was on the short end of a decision against Gary Fox. The losing streak was at 39 when he died. In 37 of those 39 fights, Smith didn't win a round.

More specifically, Smith's last 39 fights totaled 166 rounds. He won two of those rounds. Not two fights; two rounds. That's equivalent to a quarterback completing two out of 166 passes. It's a tennis player who wins two games in 39 sets. No professional sport other than boxing would tolerate a failure rate like that.

It's difficult sometimes for regulators to determine whether or not a fighter should be licensed to box. When should licensing authorities say enough is enough? Where should they draw the line?

Billy Smith was on the wrong side of the line.

There's a familiar mantra: "Oh, they know how to defend themselves. They don't get hurt."

Really? Getting hit in the head by a professional fighter doesn't hurt?

Let the officers and directors of the self-perpetuating clique known as the British Boxing Board of Control get whacked in the head a few times by each of Smith's 160 opponents.

The fact that Smith was stopped only eight times during his career indicates that he could take a punch. But when a professional boxer loses 145 fights, the line blurs between getting beaten up and getting beaten up badly.

Let me repeat what I've said many times in the past. Fighters who lose again and again are different from perennial losers in other sports. Athletes "play" sports like baseball, basketball, tennis, and golf. No one plays boxing. Fighters are punched in the head hard by men trained in the art of hurting. They're prime candidates for brain damage.

When a fighter like Billy Smith enters the ring, spectators aren't paying to watch a competitive fight. They're paying to see someone get beaten up. There's a difference.

After Smith's death, it was written that beating him was "a rite of passage" in British boxing.

Stomping an innocent victim is a rite of passage for some street gangs.

Billy Smith is entitled to be remembered with respect for the fact that he entered the ring again and again against more gifted fighters and was on his feet at the final bell almost every time. But his ring record tarnishes boxing.

Here, the thoughts of Irish middleweight John Duddy are instructive. Duddy fought professionally with bravery and honor for seven years. He won 29 of 31 fights and retired when he felt that he was no longer willing to make the sacrifices necessary to honor the craft of prizefighting.

The day after Billy Smith committed suicide, Duddy was asked for his thoughts on the tragedy.

"When a fighter has a record like that," John answered, "he's a pawn for the promoter; that's all. It's about the promoter building other fighters and filling out his fight cards. It's sad and it's wrong."

"Boxing is a debilitating sport," Duddy continued. "Every time you get in the ring, you lose a part of yourself that you can never get back. And to lose again and again like that . . ." John's voice trailed off, then picked up again. "When I was a kid, the reason I boxed is because I was good at it. That feeling and pride in what I was doing was a big part of what motivated me my whole career. Fighters know when they shouldn't fight anymore. They might not admit it, but they know."

There came a time when Billy Smith knew.

Many gyms now have someone on site who offers a direct pipeline to PED suppliers.

Edwin Rodriguez, PEDs, and Al Haymon

On October 2, 2013, Edwin Rodriguez enrolled in the Voluntary Anti-Doping Agency's 24-7-365 testing program. That means VADA can demand blood and urine samples from Rodriguez without notice anytime anywhere. In so doing, Edwin followed the lead of Nonito Donaire, who announced in early 2012 that he was unilaterally subjecting himself to year-round PED testing by VADA.

Boxing has a serious PED problem. Under the best of circumstances, trying to catch drug cheats is like designing anti-virus computer software. The cheats are always finding new ways to thwart the system.

In boxing, the system is easy to beat. Most states have drug-testing programs that a high-school student could circumvent. Testing on fight night or testing once a fight has been announced is better than no testing, but it's not enough. A fighter can use PEDs between fights and cycle off when his next fight is signed.

The Damocles Sword of testing by a qualified testing agency 24-7-365 is essential if boxing is to curtail PED use. But with rare exceptions, this testing hasn't been implemented.

Indeed, one might posit that Rodriguez and Donaire have put themselves at a competitive disadvantage. Their upcoming opponents have steered clear of 24-7-365 PED testing. That doesn't mean their opponents are dirty. But it doesn't inspire confidence that Edwin and Nonito will be in the ring against clean opposition either.

Jim Lampley was once reluctant to call for stringent measures to curtail the use of performance enhancing drugs in boxing. That changed on December 8, 2012, when Manny Pacquiao was brutally knocked out by Juan Manuel Marquez.

"I saw Manny Pacquiao lying face-down on the canvas in front of me," Lampley recalls. "I thought he might be dead. That imbued me with a sense of urgency on this issue."

One week later, on the December 15 edition of *The Fight Game*, Lampley designated Donaire as *TFG*'s "Fighter of the Year."

"He committed to random drug testing, 24-7-365 whether he is scheduled to fight or not," Lampley explained to viewers. "At a moment when, elsewhere in the sport, you can find instances of star fighters who are testing positive for performance enhancing drugs, test results which have allegedly been ignored or suppressed in favor of unobstructed commerce, enforcement efforts which get lost or fall short due to improper scheduling, inadequate testing methods, and bureaucratic incompetence; if you are looking for the ray of hope, the light in the forest, his name is Nonito Donaire."

On the same telecast, Lampley honored VADA president Margaret Goodman. After referencing VADA's "state of the art procedures" and "prominent busts" of two elite fighters (Lamont Peterson and Andre Berto), Lampley declared, "It took VADA and Margaret Goodman two fights to establish the will to enforce standards which might help to reverse what many observers now see as an onrushing tide of performance enhancing drugs in boxing. For making her point forcefully, fearlessly, and immediately, Dr. Margaret Goodman is the '*TFG* Person of the Year.'"

One can argue that it's the responsibility of state athletic commissions, legislators, and promoters to help rid boxing of PEDs. But most of all, it's the responsibility of the fighters and their camps. The fighters are the ones who are at greatest risk.

A fatality would be the most stark evidence of the crisis. But the dangers go far beyond a handful of deaths. Twenty years from now, an entire generation of fighters will have brain damage from having been hit in the head harder than would have been the case without PED use by their opponents.

Thus, it's worth focusing on Edwin Rodriguez and the laudable commitment to 24-7-365 VADA testing that he recently made.

In August of this year, Rodriguez signed with manager Al Haymon. At least three of Haymon's fighters (Andre Berto, Antonio Tarver, and J'Leon Love) have tested positive for PEDs in the past.

Another Haymon fighter (Peter Quillin) was enrolled in a USADA testing program prior to his June 2, 2012, fight against Winky Wright. Then, after blood and urine samples were taken from both fighters, Wright was told that the testing had been abandoned and the samples were destroyed.

Haymon also represents Adrien Broner.

Broner, Antonio DeMarco, Golden Boy (Broner's promoter), and the United States Anti-Doping Agency signed a contract for USADA testing prior to the November 17, 2012, Broner-DeMarco fight. But according to DeMarco, he wasn't tested by USADA for that bout, nor was Broner.

Then, on June 22, 2013, Broner fought Paulie Malignaggi.

"I wanted VADA testing," Malignaggi recalls. "And I was told, 'No, we won't do VADA. If you insist on VADA, there won't be a fight.' Finally, I said, 'Fuck it. I'm getting seven figures. I'll go ahead and fight.' Would I have been more confident that Broner was clean if there had been VADA testing? Absolutely."

Haymon's flagship fighter, of course, is Floyd Mayweather.

On June 24, 2013, at a media sit down before the kick-off press conference for Mayweather vs. Canelo Alvarez, Leonard Ellerbe (CEO of Mayweather Promotions) told reporters, "We've put in place a mechanism where all Mayweather Promotions fighters will do mandatory blood and urine testing 365-24-7 by USADA."

USADA declined a request from this writer for comment on the truth of Ellerbe's contention. Al Haymon also declined comment for this article. And questions remain regarding the issue of whether or not, several years ago, Mayweather "A" samples tested positive on three occasions.

Referencing that issue, Dan Rafael of ESPN.com stated during a November 21, 2012, online chat, "I need to see proof before I accuse somebody of something so serious. What is fact, however, is that the settlement in the Pacquiao-Mayweather lawsuit happened after the Pacquiao camp tried to get Mayweather's USADA testing records. So maybe where there is smoke there is fire."

So here's a suggestion. Why doesn't Floyd Mayweather enroll in VADA's 24-7-365 program? And let him state publicly, "Any fighter who wants to be eligible to fight me must enroll in VADA's 24-7-365 program *now*."

And let's take it a step further. In addition to Mayweather, Broner, Quillin, Berto, and Love, Al Haymon currently represents Danny Garcia,

Devon Alexander, Lucas Matthysse, Marcos Maidana, Leo Santa Cruz, Keith Thurman, Austin Trout, Omar Figueroa, Gary Russell Jr, Sakio Bika, Josesito Lopez, Erislandy Lara, Shawn Porter, Errol Spence, Chris Arreola, Seth Mitchell, and Deontay Wilder.

Let's assume that all of these fighters are clean. Let them all enter a 24-7-365 VADA testing program. I can't speak for anyone else. But that would certainly make a believer out of me.

Al and Floyd have enough money to fund it.

It's easy to talk the talk. Let's see who walks the walk.

Let's also remember the thoughts of Jim Lampley, who has warned, "Whatever is the worst thing that can happen as the result of boxers employing modern medical science to strengthen their bodies, it hasn't happened yet. But if nothing is done to further strengthen testing standards and applications, it surely will. And when it does, we won't be complaining anymore that boxing can't find its way into mainstream media. We'll be there in a big way, and in no way to our credit."

In mid-2013, I received a query from Edgar, a Dubai-based men's luxury lifestyle magazine that wanted to know if Vitali and Wladimir were "killing heavyweight boxing." My response follows.

Don't Blame the Heavyweight Mess on the Klitschkos

Wladimir Klitschko's May 4, 2013, title defense against Francesco Pianeta in Mannheim, Germany, was similar to his seventeen most recent outings dating back to 2004. Klitschko entered the ring an overwhelming favorite and won every minute of every round. He stuffed battering-ram-like jabs in Francesco's face that rendered the challenger's visage bruised and swollen. As Pianeta weakened, the champion stepped up his assault.

The only safe haven that Pianeta found came when he was sitting on his stool between rounds or lying on the ring canvas, which happened on three occasions during the bout. The carnage was stopped in round six after Klitschko knocked him down for the third time.

That has become standard operating procedure for Wladimir and his older brother, Vitali. The Klitschkos are the dominant heavyweights in boxing today and have been for some time. Their fights often seem like performances rather than competitive athletic contests. For that reason—and because the brothers will not fight each other to establish a single dominant heavyweight—there are complaints in some circles that the Klitschkos are "killing heavyweight boxing."

That's not true in Europe, where upwards of fifty-thousand fans routinely attend Klitschko fights and millions more watch on television. What about the rest of the world?

Vitali Klitschko was born in Kyrgyzstan on July 19, 1971. Wladimir was born in Kazakhstan on March 25, 1976. Their father was a career Soviet Air Force officer from Ukraine, who died of cancer twenty-five years after playing a role in the clean-up of the 1986 nuclear power plant accident at Chernobyl.

More often than not, the Klitschkos have a significant size advantage over their opponents. Vitali stands 6-feet-7-inches tall and weighs in for fights at roughly 250 pounds. Wladimir is an inch shorter and several pounds lighter.

Both Klitschkos—and Wladimir, in particular—are safety-first fighters. They've mastered the art of using their height and reach to avoid getting hit solidly on the chin and seldom take risks. Wladimir's right hand is as concussive as a train wreck. But he rarely throws it with conviction until he feels secure that his opponent has been rendered helpless by jabs.

Vitali was the first Klitschko to meet with international success in the professional ranks. He won his first 27 fights by knockout and captured the World Boxing Organization heavyweight belt in 1999. An injured shoulder forced his withdrawal after nine rounds of an April 1, 2000, title defense against Chris Byrd. Three years later, horrific cuts over his left eye led to the stoppage of his challenge against heavyweight king Lennox Lewis.

Since then, Vitali has been undefeated. He now holds the World Boxing Council heavyweight crown, and his record stands at 45 wins against 2 losses with 41 knockouts.

Wladimir won a gold medal in the super-heavyweight division at the 1996 Olympics and turned pro on November 16, 1996 (the same night as Vitali). He won his first 24 fights (23 of them inside the distance). Then he faltered, collapsing from exhaustion in the eleventh round of a December 5, 1998, bout against American journeyman Ross Puritty.

Wladimir rebounded from that loss to annex the WBO title on October 14, 2000, with a unanimous-decision victory over Chris Byrd. But twenty-nine months later, he crumbled in a second-round loss to South African Corrie Sanders. His fortitude was further questioned after a fifth-round knockout defeat at the hands of Lamon Brewster in 2005. But he has won eighteen consecutive fights since then and is currently recognized as heavyweight champion by the World Boxing Association, International Boxing Federation, and World Boxing Organization.

At age 41, Vitali is nearing the end of his ring career. Wladimir is 37 with several good years of boxing left in him. The feeling among boxing insiders is that, had they been matched against each other in their prime, Vitali would have been victorious. Wladimir is more skilled. But big brother is thought to be mentally tougher and possessed of the stronger chin.

Given their size and skill, the Klitschkos would have been competitive against any heavyweight in any era. But they're fighting at a time when there are few, if any, inquisitors who can test them. And they've tended to allocate opponents on the basis of who matches up best against whom. For example, David Haye has movement and Vitali is a bit ponderous, so Haye was matched against Wladimir. Wladimir's chin is still suspect and Shannon Briggs can whack a bit, so Vitali was the one who fought Briggs.

The primary negative with regard to the Klitschkos is that there are two of them. It breeds confusion among casual fans and precludes recognition of either man as *the* heavyweight champion of the world.

But the fact that boxing's popularity is dwindling in some areas of the world is traceable to root causes other than the Klitschkos. Their dominance isn't a turn-off to most sports fans. Traditionally, boxing has thrived when it has a dominant heavyweight champion. Joe Louis, Muhammad Ali, and Mike Tyson are examples of that.

Nor is the fact that the Klitschkos are foreigners a cause for alienation. Americans and others will happily embrace conquerors from overseas. Roger Federer, Rafael Nadal, and Rory McIlroy are proof positive.

The most pressing problem that boxing faces today isn't the Klitschkos. It's the structure of the sport.

Most sports peak in popularity as they prepare to crown a champion. Fans know who won the World Cup, the Super Bowl, the World Series, and Wimbledon. The public doesn't care much about boxing's heavyweights anymore, but it doesn't care much about the other weight divisions either. That's because people don't know who the champions are.

Once upon a time, boxing had eight weight divisions with one champion in each division. Now there are seventeen weight divisions and four world sanctioning organizations, which—for a sanctioning fee, of course—designate "world" champions, "super" champions, "diamond" champions, "silver" champions, "interim" champions, and champions "emeritus."

Also, the powers that run boxing in the United States have embraced an economic model that limits viewership to those who can afford to pay for premium cable television and spend another sixty dollars for major fights that are on pay-per-view. No other sports reduces viewership for its flagship events in that manner.

As a result of these and related factors, boxing is no longer part of the social fabric and dreams of America's underclass. It has been supplanted by other sports.

The average salary for a National Basketball Association player is roughly $5,150,000. For Major League Baseball players, it now exceeds $3,200,000. In the National Football League, the number is just shy of $2,000,000 annually.

Very few fighters make as much money in an entire career as an American team athlete makes in a single season. Also, big money comes more quickly for athletes in other sports than it does in boxing. It's no longer uncommon for elite high-school basketball stars like Kobe Bryant and Lebron James to limit their college years and enter the professional ranks as soon as possible for tens of millions of dollars.

Hall-of-fame trainer Emanuel Steward, who helped resurrect the careers of Lennox Lewis and Wladimir Klitschko, observed, "If Vitali and Wladimir had been born in the United States, with their size and coordination, they probably would have become basketball stars."

Indeed, many of the top American fighters of the past twenty-five years (Roy Jones, Oscar De La Hoya, Shane Mosley, and Floyd Mayweather) began boxing in large part because their fathers pushed them into it.

So . . . Have Vitali and Wladimir Klitschko hurt heavyweight boxing?

Let's answer that question with another query.

Where would heavyweight boxing be today without the Klitschkos?

For starters, there would probably be four so-called heavyweight "champions" instead of two. And most likely, those four would be hopelessly mediocre because it's not just the American heavyweights who are mediocre. So are all the other heavyweights in the world who aren't named Klitschko.

The Klitschkos are the only fighters who make heavyweight boxing legitimate today. Without them, the division would be a wasteland.

They're also good ambassadors for boxing.

All too often, misconduct and trash-talking are embraced as a marketing tool by television networks and promoters. Floyd Mayweather has been criminally convicted on three occasions for being physically abusive to women. Other fighters have seen their market value rise after outbursts of profanity, homophobic and misogynistic rants, and threats of physical violence outside the ring.

One never picks up a newspaper and reads about Vitali or Wladimir Klitschko being arrested for assault or carrying a concealed woman.

Both brothers are fluent in Russian, Ukrainian, German, and English. Their public comments are marked by dignity and restraint. They have worked tirelessly over the years in support of charities like UNESCO and their own Klitschko Brothers Foundation, which supports educational and health initiatives in Ukraine.

In addition, Vitali is now chairman of the Ukrainian Democratic Alliance for Reform; a political party dedicated to free speech, gender equality in all aspects of Ukrainian life, and replacing what he calls "a closed oligarchical economic system" with equal economic opportunity. In 2012, he was elected to Ukraine's parliament.

Boxing fans should celebrate the Klitschkos and appreciate them while they reign.

Shortly before his death, Emanuel Steward opined, "The elite fighters today are better athletes than fighters used to be, but they aren't as well-schooled in how to fight." To emphasize his point, Steward added, "Tommy Hearns would have destroyed Floyd Mayweather. Floyd would have given Tommy that shoulder roll, and Tommy would have broken his shoulder. And after he broke Floyd's shoulder, he would have hit him on the jaw and knocked him out."

Emanuel, of course, had a bias. He was Hearns's trainer. But his comment started me thinking about a grand possibility.

Mayweather and Pacquiao against the Greats

In recent years, there has been a lot of commentary regarding the place that Floyd Mayweather and Manny Pacquiao hold among the all-time greats. Pacquiao's admirers concede that Manny has passed his peak. Mayweather's partisans maintain that Floyd is as good as ever and mention him in the same breath as Sugar Ray Robinson. Each man is scheduled to appear in a major pay-per-view fight later this year. As those fights draw near, historical comparisons are expected to fill the air.

How good are Mayweather and Pacquiao? Or to rephrase the question the way their admirers would like it to be, "How great are they?"

To put their considerable skills in context, I chose eight fighters for a "fantasy" round-robin tournament at 147-pounds.

The fighters, in alphabetical order, are Roberto Duran, Emile Griffith, Thomas Hearns, Sugar Ray Leonard, Floyd Mayweather, Manny Pacquiao, Aaron Pryor, and Sugar Ray Robinson.

The list is limited to welterweights from Sugar Ray Robinson's championship reign to date. It doesn't include earlier champions like Mickey Walker, Barney Ross, and Henry Armstrong (each of whom competed successfully at 147 pounds). If one of the tournament participants pulled out, fans wouldn't complain if he were replaced by Jose Napoles, Donald Curry, Felix Trinidad, or Oscar De La Hoya.

All of the fighters chosen for the tournament fought at one time or another at weights other than welterweight. Roberto Duran was at his most dominating as a lightweight, although he handed Sugar Ray Leonard his first loss at 147 pounds. Aaron Pryor's peak performances were at 140. But Teddy Atlas offered his take on that recently, saying, "I don't think anyone was too big for Aaron Pryor."

Issues such as same-day weigh-ins versus day-before weigh-ins might also be considered by purists. And there's a difference between going fifteen as opposed to twelve rounds. But at the end of the day, either a fighter is very good, great, or the greatest.

Twenty-eight experts participated in the rankings process. Listed alphabetically, the panelists were:

Trainers: Teddy Atlas, Dan Birmingham, Pat Burns, Naazim Richardson, and Don Turner.

Media: Al Bernstein, Steve Farhood, Jerry Izenberg, Dan Rafael, Michael Rosenthal, and Jeremy Schaap.

Matchmakers: Jerry Alfano, Eric Bottjer, Don Elbaum, Bobby Goodman, Brad Goodman, Charles Jay, Ron Katz, Mike Marchionte, Chris Middendorf, Russell Peltz, and Bruce Trampler.

Historians: Craig Hamilton, Bob Mee, Clay Moyle, Adam Pollack, Randy Roberts, and Mike Silver.

The panelists were asked to assume for each hypothetical fight that both fighters were at the point in their career when they were the best they could be and still able to make 147 pounds.

If each of the eight fighters listed above had fought the other seven, there would have been 28 fights. And there were 28 panelists. Thus, 784 fight predictions were entered in the data base.

Every fight on this list would have been a mega-event.

Fighters were awarded one point for each predicted win and a half-point for each predicted draw (too close to call). A perfect score (each voter predicting that the same fighter would win every one of his fights) would have been 196 points.

The results have been tabulated. The rankings are:

Sugar Ray Robinson   189.5 points
Sugar Ray Leonard   156.0
Thomas Hearns   112.5
Roberto Duran   93.5
Floyd Mayweather   79.0
Emile Griffith   60.5
Aaron Pryor   59.5
Manny Pacquiao   33.5

The chart below shows how the panelists thought each fighter would fare against the other seven.

	Robinson	Leonard	Hearns	Duran	Mayweather	Griffith	Pryor	Pacquiao
Robinson	–	22.5	28	28	27	28	28	28
Leonard	5.5	–	26	21	27	25	24.5	27
Hearns	0	2	–	22.5	22	21	18	27
Duran	0	7	5.5	–	14	19.5	21.5	26
Mayweather	1	1	6	14	–	19.5	16	21.5
Griffith	0	3	7	8.5	8.5	–	17	16.5
Pryor	0	3.5	10	6.5	12	11	–	17
Pacquiao	0	1	1	2	6.5	11.5	11	–

Sugar Ray Robinson was regarded as the cream of the crop. All twenty-eight panelists said that Robinson would have beaten Duran, Griffith, Hearns, Pacquiao and Pryor. Twenty-seven of the twenty-eight panelists thought that Robinson would have beaten Mayweather. Where Robinson-Leonard is concerned, nineteen panelists picked Robinson, two picked Leonard, and seven said the fight was too close to call. That adds up to a record of 186 wins, 3 losses, and 7 draws.

Sugar Ray Leonard was the clear #2 choice. His projected tournament record was 146 wins, 30 losses, and 20 draws. Throw out his 28 fights against the original Sugar Ray, and Leonard comes in at 144 wins, 11 losses, and 13 draws.

Leonard and Thomas Hearns at their best were close to equal in the ring. But none of the electors picked Hearns over Leonard. Twenty-four picked Ray. The other four called the fight too close to call.

That said; Hearns finished third and was a clear favorite over the five fighters who finished behind him. Here it should be noted that previous fights between the participants were relevant in the minds of the panelists but not necessarily dispositive. For example, Hearns blasted out Roberto Duran in two rounds. But Hearns and Duran fought at 154 pounds, not 147. And Roberto, who was thirty-three years old at the time, was at the end of a slide that saw him lose five of ten fights. Thus, while 22 panelists picked Hearns over Duran, five picked Roberto and one had the bout too close to call.

Floyd Mayweather finished fifth in the rankings with a composite record of 75 wins, 113 losses, and 8 draws. Some of the panelists were influenced by the belief that, unlike the other fighters listed, Floyd hasn't tested himself against the toughest possible inquisitors.

"I don't see Floyd signing up for this tournament," one panelist noted.

Still, one panelist (a trainer) voiced the view that Mayweather would have beaten Sugar Ray Robinson.

"Styles make fights," the panelist explained. "Floyd might have stunk out the joint. The crowd would be booing. But I think he'd win the fight."

Twenty-six panelists thought that Sugar Ray Leonard would have beaten Mayweather. The other two called the bout too close to call.

Twenty panelists favored Mayweather over Pacquiao with the fighters at their respective peaks. Five picked Pacquiao. Three called it too close to call.

Except for Emile Griffith (60.5 points) and Aaron Pryor (59.5), there was clear separation in the rankings between each of the fighters.

Manny Pacquiao finished eighth and showed best against Griffith (11 wins, 16 losses, 1 draw) and Pryor (10 wins, 16 loses, 2 draws).

Each of the fighters in the tournament deserves to be called great. But keep in mind; there have been other fighters in other weight classes during the past half-century who are equally deserving of praise. Think, for example, of Muhammad Ali, Marvin Hagler, and Carlos Monzon.

So let's not get carried away by a wave of hyperbole when the next Mayweather and Pacquiao fights come along.

As I've said many times, common sense is uncommon in boxing

Common Sense and Scoring a Fight

A lot of people think that a judge shouldn't score a round even. Their view is that, no matter how close a round might be, there's always a basis on which to choose between the fighters. These same people often say with a straight face that, if a judge scores an extremely close round in favor of one fighter, he can always even things out by scoring the next extremely close round in favor of the other guy.

Why not score rounds honestly?

There's nothing inherently evil about the concept of even in sports. Baseball teams score the same number of runs in an inning. Football and basketball teams score the same number of points in a quarter. Golfers often take the same number of strokes on a given hole.

A fight can be scored a draw. So why shouldn't an individual round be scored even?

This doesn't mean that a judge should go overboard. Angelo Poletti, in an act of monumental indecision, scored ten even rounds in the first fight between Sugar Ray Leonard and Roberto Duran en route to a 148-147 scorecard in Duran's favor.

But a judge's scorecard is supposed to accurately reflect that judge's view of the fight. It undermines the integrity of the scoring system if a judge who is uncertain as to who won a particular round makes a decision based on a mental coin flip.

Every round in boxing starts out even. The generally used criteria for scoring each round are (1) clean punching (2) effective aggression (3) ring generalship, and (4) defense.

"In the current climate," says commentator Larry Merchant, "judges are pressured to identify a winner of each round. But once you get past the issue of who's dictating the terms and landing the most punches and doing the most damage, there are rounds that neither fighter deserves to win or lose. If I can't decide who won a round, I'm not going to make it up. I'll call the round even."

HBO's "unofficial ringside judge" Harold Lederman is in accord.

"Judges are paid to make hard decisions on close rounds," Lederman says. "But some rounds are dead even. If a judge is really undecided and can't pick the winner of a round, he should call it even. Anything else is unfair to the fans and unfair to the fighter that he decides against."

Making an arbitrary decision as to who won a round that's too close to call has the same effect as deducting a point for a foul; only here, the judge is penalizing a fighter for no good reason.

Next issue—

Just because there hasn't been a knockdown doesn't mean that a round shouldn't be scored 10-8.

A fighter can win a round in a manner that's characterized as (1) close (2) decisive, or (3) dominant.

"You don't need a knockdown for a 10-8 round," says Showtime boxing analyst Steve Farhood. "Suppose Fighter A edges Fighter B by three jabs to one. It's a 10-9 round. Now suppose Fighter A kick's Fighter B's butt all over the place but doesn't knock him down. Most judges will also score that a 10-9 round, which tells you right there that the ten-point-must scoring system is flawed in the way it's implemented. When one fighter clearly dominates another and hurts the other guy, even if there hasn't been a knockdown, that round should be scored 10-8."

"A judge doesn't need the referee to call a knockdown to score a round 10-8," adds Nevada's dean of boxing judges, Duane Ford. "When Tim Bradley fought Ruslan Provodnikov, the TV people made a big thing about how, in their view, the referee missed a knockdown and that cost Provodnikov a point. But each judge had the option of scoring that round 10-8 based on the overall action in the round if he thought that a 10-8 score was warranted. If one of the fighters is scoring effectively with power punches, hurting his opponent, and dominating the round, I'm fine with 10-8."

Or phrased differently: If a hair's breadth difference equates to a 10-9 round, shouldn't a dominant round be worth more to the winner?

That leads to a third issue. The notion that a fighter is automatically entitled to a 10-8 round simply because he knocked his opponent down is flawed.

Knockdowns are an important part of boxing and should be weighed heavily in scoring a fight. One of the main objectives in the sport is to knock an opponent off his feet.

But just because a fighter scores a knockdown doesn't mean that he's entitled to a swing of three points (from 9-10 to 10-8). If Fighter A dominates a round and is felled by a flash knockdown, shouldn't that be only a 10-9 round in favor of Fighter B? Or maybe even 10-10?

Here the thoughts of Greg Sirb (executive director of the Pennsylvania State Athletic Commission and former president of the Association of Boxing Commissions) are instructive.

"You have to score the whole round," Sirb says. "Common sense has to come into play. You can't automatically throw away two minutes fifty-five seconds of good work because a knockdown occurred. If I'm dominating a round and you score a flash knockdown, how can anyone fairly say that you're entitled to a 10-8 round? Do you really think that the judges should totally disregard the other two minutes fifty-five seconds?"

Showtime Boxing analyst Al Bernstein agrees and suggests, "Let's assess intelligently how much damage is being done. Let's distinguish between knockdowns that do serious damage and knockdowns where a fighter's glove barely touches the canvas or the fighter goes down and bounces back up. Let's also ask whether a knockdown was the result of a solid punch or a fighter going down because he was hit when he was off balance."

Too many judges are scared to turn in a scorecard that looks different from what the other judges and members of the media have constructed. But it's foolish to have a 10-point-must scoring system and put arbitrary limits on the judges' options.

As a contrast to "Fistic Nuggets," these "Notes" were on the serious side.

Fistic Notes

Teddy Brenner is widely regarded as the greatest matchmaker in the history of boxing. He began making matches in New Jersey shortly after World War II. Stints in New York at Madison Square Garden, the Coney Island Velodrome, Long Beach Stadium, Eastern Parkway Arena, and St. Nicholas Arena followed. In 1959, he returned to The Garden, where he served as matchmaker and, later, president of Madison Square Garden Boxing. He left MSG in 1978 and spent the last years of his career with Top Rank.

Brenner died in 2000. His legacy lives on in memories of the fights he made and the axioms of his trade that are now part of boxing lore. Among the words of wisdom that Brenner offered were:

★ "There's only two types of fighters: those who can fight and those who can't."

★ "A matchmaker is a guy who starts fights. Then he gets out of the way and lets other people finish them."

★ "Before I make a fight, I ask myself, 'Is this a good fight? Does the fight lead anywhere? And would I buy a ticket to watch it?'"

★ "There's heavyweight boxing. And then there's everything else."

★ "I wouldn't fix a fight for my own brother. That doesn't mean everybody in boxing feels that way."

★ "A matchmaker has to convince both sides that they can win the fight. It's a bit of a con."

★ "Managers are always suspicious that the other guy is getting a better deal."

★ "Ask a fighter who's the toughest guy he ever fought. Nine times out of ten, he'll give you the name of someone he beat."

★ "There's one thing about making boxing matches; everybody knows about them the minute they're made because it's impossible to keep a secret in boxing."

★ "It isn't easy to be a matchmaker. If a fight you make is good, the fighters get the credit. If it's bad, the matchmaker gets the blame."

★ "Fans want to see the best fights. That doesn't necessarily mean the best fighters."

★ "Matchmaking is not simply a matter of putting number one against number two. Anybody can do that."

★ "Nobody is perfect. But there's one goddamn thing I know, and that is that nobody knows more about how to make a match than I do."

★ "Guys call me up and say, 'Who do I have to see and who do I have to know?' Well, they have to see me and they have to know me."

★ "The matchmaker has to deal with people, and people are always up to something. They're always making deals and then changing their mind. People can be a lot of trouble."

★ "All I ever wanted in this game was to put on the best fights I could make."

★   ★   ★

When Bernard Hopkins defeated Tavoris Cloud, he reclaimed a portion of the light-heavyweight crown at age forty-eight. At the other end of the spectrum, Billy Conn won the whole thing at age twenty-one.

Conn grew up poor in Pittsburgh, a fact he confirmed with the observation, "Sure, I was poor. You ever see a rich kid fighting?"

On a similar note, Johnny Ray (Conn's manager), declared early in his fighter's career, "Billy is a good kid. I hope he doesn't become a gentleman until after we make some money. Being a gentleman softens you up in this business."

Conn defeated Fred Apostoli twice in 1939. His purse for the second bout was $10,467, which prompted him to say, "I'd heard there was this much money in the world, but I was always puzzled just how to get it."

More importantly, Conn's victories over Apostoli put him in position to battle Milio Bettina for the world light-heavyweight title. On July 13, 1939, he scored a fifteen-round decision over Bettina. Then, after ten more wins, he went up in weight to challenge Joe Louis for the heavyweight throne.

"Louis is a great fighter," Ray proclaimed, heralding his own fighter's chances. "But everything's got to end. The greatest athletes in every sport fade eventually. Around Pittsburgh, you'd of had your head broke if you said that someday Honus Wagner would be just another bum at shortstop. But champions always collapse."

Conn came close against Louis. When they met in the ring on June 18, 1941, he was leading on the scorecards going into the thirteenth round. Then the Brown Bomber rallied to knock him out. Five years later, they fought again, but Conn was a shell of his former self. Louis dominated throughout their rematch en route to an eighth-round knockout.

Years later, Conn would say of his conqueror, "Joe Louis is the only guy I know who never rapped anyone, never said a bad word about anyone."

★ ★ ★

Boxing has been under fire since—well, since forever—for biased and incompetent judging.

People often ask, "Who are these judges?"

One of them is Ted Gimza.

The WBA appointed Gimza as a judge for the October 5, 2013, title unification fight in Moscow between Wladimir Klitschko and Alexander Povetkin. Povetkin was so hopelessly outclassed that that each judge had him losing all twelve rounds. Still, Gimza's credentials were of special note.

Reporting on Gimza in April 2013, the Fox News website in Chicago wrote, "Gimza, a two time felon who has a long criminal history dating back to 1975, had his most recent run-in with the law in February of 2012. He was pulled over in Buffalo Grove for speeding and subsequently charged with DUI, unlawful possession of a 38 caliber handgun, no firearm identification card, as well as possession of a switchblade. This, while also being on probation for a previous DUI in 2010."

On July 29, 2013, Gimza pled guilty to a felony weapons charge and was sentenced to two years probation, which included home confinement and the requirement that he wear an electronic ankle bracelet for 160 days. Gimza then applied to the court for special permission to leave the United States and travel to Moscow for "for employment purposes" to judge the Klitschko-Povetkin fight. Permission was granted.

These are not good credentials for a judge.

★   ★   ★

Lou Duva has been in less-than-good health lately. But on occasion, the venerable trainer's voice echoes through my mind. Among the thoughts he shared with me over the years are:

★ "Fighters! You bring them up. You teach them everything. Then they leave you."

★ "The way the business is now, you've got to be a con man to succeed in boxing."

★ "When I was young, I fell in love with fighters who had talent. Now I fall in love with fighters who have character."

★ "Nobody but nobody, I don't care who it is, knows completely what boxing is all about."

★   ★   ★

Eric Drath is a fine filmmaker. His credits include *Cornered* (a 2008 documentary about the fight between Billy Collins and Luis Resto that became infamous because of trainer Panama Lewis's doctoring of Resto's gloves) and *Renee* (a riveting 2011 documentary about the transformation of Richard Raskin into Renee Richards).

Drath's latest venture—*No Mas*—focuses on the first two fights between Sugar Ray Leonard and Roberto Duran and is part of ESPN's *30 For 30* series.

Leonard, in 1980, was well on his way to becoming boxing's premiere attraction. After winning a gold medal at the 1976 Olympics, he'd won 27 consecutive pro fights and knocked out Wilfred Benitez to claim the WBC welterweight crown.

Duran had compiled a 71-and-1 record and was on the short list of greatest lightweights of all time, having earned recognition as the 1970s "Fighter of the Decade."

Among the adjectives applied frequently to Roberto were "savage, relentless, brutal, and demonic." At a press conference prior to Leonard-Duran I, he flashed his middle finger in the direction of Ray's wife and offered to have sexual relations (although he expressed it in cruder terms) with Ray's mother.

Leonard told Drath, "I'd never faced anyone who was so nasty and angry."

Leonard-Duran I featured two great fighters with contrasting ring styles who were in their prime. Duran won by a razor-thin margin when Leonard inadvisably chose to brawl rather than box with him.

Five months later, they met in the ring again. Duran was not in the best of shape, which meant that he fought at a slower pace. In round seven, Leonard began showboating and taunting him. Trailing by a slender margin on each of the judges' scorecards, Duran quit in round eight. He might not have spoken the words "no mas" as legend has it. But by waving his hand, turning his back, and walking away from the action, he clearly told referee Octavio Meyran, "This fight is over. I've had enough."

"This is the most inexplicable thing I have ever seen in the ring," blow-by-blow commentator Howard Cosell told a national television audience.

The boxing community and fight fans everywhere agreed with him.

No Mas features contemporary interviews with Leonard and Duran interspersed with talking heads. The best of the latter are Mike Tyson (who describes Leonard as "a pit bull with a pretty face") and the always reliable Steve Farhood.

There's also some good archival footage, including action from both fights and a wonderful scene where Ray Charles (whom Ray Charles Leonard was named after) sings *America the Beautiful* in the ring before the second Leonard-Duran bout. But the film doesn't capture the underlying personal drama that Drath so adroitly conveyed in his earlier sports documentaries.

There's some transparently manipulative footage of Leonard and Duran together in a boxing ring that was shot earlier this year. But Leonard is never asked on camera for a nuanced explanation of why he thinks Duran quit. And Duran says simply, "I don't regret anything."

One of the sad things about the "no mas" fight is that people forget how good Leonard was that night. All they remember is Duran's surrender. The headline was "Duran Quits," not "Leonard Wins." That leaves a frustrated Ray Leonard telling Drath, "It was all about why he quit. And I'm saying, 'Because of me.'"

Meanwhile, the question of what motivated Duran's actions that night remains unanswered. Was he suffering from stomach cramps? Did

Leonard's showboating humiliate him to the point of wanting out? Did he say to himself, "This guy is making me look silly. I'm physically depleted. I'm not beating him tonight. Fuck it."

Duran has never conclusively answered that question. One wonders if he even knows the answer.

★   ★   ★

In his heyday, Iran Barkley guaranteed a war every time out. "The Blade" fought like Arturo Gatti but with less finesse. A lot of fighters being groomed for stardom—James Kinchen, Michael Olijade, and Darrin Van Horn, to name a few—were derailed by his fists. And there were wars with the likes of Roberto Duran, James Toney, Michael Nunn, Nigel Benn, Robbie Sims, Wilford Scypion, Mike Tinley, and Sanderline Williams,

"[Top Rank matchmaker] Teddy Brenner matched me tough every time out," Barkley recalls. "Teddy Brenner didn't make fights. He made wars. If Teddy Brenner was alive today, a lot more fighters would be punch drunk."

The high point of Barkley's career came on June 6, 1988, when he challenged Thomas Hearns for the WBC middleweight crown. Bleeding badly from a cut above his left eye, Iran launched a desperation right uppercut in round three and knocked out Hearns.

"I wasn't supposed to win that fight," Barkley says. "Nobody gave me a chance except me and my mother. The fight was all about Tommy. But as far as I was concerned, it was all about me. Tommy had experience, but I had experience too. Tommy had a big punch, but I had a big punch too. When I won, it upset a lot of people. Bob Arum [who promoted both fighters] didn't pat me on the back and say 'great fight.' I had to pay for my own victory party. People said afterward that it was a lucky punch, but there's no such thing in boxing. And to prove it, I beat Tommy on a decision when we fought again [in 1992]."

Barkley is fifty-two years old now. His career ended on six straight losses, the last of which was fourteen years ago.

"I'm still hoping I can get a big money fight," Iran says. "But no one wants to fight me. Maybe me and Tommy can do it again."

*   *   *

Do you remember when Manny Pacquiao was criticized in some circles because he supposedly was avoiding "slick African American fighters" as opponents?

Floyd Mayweather has fought one African American opponent (an aging Shane Mosley) since April 2006. And Adrien Broner, who's being touted as Mayweather's heir apparent, has faced only one African American (John Redish) in his last fourteen fights. In fact, as best I can tell, "The Problem" has fought only five African Americans (Henry White Jr, Eric Ricker, Terrance Jett, and Allante Davis being the others) in his entire 26-bout pro career. As of this writing [on March 1, 2013], those five Broner opponents have a composite ring record of 21 wins in 69 fights.

*   *   *

The Nevada State Athletic Commission embarrassed itself on February 28, 2013, when it fined Julio Cesar Chavez Jr $900,000 and suspended him for nine months because he tested positive for marijuana use after his September 15, 2012, fight against Sergio Martinez.

Chavez, of course, started the idiocy when he smoked grass and, after testing positive, proclaimed, "I have never smoked marijuana. For years, I have had insomnia, so I went to the doctor and he prescribed some drops for me that contained cannabis. I stopped taking them before the fight with Martinez, and I didn't think I was going to test positive."

Then the grandstanding WBC got into the act, announcing on October 3, 2012, that it had fined Chavez $20,000 and ordered him to enter a drug rehabilitation center.

Chavez responded, "I do not condone what the World Boxing Council said about their desire to send me to rehab. That's for drug addicts, and I'm not. The Council has not even seen me. How can they say that?"

Perhaps some of the people who pull the strings at the WBC could enter an eating disorder clinic.

But back to Nevada.

Last week, Chavez belatedly and penitently explained his marijuana use to the Nevada State Athletic Commission as follows: "I was told it would help my stress. I was tense for the fight and someone mentioned it to me and that's why I did it eight or nine days before the fight. I couldn't tell you the exact reason why I did it. I just can tell you I was under a lot of stress and had family problems, a lot of things going on in my life. It was the biggest mistake and I'll never do it again."

Chavez also told the commission that he hadn't smoked marijuana before any other fight, but declined to say whether he'd smoked marijuana at any time in his life other than "eight or nine days" before the Martinez fight.

Nine hundred thousand dollars? For smoking marijuana?

Let's get real! What do you think would happen if all NSAC commissioners and commission employees were subjected to random testing for recreational drug use?

★   ★   ★

After losing to Joe Frazier on March 8, 1971, Muhammad Ali embarked on a tour that saw him fight in Canada, Switzerland, Japan, Indonesia, and a half-dozen cities in the United States before journeying to Zaire to reclaim the heavyweight throne. One of the stops on his tour was Ireland, where he fought Al "Blue" Lewis on July 19, 1972.

When Ali Came to Ireland is a fifty-minute documentary that recounts the events leading up to and during that fight.

Ali has Irish blood in him. One of his maternal great-grandparents, Abe Grady, immigrated to the United States from County Clare soon after the Civil War and married a woman listed on the census rolls as a "free colored woman."

That said; when Ali arrived on the Emerald Isle, he announced, "I don't know much about Ireland. All I know is that there's a lot of green here."

The promotion of Ali-Lewis was chaotic from the start. Promoter Butty Sugrue (a pub owner and former circus strongman) was strapped for cash and found it difficult to meet his pre-fight financial obligations. Then, on the day of the fight, thousands of spectators crashed the gates rather than pay for tickets.

Al "Blue" Lewis had been sentenced to thirty-years in prison for beating a man to death in a Detroit street robbery. He'd learned to box behind bars and, after five-and-a-half years incarceration, was given early parole for helping to mediate an end to a prison riot during which the warden had been held hostage. Lewis gave it his all against Ali but was knocked out in the eleventh round.

When Ali Came to Ireland doesn't explore the big picture of Ali's life in or out of the ring. It focuses on one fight in one locale. Vintage footage (some of it not previously seen commercially in the United States) is mixed with "talking heads" to tell the tale. It's an engaging look. And there's poignancy in seeing Ali when he was healthy and young, surrounded by people like Angelo Dundee, Harold Conrad, and George Kimball, who are now gone.

★   ★   ★

I attended a screening of *Grudge Match* with a group of high school students. At the end of the film, one of the students said to a friend, "Man; that was good until the end, which was stupid."

My sentiments exactly.

I'm hard-pressed to think of an actor who owes more to a single role than Sylvester Stallone owes to *Rocky*. For Robert DeNiro, his role as Jake LaMotta in *Raging Bull* is one in a long line of celebrated performances.

In *Grudge Match,* the two actors team up to tell the story of Henry Sharp (Stallone) and Billy McDonnen (DeNiro), ex-fighters in their sixties who split two bouts thirty years ago and are forced by circumstances into a rubber match.

Grudge Match doesn't take itself too seriously. It's funny with poignancy and some drama. The screenplay and performances are good enough that it's easy to suspend disbelief. There's suspense as to who will win the climactic bout.

Then the fight starts and the film devolves into silliness.

On a snowy Saturday in December, Stallone and DeNiro were at the Ritz-Carlton Hotel in Manhattan to talk about *Grudge Match*. For forty minutes, they and cast members Kevin Hart, Alan Arkin, and Kim Basinger answered questions from the media.

DeNiro had the look of a man who's really bored at press conferences. Listening to him talk, one had the feeling that he approached *Grudge Match* tongue-in-cheek while Stallone approached it as high drama. Both men expressed genuine respect for boxing and boxers.

Asked to comment on the respective merits of *Rocky* and *Raging Bull*, Stallone spoke effusively about DeNiro's towering performance as Jake LaMotta. When it was DeNiro's turn to answer, he said simply, "They're two different styles of films."

Kim Basinger looked very pretty.

★   ★   ★

Boxing has traditionally been a young man's game. John L. Sullivan won the world bare-knuckle heavyweight championship at age twenty-three and the first gloved crown three years later. James J. Corbett was six days past his twenty-sixth birthday when he dethroned Sullivan in 1892.

Bob Fitzsimmons broke the mold.

"I am thirty-four years of age now," Fitzsimmons acknowledged before meeting Corbett in the ring on March 17, 1897. "And I don't think I am as vicious as I used to be. I don't have the same thrill now when I see a man sinking to the floor. I hate to smash a man and see him bleed. My only desire is to put it on his chin and knock him hard enough to lay him out for a little more than ten seconds."

That said; there was still bad blood between Fitzsimmons and Corbett before they fought.

"I read in the papers that Mr. Corbett intends to give me the worst licking I ever got in my life," Fitzsimmons declared. "Notwithstanding his enormous output of braggadocio, I will be in the ring to receive all he can give to me. Many believe him invincible. I do not. Corbett, heretofore, has fought men who are my inferiors as fighters. And I believe no one knows it better than Corbett himself."

When the hour of reckoning came, the champion dominated the early going. But Fitzsimmons survived and, in round fourteen, scored a brutal one-punch knockout with what has been memorialized in boxing lore as Ruby Robert's left hook to Gentleman Jim's solar plexus.

"I can't believe it," Corbett said in the ring afterward. "I am defeated. How can it be?"

Decades later, in his 1925 autobiography, Corbett elaborated on his loss to Fitzsimmons and observed, "My hat is off to anyone who reaches the top. It will always be a struggle, taking ambition and courage and willpower to win. It is for these things that the prize ring, with all the brutality and faults that go with it, still is of importance in life." And he added poignantly at the close of his book, "The roar of the crowd is no longer for me. I am one of them."

★ ★ ★

SOME WORDS OF WSDOM FROM GREAT FIGHTERS

Tom Sayers of England (to John Heenan of the United States, as the two men shook hands before doing battle on April 17, 1860): "A fine morning this. If a man can't fight such a day as this, he can't fight at all."

James Corbett: "The mental attitude must be preceded by a determined effort of the will. One has first to clench his mental muscles and set himself with determination; then follow with calm deliberate poise. I willed myself into this state during the long months preceding the fight. One thing was on my mind at all times: 'You can't win this fight if you lose your nerve. Worry will weaken you.'"

George Byers (who reigned as "world colored heavyweight champion" from 1898 to 1901), giving advice to the young Sam Langford: "Always remember; the best thing in this fight game is to not get hit. It doesn't matter if you hit hard enough to knock down a building if you can't avoid getting hit."

★ ★ ★

I was going through some notes on my computer recently and found a story that I think is worth sharing.

On June 5, 2010, Yuri Foreman fought Miguel Cotto at Yankee Stadium. Foreman injured his knee in round seven. The state athletic commission inspector assigned to Foreman's corner advised referee Arthur Mercante Jr that Yuri's trainer, Joe Grier, wanted to stop the fight. Defying logic and a hundred years of ring precedent, Mercante insisted that the fight go on. A severely compromised Foreman was TKO'd in round nine.

In the aftermath of the fight, Grier was upset. He felt that he'd somehow failed his fighter. Then, five days after the bout, he received a telephone call from Cotto's trainer, Emanuel Steward.

Steward imparted some choice words regarding the referee's handling of the contest. He also told Grier that he admired the job Joe had done in developing Foreman as a fighter and the way he'd handled himself on fight night.

"Emanuel was so nice," Grier said afterward. "I never thought I'd hear from him. I thought it would be like, he's a big trainer, his guy won, and he'd go on his way without ever looking back. The fact that he took the time to call and the things he said made me feel so good."

That was Emanuel Steward.

There was a time when some boxing fans called Riddick Bowe "the next Ali." It would be a shame if health issues proved them right.

Riddick Bowe's Plight

Hall-of-fame trainer George Benton once said, "I've never seen an old fighter come back without it being for money."

More recently, writer Bart Barry observed, "Prizefighting finds its participants in unfortunate situations, elevates them too high, and then drops them back on their original paths—with brain damage."

Sadly, those two thoughts describe the plight of forty-five-year-old Riddick Bowe.

Twenty years ago, Bowe was the undisputed heavyweight champion of the world.

Last Friday night (June 14, 2013), Bowe, weighing three hundred pounds, was knocked down five times in less than two rounds of a Muay Thai (kickboxing) bout in Thailand. As reported by Jocelyn Gecker of the Associated Press, "The fight was one of a dozen at the venue, which had the atmosphere of a village fairground with loud music and amusement park rides nearby. Promoters had said they hoped to draw about 20,000 people, but a crowd closer to 1,000 turned up even though admission was free. On a sweltering night, Bowe sat and sweated for hours as he waited his turn to fight. The venue had no changing rooms, so Bowe and other fighters stripped down and changed in open air tents beside the stage."

Bowe took a beating. He did not land a single punch or kick during the bout. Discretion being the better part of valor, he stayed on the canvas after the fifth knockdown.

In his prime, Bowe was a supremely gifted boxer. He won the heavyweight crown in 1992 with a unanimous-decision triumph over Evander Holyfield. Successful defenses against Michael Dokes and Jesse Ferguson followed. He lost his championship by majority decision in a 1993 rematch against Holyfield. But he rebounded to beat Larry Donald, Herbie Hide, and Jorge Luis Gonzalez before knocking Evander out in the eighth round of their 1995 rubber match.

What Bowe didn't do was train properly. He got lazy and squandered his immense talent. The last two bouts of his legitimate ring career were against Andrew Golota in 1996. On each occasion, Golota was disqualified for low blows. But both times, Riddick took a beating. After the second Golota fight, he was slurring his words badly.

In January 1997, Bowe announced that he was retiring from boxing to join the United States Marines. It was, he said, the fulfillment of a lifelong dream. His record at the time was 40 and 1 with 32 knockouts.

Eleven days after Bowe enlisted, he was granted a discharge from the Marines. Everyone involved (including the Marines) understood that it wasn't going to work out.

A downward spiral followed. Bowe hit rock bottom on February 25, 1998, when he kidnapped his estranged wife (Judy) and their five children in a frightening and irrational attempt to reunite his family.

Scott Shaffer later reported, "According to court records, Bowe borrowed a Lincoln Navigator and placed a bag in the vehicle that contained a flashlight, duct tape, pepper spray, and handcuffs. He was also armed with a buck knife. He then drove with his brother [to Judy's home in North Carolina]. After the Bowe's three oldest children left the home, he ordered the children to get into the Lincoln Navigator. When children complied, he drove the vehicle onto Mrs. Bowe's driveway. While his brother remained in the vehicle with the children, Bowe ran to the front door and forced it open. He pushed Lynette Shaw, Mrs. Bowe's cousin, back inside the house and motioned her to be quiet. He asked Ms. Shaw to tell him where Mrs. Bowe was located. With hand gestures, he indicated that he would hit Ms. Shaw if she did not disclose Mrs. Bowe's whereabouts. Ms. Shaw led Bowe to Mrs. Bowe's bedroom. He shoved the door open, removed the bed covers, and ordered Mrs. Bowe to get up. He gestured that he would hit her if she did not comply. He demanded that she prepare herself and the two youngest children to leave immediately for [the former marital residence in] Maryland. En route, Bowe displayed the flashlight, duct tape, pepper spray, and handcuffs to Mrs. Bowe and told her, 'I came prepared.' He also informed her that, if he had found her with another man, he would have killed both of them. At one point, he stabbed Mrs. Bowe on her left breast through a heavy jacket that she was wearing. Although Mrs. Bowe said she was not seriously injured, she did bleed from the resultant wound. He also slapped her. In addition, Bowe ordered his wife to call her attorney and instruct him to suspend their divorce proceedings. Mrs. Bowe dialed her attorney and her brother on a cellular phone. Her attorney's secretary informed her that her attorney was not available. Her call to her brother was unanswered. When the vehicle stopped at a restaurant in Virginia, Mrs. Bowe went to the ladies restroom. Bowe stood guard outside the door. While in the restroom, Mrs. Bowe called Ms. Shaw in North Carolina to notify her of the location of the restaurant. Mrs. Bowe also asked two elderly women who were in the restroom to contact the police to inform them that she was being kidnapped. Shortly after they left the restaurant, local police officers stopped the Lincoln Navigator and arrested Bowe."

After lengthy pre-trial maneuvering, Bowe pled guilty to criminal charges and was imprisoned for seventeen months. Upon his release from prison, he announced his intention to resume his ring career.

But there was a roadblock. In conjunction with Bowe's plea bargain and sentencing, his attorneys had submitted evidence to the court stating that Riddick's conduct had resulted from brain damage sustained as a consequence of boxing.

More specifically, Dr. Neil Blumberg interviewed Bowe at length, studied the results of an MRI and various cognitive tests, and stated the belief that Bowe suffered from a brain impairment known as frontal lobe syndrome.

Blumberg's report declared in part, "As a result of my forensic psychiatric evaluation, it is my opinion to a reasonable degree of medical certainty that, at the time of the [kidnapping] offense and at the present time, Riddick Bowe was and is suffering from personality change due to frontal lobe brain syndrome. Common manifestations of personality change include affective instability, poor impulse control, outbursts of aggression or rage grossly out of proportion to any precipitating psycho-social stressor, marked apathy, and suspiciousness or paranoid ideation. As an example, injury to the frontal lobes may yield such symptoms as lack of judgment or foresight, disinhibition and euphoria. This type of impairment is not uncommon, especially in individuals who spent the majority of their lives in the boxing profession. Despite the defendant's success as an amateur and professional boxer, he sustained enough significant blows to the head to create this brain damage which has led to a gradual but progressive worsening in his impulsivity, judgment, and behavioral controls. Although Mr. Bowe's personality change due to frontal lobe brain syndrome is not curable, it is treatable [with] outpatient cognitive remediation, which should be continued on a long-term basis. Treatment with antidepressant, anticonvulsant and/or mood stabilizing agents may also be useful and effective in dealing with the specific behavioral and emotional difficulties that can occur with this disorder."

The court accepted Dr. Blumberg's finding, in part because of the bizarre nature of Bowe's experience with the Marines.

When Bowe announced his intention to return to boxing, he told British writer Anthony Evans, "I missed it all so much. I never wanted to retire, but my manager at the time convinced me to. I knew all I needed was a rest, but I got talked into a retirement situation. Once I retired, I became so frustrated and my life kept going downhill. I'd be sitting alone at home, watching fights on TV, and I'd miss it so bad I'd just burst out crying. A lot of people are telling me I shouldn't fight, but you should be able to do what you want to do. Let me do what makes me happy. If it wasn't for boxing, what else would I do?"

As for the court's acceptance of the finding that he had brain damage, Bowe told Evans, "Let me tell you something, when I went to court, they tried to make it into a big deal, and it wasn't. It was just a lawyer's idea, a trick, that is now backfiring on me."

Dr. Margaret Goodman (former chief ringside physician and chairperson of the Nevada State Athletic Commission's medical advisory board) took a contrary view. Goodman, who had followed the Bowe proceedings from afar, declared, "If a fighter has been documented to have brain damage, game over. Brain damage doesn't disappear. Some of the clinical manifestations such as slurred speech can improve, but there are many other symptoms and signs. Refraining from getting hit in the head will improve someone clinically, but it doesn't cure the problem. You can't rest or train away brain damage. You can improve the symptoms from lack of exposure. So any jurisdiction allowing him to continue is drastically increasing the fighter's risks. I heard Mr. Bowe went for extensive speech therapy. That's great. He should do that. But getting hit in the head will wipe out any improvements he has made."

On September 25, 2004, Bowe returned to the ring in Shawnee, Oklahoma, with a second-round knockout of Marcus Rhode (who was on a seven-fight losing streak during which he was knocked out six times).

Then, in March 2005, Bowe signed a promotional contract with Goossen Tutor Promotions.

Asked if he had detected any slurring of words in Riddick's voice, Dan Goossen distinguished himself by saying, "I'm not training him to do *Othello*. I just want him to beat people up."

On April 7, 2005, Bowe eked out a ten-round split-decision over stepping-stone-for-heavyweight-prospects Billy Zumbrun. Three years and one fight later, he retired from boxing.

Boxing fans talk about how sad it is that Joe Louis was reduced to participating in staged professional wrestling matches after his boxing career was over. At least Joe Louis wasn't getting beaten up.

*The floodgates are open now with regard to PED use in boxing. It's a
problem.*

PEDs: When the Lawsuits Come

On December 8, 2012, Manny Pacquiao fought Juan Manuel
Marquez at the MGM Grand in Las Vegas. It was the fourth time that the
two men had met in the ring. In thirty-six previous rounds, Marquez had
been unable to knock Pacquiao down.

Marquez had a new look when he faced Pacquiao in their fourth
encounter. Having trained under the supervision of Angel "Memo"
Heredia (a/k/a Angel Hernandez), Juan Manuel was sporting a dramati-
cally altered physique. To some, even his head seemed differently shaped.

Heredia's résumé includes a stint as a steroid dealer who cooperated
with prosecutors after being ensnared in the BALCO drug scandal.

In round six, Marquez knocked Pacquiao unconscious with one
punch. The image of Manny pitching forward and lying face-down on
the canvas lingers in the mind. He lay there for a long time.

The floodgates are open now. Whether or not Marquez used illegal
PEDs, a lot of fighters think that he did. And they'll use them to further
their own ring aspirations.

Pacquiao, like Marquez, has been suspected of PED use in the past
and scored his share of brutal knockouts. Neither man has ever tested positive for illegal performance enhancing drugs. But it's a matter of record
that elite fighters like Fernando Vargas, James Toney, Antonio Tarver, Andre
Berto, and Lamont Peterson have. Shane Mosley never tested positive, but
his name surfaced in the BALCO investigation and he ultimately admitted using PEDs. Other fighters like Evander Holyfield, Jameel McCline,
and Yuriorkis Gamboa have been linked to PED use by clinic records.

As I wrote nine months ago, "PED use is more prevalent in boxing
now than ever before, particularly at the elite level. Fighters are reconfig-
uring their bodies and, in some instances, look like totally different physical beings. In a clean world, fighters don't get older, heavier, and faster at
the same time. But that's what's happening in boxing. Improved perform-

ances at an advanced age are becoming common. Fighters at age thirty-five are outperforming what they could do when they were thirty. In some instances, fighters are starting to perform at an elite level at an age when they would normally be expected to be on a downward slide. PEDs offer more than a shortcut. They take an athlete to a place that he, or she, might not be able to get to without them. When undertaken in conjunction with proper exercise and training, the use of PEDs creates a better athlete. The use of PEDs is also illegal, gives an athlete who uses them an unfair competitive advantage, and endangers other fighters who are getting hit in the head harder than before by opponents."

Suppose Pacquiao hadn't gotten up, ever, after being knocked out by Marquez? Suppose he had lapsed into a coma and died? Or suffered serious irreversible brain damage?

To repeat; I'm unaware of evidence proving the proposition that Juan Manuel Marquez has used illegal PEDs.

That said; many fighters are using PEDs. And it's inevitable that there will be lawsuits over that use; lawsuits brought by fighters who have lost fights and suffered injuries at the hands of users.

Boxing is legalized assault. It consists of conduct that would be a crime had it not been sanctioned by the state.

Fighters—in legal terms—assume the risk of being hurt every time they step into the ring. A fighter consents to being hit by an opponent who has honed his skills and gotten into the best condition possible. But—and this is a big but—the opponent must prepare for the fight and conduct himself during the fight within the rules.

The rules and regulations that govern boxing have the force of law. Many of them are in place to protect the health and safety of fighters. One of these rules is that a boxer may not use certain designated drugs. Violating these rules can give rise to a cause of action in a civil lawsuit for battery.

Would a fighter have a cause of action for battery if he were hurt by an accidental low blow or accidental head butt? No. That risk is assumed when a fighter enters the ring. It's understood that the remedy will be a warning, a points deduction, or disqualification at the discretion of the referee.

The same also likely holds true for intentional low blows, intentional head butts, and fouls of that nature. These transgressions are anticipated in boxing and are dealt with by the rules.

But then we go to more egregious conduct that is not reasonably anticipated during the conduct of a fight . . . such as ear biting.

For many years, Jim Thomas was Evander Holyfield's attorney. Thomas recounts, "I remember very clearly talking with Evander on the morning after Mike Tyson bit off part of his ear. I told Evander that no one can say anything with certainty when it comes to litigation, but that I thought he had a claim against Mike that was as close to a sure thing as anything I'd ever seen. I was willing to pursue that lawsuit. But Evander felt it was important for him to forgive Mike, and suing Mike would have been inconsistent with that forgiveness. I remember Evander telling me, 'I made thirty-four million dollars for three rounds last night. That's enough.'"

In some ways, using illegal PEDs is more egregious than a foul committed in the heat of battle. It's premeditated, scripted, and implemented over a long period of time.

Who could be sued for illegal PED use?

The most obvious potential defendants are the offending fighter and anyone who facilitated his use of PEDs.

An entity such as USADA that was responsible for administering drug tests prior to the fight and was negligent or otherwise culpable in failing to detect or report the presence of illegal substances might also be named as a defendant. In some instances, the governing state athletic commission would be vulnerable to suit. But many states have a doctrine of "sovereign immunity" that precludes such claims.

A plaintiff would have to prove three things to prevail at trial. On each issue, the level of proof required would be a "preponderance of the evidence."

First, the fighter (or his estate if the fighter had died) would have to convince the jury that it was more likely than not that the opponent had used illegal performance-enhancing drugs.

A positive drug test would be the best proof on this issue. But other evidence would be admissible. It's worth remembering that Lance Armstrong, Marion Jones, Barry Bonds, Alex Rodriguez, Shane Mosley, and other high-profile athletes tested "clean" before they were undone by investigations and collateral legal proceedings.

The plaintiff could take depositions of the opposing fighter, his conditioner, trainer, manager, friends, and the alleged PED supplier. It's one thing for a fighter and his camp to deny PED use to the media. It's another thing to deny knowledge of PED use under oath. The latter can lead to a charge of perjury. Criminal prosecutions for lying under oath in a civil case are rare. But in a case of this nature, the authorities might be watching.

Second, the plaintiff would have to prove by a preponderance of the evidence that there was a causal connection between the illegal PED use and the damages suffered by plaintiff in the fight. In other words, it would require a finding on the part of the jury that something different would likely have happened without the use of illegal PEDs.

That's not easy to prove. Boxing is a violent sport. By it's nature, bad things happen. No one suggests that Ray Mancini used illegal PEDs before he fought Deuk-Koo Kim or that Emile Griffith used illegal PEDs before bludgeoning Benny "Kid" Paret to death.

But the plaintiff wouldn't have to prove that illegal PED use was the sole cause of the damages suffered; only that it was a contributing factor.

If someone is driving drunk and the car skids out of control on an icy road killing a pedestrian, the car might have skidded out of control anyway because of the ice. But the fact that the driver was drunk will weigh heavily in determining whether or not there was a causal connection.

If someone who previously suffered a stroke has a cerebral hemorrhage after being punched in the head in a bar fight, the defendant can't escape legal responsibility by simply saying, "He might have had a cerebral hemorrhage anyway."

A fighter wins by inflicting physical damage on his opponent. Hurting an opponent more seriously than he would otherwise have been hurt is not just a foreseeable result of PED use. It's the goal of PED use. When a fighter artificially enhances his power, speed, and stamina, it becomes more likely that he will injure his opponent.

And third; to receive compensation, the plaintiff would have to prove the extent of the damage suffered. This could lead to compensation for pain and suffering from physical injuries and also lost economic opportunity (such as being unable to fight for a given period of time due to injury or the difference in economic terms between winning and losing the fight). These calculations would be highly speculative. But that's what juries are for.

Under certain circumstances, the jury might also award punitive damages.

Emotion plays a significant role in jury verdicts. The plaintiff's case would be more compelling if he'd suffered a serious injury in the fight. A ring death would particularly incentivize the lawyers.

The jury would have the right to draw its own conclusions from the evidence presented to it. As with most cases, the outcome would depend in significant measure on which side had the better lawyers and more convincing expert witnesses.

A lawsuit of this nature would not be without precedent. On April 30, 2005, James Toney outpointed John Ruiz at Madison Square Garden to annex the World Boxing Association heavyweight crown. Thereafter, Toney tested positive for the banned steroid, Nandrolone. He was fined and suspended by the New York State Athletic Commission and the result of the fight was changed to "no decision." But there was more to come.

On December 13, 2005, Ruiz filed a civil lawsuit for battery and other minor claims against Toney in the United States District Court for the Southern District of New York. The heart of his complaint read, "Ruiz did not consent to fight a boxer whose skills, strength, and abilities were artificially augmented by the use of Nandrolone. Furthermore, Ruiz did not have knowledge of Toney's use of Nandrolone, either actual or implied, as use of that drug violates federal law and is forbidden by the rules of the sport of boxing."

Ruiz had a strong case in many respects. His Achilles heel was damages. After Toney tested positive for Nandrolone, John got his belt back and the loss was expunged from his record. He hadn't suffered any broken bones or a bad beating in the fight. And in his next outing, he received a seven-figure payday to defend his title against Nikolay Valuev. The case was settled pursuant to a confidentiality clause whereby each side agreed to not discuss publicly the terms of the settlement.

Civil lawsuits brought by wronged individuals have been a driving force for reform in many areas of American life. At present, it's painfully clear that state athletic commissions aren't dealing effectively with the widespread use of illegal performance-enhancing drugs in boxing. Maybe private litigants will.

The lawsuits will come. The key questions are when, who will bring them, and how will they end?

Boxing's literary history is part of what keeps it alive.

Leon and Michael Spinks: Boxing's Improbable Heavyweight Champions

Leon and Michael Spinks are in danger of slipping through the cracks of history and being remembered largely as appendages to other fighters. They were the first brothers to win gold medals in boxing at the same Olympic games. Later, they became the first brothers to claim the heavyweight championship of the world.

Leon's 1978 triumph over Muhammad Ali and Michael's 1985 victory over Larry Holmes are two of the biggest upsets in boxing history. But Michael (who is also on the list of elite light-heavyweight champions) is best remembered for being obliterated by Mike Tyson in ninety-one seconds. And Leon . . . Well, Leon is remembered for being Leon.

One Punch from the Promised Land: Leon Spinks, Michael Spinks, and the Myth of the Heavyweight Title by John Florio and Ouisie Shapiro (Lyons Press) gives the brothers the attention they deserve.

Leon and Michael Spinks were born in St. Louis and spent their formative years in a single-parent home in the crime-ridden Pruitt-Igoe housing project.

Leon grew up fighting outside the ring as often as he fought in it. John Crittenden (a school classmate) told Florio and Shapiro that Leon was "not a bright guy at all" and recalled, "We had seventh and eighth grade together, and he was way below the level of the eighth grade. I can remember him writing his name on the blackboard, and he had the 'e' in Leon backward."

Kay Spinks (Leon's mother) told the school principal, "I know my boy doesn't always follow the rules. I try to make a good world for him at home, and you do the same here. But in between, we have to turn him over to that other world."

Leon, the authors recount, "had only two speeds—turbo and sleep."
To call him "undisciplined" would be putting it mildly.

In 1973, at age nineteen and without a high-school diploma, Leon
enlisted in the Marines. He took poorly to military life, went AWOL from
time to time, got into fistfights with drill instructors, and spent considerable time in solitary confinement. His saving grace was that he was good
with his fists. Ultimately, the Marines assigned him to special services: the
Camp Lejeune boxing team.

Fighting as a light heavyweight (178 pounds), Leon compiled an
amateur record of 178 wins against 7 losses with 133 knockouts. He was
a three-time National AAU light-heavyweight champion and won a silver
medal at the Pan American games. In 1976, he and Michael (who fought
at 165 pounds and was three years Leon's junior) made the United States
Olympic boxing team.

Leon fought with a ferocity uncommon in the amateur or professional
ranks. Think young Mike Tyson without technique. His style was to come
forward throwing punches, get hit, and keep coming forward. George
Foreman, who'd won a gold medal at the 1968 Olympics, voiced the opinion, "Spinks isn't a boxer, but he's the best street fighter I've ever seen."

The street fighter and his brother joined Sugar Ray Leonard, Howard
Davis Jr, and Leo Randolph as gold medalists in Montreal. After Leon
won his medal, he was given an early discharge from the Marines. He
wasn't a soldier. Not really. And the military brass understood that
Olympic gold would bring closer scrutiny of Leon's conduct by the world
at large.

Suzanne Wheatley (an administrative officer at Camp Lejeune when
Leon was stationed there) told the authors, "My superiors wanted to get
him out before he became an embarrassment to the Marine Corps."

Leon turned pro on January 15, 1977. In his eighth professional bout,
he was matched against Muhammad Ali. It was a "gimme" for Ali; an easy
fight for the aging champion against a crude novice fighter. Few people
in the boxing community took the bout seriously. But Ali's skills had
eroded badly, and he didn't train seriously for the novice. Spinks emerged
with a fifteen-round split-decision triumph.

No one could have succeeded Ali and been fully accepted by the
public. Larry Holmes found that out. Leon was particularly ill-suited to
the task.

"It was evident," Florio and Shapiro write, "that Leon had no plans to become any kind of role model. Maybe he didn't know how. Or maybe he didn't want the responsibility. More likely, he never even considered it. The one thing that's certain is that ghetto culture had attached itself to his DNA. Nobody was able to stop Leon from being Leon."

Far from representing black pride, Leon was the all-too-visible embodiment of a stereotype that fed into a demeaning portrait of African Americans. In the seventh months after beating Ali, he was arrested five times for offenses ranging from driving the wrong way on a one-way street to possession of cocaine. Comedians from Johnny Carson to Richard Pryor made him a staple of their humor.

Bob Arum (who promoted both Ali-Spinks fights) later recalled, "Leon never had any sense. He was just not very smart. And he was totally and completely irresponsible."

Leon had been a drinker, smoked marijuana regularly, and indulged in cocaine throughout his life. His choice of substance abuse depended on who he was with and how much money he had at the time.

Roger Stafford (who befriended Leon in the Marines) told the authors about being with the fighter in Las Vegas several days before Ali-Spinks I.

"I tried to keep him in line," Stafford recounted. "These pimps in Las Vegas had these houses and lots of girls and a lot of drugs. They told Leon they were having a get-together and they invited him. Leon couldn't pass the drugs by. Leon got tore up; he was so intoxicated. And this was two days before he fought Ali. All he was thinking about was getting drunk and full of drugs."

Training for his September 15, 1978, rematch against Ali, Leon continued binging on alcohol, marijuana, and cocaine. He went AWOL from training camp for days at a time. Three days before the fight, Arum saw him dead drunk, staggering into the hotel elevator as the promoter was going to breakfast.

Florio and Shapiro report, "Leon spent the day before the rematch downing booze, smoking pot, snorting cocaine, and screwing woman. [His] activities on the day of the fight are sketchy, but the facts that can be gathered don't paint a picture of sobriety."

Ali was a shell of his former self for Ali-Spinks II. But that was enough to reclaim the crown by unanimous decision against the dissipated pretender.

From that point on, Leon was a punching bag for the stars and, eventually, a punching bag for club fighters.

His money quickly vanished. After beating Ali, he was surrounded by an army of leeches and spent money like it was water. He was married to the former Nova Bush, who stood 6-feet-1-inch tall, weighed 200 pounds, and had a bleached blonde Afro. Nova was the oldest of nine children. Her mother had served time in prison after stabbing Nova's father to death.

"From the moment Leon won the championship, it's been hell," Nova told *People* magazine. "Have you ever seen two or three dogs pulling on a rag. Well, Leon's the rag."

Leon and Nova were divorced in 1982. By that time, he had three children by an old girlfriend named Zadie Mae Calvin.

Over the last ten years of his career, Leon compiled a 9-13-1 record. His early training regimen had been described as "hard work and harder partying." Now the hard work part went by the wayside. Most of the opponents he faced during his later years weren't even good club fighters. But Leon's skills had deteriorated to the point where he lost a decision to a fighter named James Wilder, who was 2-34-1 at the time.

Emanuel Steward, who trained Leon briefly on the downside of the fighter's career, recalled going to Leon's hotel room the night before a 1986 WBA cruiserweight title bout against Dwight Muhammad Qawi and finding his charge lying in bed naked with a woman amidst a garbage dump of beer bottles and fried chicken containers.

"I never in my life experienced a fighter that did this stuff," Steward told Florio and Shapiro. "Even today, nobody tops Leon. [But] you gotta remember where he came from: the projects. He got started there early and it became part of his genetic makeup. Smoking weed, drinking beer. Some people outgrow it and are able to control it. He was never able to control it. He never did feel comfortable in a nice environment. He's comfortable in a ghetto low-income-type place. He has a low image of himself."

When Leon finally retired at age forty-two, his ring ledger stood at 26 wins, 17 losses, and 3 draws with 9 KOs by. One year later, he was living in a homeless shelter in St. Louis and working part-time for minimum wage in janitorial services at the Kiel Auditorium. He married twice more and now lives with his third wife in Henderson, Nevada. On occasion, he's paid for autograph signings. But he suffers from dementia—most likely the result of heavy substance abuse and blows to the head—and is unable to fully care for himself.

Michael Spinks was markedly different from his older brother in ability and temperament.

"Michael always seemed so logical compared to Leon," Bob Arum told Florio and Shapiro. "Michael had some sense."

Michael didn't want to fight professionally. After winning a gold medal at the Olympics, he took a job cleaning offices at the Monsanto Chemical Plant in St. Louis. But financial reality intervened.

The younger Spinks turned pro on April 16, 1977. He won the WBA light-heavyweight crown on July 18, 1981, by unanimous decision over Eddie Mustafa Muhammad and unified the title by besting Dwight Muhammad Qawi on March 18, 1983. Then, on September 21, 1985, he moved up in weight to challenge Larry Holmes for the heavyweight throne.

Prior to Holmes-Spinks, nine reigning light-heavyweight champions had tried on thirteen occasions to annex the heavyweight crown. All of them (including Billy Conn and Archie Moore) had failed. But Holmes (like Ali) was well past his prime. Michael won a fifteen-round decision to claim the lineal heavyweight championship. A questionable points victory over Holmes in a rematch followed. Then Michael knocked out Steffen Tangstad and a faded Gerry Cooney before being obliterated by Mike Tyson on June 27, 1988. That was Michael's last fight. He retired with 31 victories against a single loss.

Throughout his ring career and afterward, Michael conducted himself with dignity and restraint. Unlike Leon, he lived within his financial means and made a serious effort to save his money. Unfortunately, he trusted the investment of that money to Butch Lewis.

Lewis died of a heart attack on July 23, 2011. Several weeks later, Michael learned that the man he'd trusted to oversee his financial portfolio had stolen most of it. He sued Lewis's estate but was able to achieve only partial recovery.

Florio and Shapiro do a good job of recounting the Spinks saga. The world of abject poverty that Leon and Michael came from is recounted in detail and with feeling. The writing flows nicely and the big fights are well-told.

There's some unnecessary hyperbole. After Leon beat Ali, Leon was not, as the authors claim, as famous as the president of the United States. And there are some nagging factual errors. For example, the attendance for Ali–Spinks II was 63,350, not 70,000. And the authors say the fight was "nearly a shutout," which is sloppy writing given the fact that they later note that the decision was 10-4-1, 10-4-1, 11-4 in Ali's favor.

Neither Leon nor Michael was interviewed for the book. Florio and Shapiro tried. But Leon's cognitive difficulties have progressed to a point where he is, as the authors put it, "an unreliable witness to his own story," And Michael, through his attorney, made "several unrealistic demands, including a sizable interview fee."

That latter omission is unfortunate. Michael is an enigmatic and private person. It would be nice to know more about what he's like. But authors work with what they have.

Like its subject, Mike Tyson's autobiography is fascinating but flawed.

Mike Tyson: Undisputed Truth

Tommy Brooks, who trained Mike Tyson briefly late in the fighter's career, told Mike, "Man, you're going to be in a wheelchair and people are still going to be wondering what you're up to."

Tyson's autobiography—*Undisputed Truth* written with Larry Sloman (Blue Rider Press)—helps satisfy that curiosity.

The book's title is a misnomer since some of what Tyson says in it is very much in dispute. For example, one can believe or disbelieve Mike when he states that he didn't rape Desiree Washington and that his conviction was a miscarriage of justice. I've come around to the view that, in Tyson's mind, he was innocent of the charge. But a twelve-person jury disagreed with his version of events.

That said; *Undisputed Truth* is worth the read.

The book begins with a chilling re-creation of the depraved and degrading environment that Tyson came from. He grew up in the Browns-ville section of Brooklyn surrounded by violence. For many of his child-hood years, the family (which consisted of Mike, his mother, brother, and sister) lived in abandoned buildings. His biological father, who sired sev-enteen children by various women, was absent.

Tyson began drinking at age ten and using cocaine at eleven. He slept in the same bed with his mother until he was in his teens, sometimes with one of her lovers beside them.

Much of the book is a recitation of the craziness and exploration of personages that the world already knows: Cus D'Amato, Don King, the managerial team of Jimmy Jacobs and Bill Cayton, Robin Givens, Desiree Washington, and others. There's Mike biting Evander Holyfield's ear and his self-justification because Holyfield had repeatedly headbutted him.

The most vivid portrait is of the man whom one might call Tyson's "creator"—Cus D'Amato.

"Cus wanted the meanest fighter that God ever created," Tyson says. "Someone who scared the life out of people before they even entered the ring. I was the perfect guy for his mission; broken home, unloved, and destitute; hard and strong and sneaky. He trained me to be totally ferocious, in the ring and out. To Cus, my opponents were food. Nourishment. Something you had to eat to live."

There's a lot of graphic sex in *Undisputed Truth*—with prostitutes, with groupies, and in adult clubs.

Tyson admits to having been a substance abuser for most his life and calls himself a "quintessential addict." After beating Trevor Berbick to win the WBC heavyweight crown, he was featured in a "just say no to drugs" television and print-advertisement campaign. At the same time, he was using drugs and financing a crack enterprise in Brownsville.

"Jimmy [Jacobs] and Bill [Cayton] were intent on stripping away all the Brownsville from me and giving me a positive image," he notes. "But I was a fake fucking Uncle Tom nigga. I felt like a trained monkey. I didn't become champ of the world to be a submissive nice guy. They wanted me to be a hero, but I wanted to be a villain."

Regarding his three-year incarceration after a jury found him guilty of rape, Tyson acknowledges, "Prison doesn't rehabilitate anyone. It debilitates you. I don't care how much money you earn when you get out, you're still a lesser person than when you went in. Prison took the whole life out of me."

And there's the financial fleecing of Tyson at every level; by his women, by Don King, and by others he trusted. There are people who hustled Mike and he still doesn't know it. The ultimate irony might be that Mike Tyson, who came from the streets, didn't have street smarts.

Undisputed Truth is infused with self-loathing.

Tyson references himself as "stupid . . . wretched . . . a miserable person . . . a selfish pig . . . a bum . . . a sewage rat . . . an ignorant monster . . . a piece of shit."

Among the thoughts he shares are, "My baseline normal is to destroy myself . . . You could put me in any city in any country and I'd gravitate to the darkest cesspool . . . My social skills consisted of putting a guy in a coma . . . I had the biggest loser friends in the history of loser friends . . . I couldn't understand why anyone would want to be with me . . . There's no doubt that I have some self-hatred issues . . . Sometimes I don't know if I was even made for life."

Sloman put a lot of time and effort into *Undisputed Truth*. The book is 580 pages long and clearly the product of a huge amount of work.

Tyson's voice is nicely captured in the early chapters. But about halfway through, there are places where the book begins to sound more like a collaborator piecing together newspaper articles and other public sources than Tyson himself.

The narrative is remarkably compelling at times. But there are also a lot of nagging errors that fact checking should have discovered and corrected.

For example, Big Fights Inc was created and, for decades, wholly-owned by Bill Cayton, who hired Jimmy Jacobs as a salaried employee. The book misstates that the company was formed by both men. HBO commentator Barry Tompkins is referred to as "Barry Watkins." Bobby Czyz did not "beat the shit" out of Evander Holyfield before Evander stopped him in round ten. In the real world, Evander was ahead in the fight when Czyz retired on his stool after five rounds.

More significantly, most of the mea culpas in *Undisputed Truth* relate to misdeeds that the world already knows about. There are some unexplored issues that Mike doesn't deal with.

Over the years, Tyson has talked at length about having read Plato, Tolstoy, Shakespeare, and others. Perhaps he should read Ovid, the Roman poet, who lived from 43 BC to 18 AD and wrote, "It is the privilege of beasts to rage about furiously. It is the duty of man to control himself."

One of the saddest things about Tyson's life is that all the craziness has obscured how good a fighter he was when he was young.

Talking about "boxing Gods" like Jack Johnson, Jack Dempsey, and Joe Louis, Tyson declares, "I was never really one of those guys. I wish I was, but I wasn't."

He could have been.

"Life is short; we get old so fast. It doesn't make sense to waste time on hating."　　　　　　　　　　　　　　　　*—Muhammad Ali (1995)*

Hate and Sochi

Everyone in boxing is part of the larger sporting community and society as a whole. Thus, it's worth looking at an issue that has gathered significant attention in recent months.

Earlier this summer, Russian president Vladimir Putin signed a law that allows the government to prosecute, imprison, and fine individuals if they engage in "propaganda of non-traditional sexual relations" that is likely to be heard or read by minors. In practice, the law bars the public advocacy of gay rights and gay relationships anywhere that those under the age of eighteen might hear or read about the discussion (for example; in schools, on the streets, or in the media).

One might ask what the reaction would be if a similar law barred the teaching of Judaism or tolerance of Judaism.

Or Christianity.

Homophobia is rampant and codified into law in many parts of the world today. Our own nation has confronted the issue of gay rights in recent decades. But unlike Russia, the United States has been moving toward a position of tolerance and understanding.

The 2014 Winter Olympics are scheduled to be held in Sochi on the coast of the Black Sea in Russia from February 7 through February 23.

Soon after the law in question was signed by Putin, Vitaly Mutko (Russia's minister of sports) declared, "An athlete of non-traditional sexual orientation isn't banned from coming to Sochi. But if he goes out into the streets and starts to propagandize, then of course he will be held accountable."

Then Alexander Zhukov (head of the Russian National Olympic Committee) stated that gay athletes could participate in the Winter Olympics without fear of reprisal as long as they didn't promote a gay lifestyle.

There are many ways that the United States can respond to Russia's anti-gay legislation. Or it can choose not to respond at all.

One suggestion has been that the United States boycott the Sochi Olympics. Would that boycott be appropriate?

The United States boycotted the 1980 Summer Olympics in Moscow to protest the Soviet invasion of Afghanistan without significant result. China has a long history of ignoring human rights, but the United States Olympic team was in Beijing in full force in 2008.

And let's be honest; there's division within the United States on the issue of gay rights. Indeed, when the Summer Olympics (Atlanta, 1996) and Winter Olympics (Salt Lake City, 2002) were last held here, homosexual acts between consenting adults were crimes punishable by imprisonment in Georgia and Utah.

John Carlos won a bronze medal in the 200-meter dash at the 1968 Olympics in Mexico City. He and gold-medal winner Tommie Smith (a fellow U.S. Olympian) became indelibly etched in the consciousness of the civil rights movement when they silently raised black-gloved fists during the medal presentation ceremony.

Carlos opposes a boycott of the Sochi Olympics. Last month, he told writer Dave Zirin, "If you stay home, your message stays home with you. To be heard is to be greater than a boycott. Had we stayed home, we'd never have been heard from again."

Carlos's thoughts echo those of Arthur Ashe (the greatest African American male tennis player ever). Twenty-four years ago, I spoke with Ashe about a similar decision that he'd faced.

"In 1967," Ashe reminisced, "the Davis Cup draw came up. And lo and behold, the United States was supposed to meet South Africa in the third round. I was thinking to myself, 'Oh, my God. Just three months ago, Muhammad Ali refused [induction into the United States Army]. And here I am, the only black player in tennis, the main member of the Davis Cup team.' Fortunately, the president of the United States Tennis Association then was Robert Kelleher, a wonderful man. We talked about it, and he suggested that the most effective way to deal with the situation would be for us to give up the home-court advantage. We had what was known as choice of ground. Kelleher told me, 'Let's do something that has never been done in the history of Davis Cup competition. Let's offer to play South Africa in South Africa and go down there and beat the crap out of them. Let South Africa see a black person win in their own backyard.'"

That moment never came. South Africa was ousted from the Davis Cup competition by West Germany in the second round. But Ashe's point is well taken.

It's the same point that was made by Barack Obama on August 9 when he declared, "One of the things I'm really looking forward to is maybe some gay and lesbian athletes bringing home the gold or silver or bronze, which I think would go a long way in rejecting the kind of attitudes that we're seeing there."

So let me offer a suggestion. The United States Olympic team should compete in Sochi on two conditions.

First, the United States Olympic Committee should design the jackets worn by our athletes during the opening and closing ceremonies and also the uniforms worn in competition so that the clothing has a clearly visible symbol of respect for all people regardless of their race, color, religion, or sexual orientation. A rainbow would be nice.

And second, the flag-bearer who leads the United States delegation into the stadium at the opening ceremonies should be an openly gay athlete.

There's a quotation in silver letters on a gray wall at the United States Holocaust Memorial Museum in Washington, DC. It reads as follows:

> *First they came for the socialists.*
> *And I did not speak out because I was not a socialist.*
> *Then they came for the trade unionists.*
> *And I did not speak out because I was not a trade unionist.*
> *Then they came for the Jews.*
> *And I did not speak out because I was not a Jew.*
> *Then they came for me.*
> *And there was no one left to speak for me.*

The ritual "ten count" tolled for some good boxing people in 2013.

In Memoriam

Johnny Bos, who died on May 11, 2013, at his home in Florida at the much-too-young age of sixty-one, was a Runyonesque character.

Bos was a large man with shaggy dirty-blond hair, six-feet-three-inches tall, whose weight fluctuated between 225 and 300 pounds. He was partial to long fur coats and bore a faint resemblance to Hulk Hogan.

Johnny was a boxing guy. Other boxing insiders describe him as one of the most knowledgeable boxing people they ever met. "The go-to guy for a lot of people," Hall of Fame matchmaker Bruce Trampler called him.

Bos fit between the cracks of what other people do in boxing. He was part matchmaker, part manager, and part booking agent. "I manage the managers," was how he described his role.

Mike Jones and Dennis Rappaport relied on Bos to select opponents for Gerry Cooney and Billy Costello. Bill Cayton and Jim Jacobs used him for the young Mike Tyson. Mickey Duff and Jarvis Astaire trusted him on imports to England. Tracy Harris Patterson and Joey Gamache traveled roadmaps to championships courtesy of Bos.

Johnny worked his magic before Boxrec.com and YouTube made fighter videos and fight results readily available at the click of a mouse. He knew who the fighters were and how their styles matched up. The opponents he found didn't pull out of fights at the last minute and were what they were supposed to be when they showed up.

"He was my first mentor," matchmaker Ron Katz says. "I was a kid doing shows in White Plains when Johnny took me under his wing. Night after night, we were on the phone until the wee small hours of the morning, talking boxing."

"Johnny was one of my teachers," adds promoter Lou DiBella. "There are matchmakers all over the world who were influenced by him. He loved boxing. He loved fighters. He was a hardcore blue-collar boxing guy. And he was incredibly generous with his knowledge."

"He'd do anything to be part of boxing," recalls Bob Goodman (whose résumé includes stints as Don King's right-hand man and president of Madison Square Garden Boxing). "He loved boxing so much."

I met Bos in 1984 when I was researching a book about the sport and business of boxing entitled *The Black Lights*. We got together for lunch at a diner near his home to talk about the sweet science.

"I'll have the usual," Johnny told the waitress.

I don't remember what I had for lunch that day. I do remember what Johnny ate. "The usual" was four hotdogs with sauerkraut.

At the same meal, Johnny told me that he refused to eat vegetables because they gave him indigestion. "I don't consider sauerkraut a vegetable even if it was once cabbage," he noted.

Johnny ate too much, drank too much, and partied too much. There were too many drugs.

"I started taking care of myself," he told me years later. "But I started too late."

He was also independent, possibly to a fault. He wasn't the sort of person who fits within a structure and, as a result, never found a long-tenured position with a promoter.

"And Johnny was a terrible businessman," adds Ron Katz. "He took people at their word instead of asking them for a written contract. Some of the people he dealt with were straight with him, but others screwed him."

For years, Bos was an integral part of the New York boxing scene. In the mid-1990s, he fell on hard times, economically and in terms of his health, and moved to Florida. Things didn't work out in the Sunshine State so he returned to the Big Apple and helped build the careers of Paulie Malignaggi and Yuri Foreman.

Then things turned sour again.

"I love New York, but New York don't love me," Johnny said.

In 2008, the struggle to make ends meet and congestive heart failure forced him back to Florida.

"I knew he was in poor health," Katz says. "But his death is a real shock. Johnny was like a cartoon superhero to me. And cartoon superheroes aren't supposed to die."

Johnny Bos might not be missed by a lot of people. But the people who miss him will miss him a lot.

★   ★   ★

Emile Griffith, who died on July 23, 2013, at age seventy-five, was a terrific fighter.

Griffith fought in an era when there was one recognized champion in each weight division. He won his first world title at 147 pounds with a thirteenth-round knockout of Benny "Kid" Paret in 1961. Five years later, having moved up to 160, he decisioned Dick Tiger to claim the middleweight throne.

How formidable was Tiger? After losing to Griffith, he defeated Jose Torres in his next bout to claim the light-heavyweight crown.

Emile was always willing to go in tough. He'd fight anyone. During the course of his career, he beat Paret twice, Tiger twice, Nino Benvenuti, Benny Briscoe, Gypsy Joe Harris, and Luis Rodriguez (three times).

For years, he was a fixture at Madison Square Garden, where he fought twenty-eight times. His career spanned almost two decades (from June 2, 1958, to July 30, 1977). In 111 fights, he was knocked out twice. All told, he boxed 1,122 rounds in his pro career. By contrast, Sugar Ray Leonard tallied 306 rounds; Thomas Hearns, 380.

Griffith is best remembered today for his March 24, 1962, fight against Benny Paret. After beating Paret for the title, he'd lost a split-decision in a rematch six months later.

Griffith-Paret III was contested at Madison Square Garden. At the weigh-in prior to the bout, Paret made crude sexual remarks and taunted Griffith about his sexuality. Emile was presumed to be gay at a time when the stigma that attached to homosexuality was ugly and overwhelming. That night, Griffith pinned Paret in a corner and battered him into submission. The beaten fighter lapsed into a coma and died ten days later. It was the first ring death to be witnessed live in the United States on national television.

"I was never the same fighter after that," Emile later acknowledged. "After that fight, I did enough to win. I would use my jab all the time. I never wanted to hurt the other guy. I would have quit, but I didn't know how to do anything else but fight."

For the rest of his life, Griffith would dance around the issue of his sexual orientation. He had come of age before Stonewall lit the flame that kindled the gay rights movement.

"I've chased men and women," Emile would tell writer Gary Smith in what was as close to a public acknowledgement of his sexuality as he ever came. "I like men and women both. But I don't like that word: homosexual, gay, or faggot. I don't know what I am. I love men and women the same."

In 1992, as Griffith was leaving Hombre (a gay bar near the Port Authority Bus Terminal in New York), he was attacked by a gang of thugs and viciously beaten. During the two-month hospitalization that followed, he suffered kidney failure, severe infections, and memory lapses. After his release, dementia set in.

The decline in Emile's quality of life was painful to all who knew him. Outside the ring, there had always been a childlike quality about him. He was playful and gentle with a lyrical lilting voice and warm smile that lit up his face.

"He was a joy to work with," former Madison Square Garden Boxing president Bobby Goodman recalled upon hearing of Emile's death. "Whether you were a matchmaker, a promoter, a publicist, a writer; he was friendly to everyone. You couldn't find a nicer guy."

"I knew him since 1960," trainer Don Turner said. "That's fifty-three years. He was a great fighter and he was always nice to me. It's sad that he's gone."

On a personal note; I met Griffith at the Times Square Gym in 1983. I had just begun researching *The Black Lights*, which was my initial foray into boxing writing. Emile was training fighters there. We talked at length.

Thereafter, a ritual greeting developed between us. Whenever I saw Emile, my jaw would drop. Then I'd point in his direction and blurt out, "Sugar Ray Robinson!"

Emile would laugh and hug me. We must have done it fifty times.

Several years ago, I saw Emile at a club-fight card in New York. My jaw dropped. I pointed in his direction and blurted out "Sugar Ray Robinson!"

A look of consternation crossed Emile's face.

"No, no, no!" he cried out. "Emile Griffith."

The tragic end game had begun.

★ ★ ★

The death of Nelson Mandela on December 5, 2013, engendered a global outpouring of remembrance and love.

Mandela was a worldwide symbol of dignity, perseverance, and equality for all. People from all walks of life looked upon him as one of their own. That's true of the boxing community as well.

Mandela boxed as an amateur and was a devotee of the sweet science throughout his life. Over the years, he met with Muhammad Ali, Joe Frazier, Lennox Lewis, Ray Leonard, Marvin Hagler, Mike Tyson, and Evander Holyfield among others.

The leads to a whimsical remembrance.

Mandela sometimes gave visitors a T-shirt bearing the prison number he wore during his twenty-seven years of incarceration: 46664.

When Don King met Mandela, he gave "Madiba" a similar gift: a T-shirt emblazoned with the number that Don wore for four years at the Marion Correctional Institute in Ohio.

Some tragedies in boxing are unavoidable. But others aren't.

Magomed Abdusalamov and the Dark Side of Boxing

At 10:00 PM on November 2, 2013, Russian heavyweight Magomed Abdusalamov entered the ring at Madison Square Garden to fight Mike Perez. The following morning, Abdusalamov was in a coma following the removal of a portion of his skull and other surgical procedures to treat bleeding and swelling in his brain. As of this writing, doctors don't know whether or not he will survive. If he does, it's possible that he will never talk, see, or walk again.

Everyone agrees that what happened to Abdusalamov is a tragedy. How it happened has been distorted in the retelling.

An unnamed source at the New York State Athletic Commission (which had jurisdiction over the fight) told the *New York Daily News*, "We did everything we were supposed to do that night. He never said anything was wrong. After the fight, he went back to the audience and was watching the main event."

The Wall Street Journal reported that Abdusalamov congratulated Perez and then "was whisked off to Roosevelt Hospital to get patched up."

As questions proliferated, the New York State Inspector General's Office launched an investigation to determine whether state athletic commission officials handled the fight and its aftermath properly. The interview notes from the investigation are likely to read like *Roshomon,* with participants offering alternative, contradictory, and self-serving versions of the same events.

When a tragedy of this nature occurs, there's a need to examine what happened with an eye toward asking whether proper procedures were in place and whether those procedures, if appropriate, were properly implemented.

This writer has interviewed twenty-two people who were involved in the events of November 2. Some of them, including five individuals affiliated with the New York State Athletic Commission, spoke on condition of anonymity. Others were willing to go on the record.

This is what happened.

Magomed Abdusalamov was born on the western shore of the Caspian Sea on March 25, 1981. After turning pro in 2008, he moved to Florida, where he lived with his wife and three daughters. He learned some English but only enough for limited conversation.

In his first five years as a fighter, Abdusalamov compiled an 18-and-0 record against undistinguished opponents. All of his wins were by knockout. Mike Perez was undefeated in nineteen bouts against comparable opposition.

Osric King (who is board certified in family medicine) was the ring doctor assigned to Abdusalamov's corner on November 2. Anthony Curreri (an ophthalmologist) was in Perez's corner.

The bout began with both fighters throwing heavy punches and Perez getting the better of it. With eighty seconds left in round one, Perez landed what has been referenced in fight reports as a straight left hand that appeared to break Abdusalamov's nose. A look at the replay in slow motion suggests that it was a forearm to the face, not a legal punch, that caused the damage.

Had referee Benjy Esteves called a foul, subsequent events might have unfolded differently.

Accidental foul, broken nose. At that point, Abdusalamov could have said that he was unable to continue and the bout would have been ruled "no contest."

That didn't happen. The full extent of the damage caused by the blow to Abdusalamov's nose is unclear. What's very clear is that he acted strangely thereafter.

At the end of the first round, Abdusalamov walked slowly to his corner but did not sit on his stool. Instead, he stood for a full thirty seconds, touching the already swollen left side of his face with his glove and asking (in Russian), "Did he break my nose?"

Finally, he sat. That would have been a good time for the commission doctor assigned to Magomed's corner to increase his vigil.

Thereafter, Abdusalamov was slow getting off his stool and moving to the center of the ring at the start of each round. After the second stanza, he gestured for his corner to put an icepack on the back of his head. After round four, he looked to be in distress, gestured again for the icepack, and slumped on his stool to the point where trainer John David Jackson told him, "Sit up." When the one-minute break ended, Magomed grabbed onto the ring ropes to pull himself up off his stool.

The fight was competitive through four rounds. In round five, Abdusalamov began to fade. After that round, Jackson asked his charge, "How do you feel?"

Magomed didn't answer.

"Good?" Jackson pressed.

Again, no answer.

"I didn't hear from you," Jackson said.

But the fight went on.

After round six, Magomed stood for a full fifteen seconds before sitting on his stool.

After round seven, Jackson asked, "Are you okay?

There was no response.

"How do you feel?"

No answer.

"You gotta let your hands go," Jackson told him.

Meanwhile, the left side of Abdusalamov's face was becoming increasingly disfigured, and what had once been a good action fight was turning ugly.

On at least two occasions, Dr. King stood on the ring apron near Abdusalamov's corner and looked on between rounds. But he was standing outside the ropes to Magomed's left, and the fighter's head was turned to the right so he could hear one of his cornermen (Boris Grinberg Jr) translate Jackson's instructions into Russian. Thus, Dr. King could see little more than the back of the fighter's head. There is no indication that he tried to communicate verbally with the fighter.

Adbusalamov fought courageously after the bell rang to start each round. There was never a time in the fight when he seemed defenseless. That said; by round eight, he was clearly a beaten fighter. His face was horribly swollen. There was a gash on his left eyelid. It appeared as though his nose, cheekbone, and jaw might be broken.

The fight went the full ten rounds. Perez won a unanimous decision.

After the fight, Abdusalamov was examined cursorily in the ring by Dr. King and Barry Jordan (a neurologist who serves as chief medical officer for the New York State Athletic Commission). Then he went upstairs to his dressing room. His father, brother, John David Jackson, cutman Melvin "Chico" Rivas, manager Boris Grinberg, Boris Grinberg Jr, and promoter Sampson Lewkowicz were with him.

"Everybody was sad," Boris Jr (who is fluent in English and Russian) recalls. "Mago looked at his face in the mirror and said, 'Oh, man.' The doctor [Gerard Varlotta, an orthopedic surgeon] checked him out. He took some time with him; it wasn't quick. The doctor checked Mago's nose and the bones in his face and asked Mago if he was in any pain. Mago told him his head hurt a little. Then the doctor gave him a test with numbers on cards. Mago did it quickly. But on the first card, he missed two numbers and, on the next card, he missed three numbers. Then another doctor [Dr. Curreri] came in and stitched Mago up. While he was stitching, Mago started crying. When that was done, the doctor who did the stitching told Mago to get the stitches taken out in a week and his nose was broken and there might be other bones broken, and he should see a doctor to check it out. None of the doctors said to go right away to the hospital."

Lewkowicz has a similar recollection and says that one of the doctors told him that Magomed had "a broken nose for sure" because there was blood in both nostrils.

The best indications are that Dr. Varlotta's post-fight examination was conscientiously administered and that Abdusalamov was alert and responsive with one open issue.

The "test with numbers" that Boris Jr referred to is known as the "King-Devick test." It's a short exercise that requires a person to read single-digit numbers displayed on several differently formatted cards. The examining physician then compares the speed with which the subject has read the numbers to the time taken on a baseline test (in this case, a test administered at Abdusalamov's pre-fight medical examination). If the time needed to complete the test is significantly longer than the person's baseline test time, the person is presumed to have suffered some type of head trauma that requires further observation.

No one at the New York State Athletic Commission has offered an explanation regarding the "missed numbers."

There are also conflicting accounts as to whether Abdusalamov was advised to go to the hospital that night.

One commission source has aligned with the fighter's camp and says that Magomed was told he should go to the hospital because of his nose and other possible fractures, but that he was not told it was important to go immediately.

Whatever advice was given, there appears to have been little urgency attached to it. Nor was there an offer of help regarding transportation.

"I'm one hundred percent sure that he was told to go to the hospital that night," another commission source says. "How would he have gone to the hospital? You don't need an ambulance for a broken nose. You need an ambulance for an acute injury, which no one knew he had at the time."

Magomed's cutman, Melvin "Chico" Rivas, says, "It was like, probably, you should go to the hospital tonight. But do it on your own. No ambulance or anything like that."

At the close of Dr. Varlotta's examination, he gave Abdusalamov's camp the paperwork detailing insurance coverage that would be applicable if Magomed went to the hospital or an independent doctor that night or at a later date.

Meanwhile, because of dehydration, Magomed was unable to give the required post-fight urine sample, which was to be collected as a matter of course by the commission inspector assigned to the fighter's dressing room.

The inspector was Matt Farrago, a former fighter. Farrago waited until Abdusalamov had showered and asked him to try again. This time, Magomed was able to urinate.

Boris Grinberg Jr recounts what happened next.

"The inspector looked at the urine and told us, 'There's a lot of blood in his urine. There might be some kind of internal problem. You should take him to the hospital now.' I asked, 'How do we get to the hospital? Where is the nearest hospital?' The inspector said, 'I don't know. Let me find out.' He left the locker room and came back and said, 'I couldn't find anyone to ask. Take a taxi. The driver will know.' I asked Mago, 'So, Mago; what do you think? Should we go to the hospital?' Mago said 'Yes.' That was when we decided to go to the hospital. The inspector was the only one from the commission to tell us to go to the hospital now. And we didn't even know where to go."

There was still no sense of urgency. Abdusalamov's face was now grotesquely swollen as the beating he'd taken began to fully show. But he'd answered questions cogently, showered, and dressed himself after the fight. At no time did he seem to be struggling mentally.

"We walked down the stairs that go onto the stage and then down some more stairs to where the ring is," Boris Jr recalls. "Mago started having a little trouble walking then, so we stopped for a moment. There was a fight going on, but Mago wasn't watching it. Then we went out onto the street to look for a taxi."

Sampson Lewkowicz picks up the narrative.

"When the doctors said that Mago was all right, I went downstairs to watch the next fight [Gennady Golovkin vs. Curtis Stevens]. Then Boris [Boris Grinberg Sr] came to me and said, 'We should take Mago to the hospital.' I went to Melvina [New York State Athletic Commission chairperson Melvina Lathan] and said, 'We need to take Mago to the hospital. He doesn't feel well.' Melvina told me, 'Talk to Dr. Jordan.' So I went to Dr. Jordan. And while we were talking, I got a call from Boris [Sr], saying he was outside with Mago on the street. I went outside. We stopped a cab. While we were there, Mago threw up. The cab driver told us that Roosevelt Hospital was the nearest hospital, and Dr. Jordan on the phone said the same thing. So Mago, his brother, and Boris Jr got in the cab and went to the hospital."

When Abdusalamov arrived at Roosevelt Hospital, he was told to wait in line at a receiving window before he was treated. Boris Jr tried to explain the urgency of the situation and was advised that, if he went outside and dialed 911, an ambulance would then pick Magomed up and bring him to another admitting station where he could be treated more quickly.

Boris Jr went outside to make the call. Meanwhile, Boris Sr had arrived at the hospital, and Magomed vomited again. Boris Sr shouted, "He is fighter from Madison Square Garden." Finally, the hospital staff began to move quickly.

Abdusalamov was given a CT scan that revealed swelling and bleeding in his brain. The doctors operated and placed him in a medically induced coma. The following day, he suffered a stroke and his temperature rose to 104 degrees. He has been kept alive by life-support machines since then.

There are numerous issues to be addressed in examining what happened on the night of November 2. The threshold issue is whether the fight should have been stopped before the full ten rounds were contested. If Abdusalamov had been healthy after the fight, there would be little discussion regarding that issue. But he's not healthy; he's hovering near death. Thus, it's imperative to ask whether proper procedures were in place to determine whether the fight should have been cut short and, if so, were those procedures properly implemented.

Fighters are expected to go out on their shield. That standard runs counter to self-preservation and common sense, but it's part of boxing. If Abdusalamov had opted out of the fight, he would have been derided by many fans and members of the media as a quitter.

Given that reality, there are three lines of defense to protect a fighter when he crosses over the line that separates bravery and courage from unacceptable risk: (a) the referee (b) the ring doctor, and (c) the fighter's corner.

The referee is the first line of defense. He can intervene to stop a fighter from taking punishment on split-second notice. The referee shouldn't become overly involved in the flow of a fight. But he is more than a spectator.

In New York, a ring doctor as well as the referee can stop a fight. Unfortunately, some referees take this to mean that stopping a fight because a fighter has suffered sustained punishment is no longer their call. Meanwhile, some ring doctors believe that, absent a dangerously placed cut or apparent neurological impairment, it's the referee's call. The fighter falls through the cracks.

Here, it's worth noting that Benjy Esteves (who refereed Abdusalamov-Perez) also refereed the February 26, 2000, fight at Madison Square Garden between Arturo Gatti and Joey Gamache. That fight resulted in two first-round knockdowns, a brutal second-round knockout, and career-ending brain trauma for Gamache.

A fighter's trainer also has the responsibility to stop a fight when risk outweighs possible reward. After the fact, cutman Melvin "Chico" Rivas recalled, "Mago was responding to everything we were saying. We never felt like we had to ask him if he wanted to continue. He's such a warrior."

John David Jackson should have asked. And more important from a procedural point of view, the referee and ring doctor should have been more proactive insofar as Abdusalamov's physical condition and state of mind were concerned.

Often, a fighter doesn't say directly that he wants to quit. But it shows in his face and body language in the corner between rounds. After the first round, and after many subsequent rounds, Abdusalamov looked like a man who would have been happier if someone said, "That's enough." All one had to do was look at his face. Not the swelling and bruising, but the haunting "I don't want to be here" look in his eyes. Yet round after round, the corner kept sending him out to fight while the ring doctor and referee passively looked on.

After round one, Dr. Osric King should have stepped onto the ring apron to ascertain precisely why Abdusalamov wasn't sitting on his stool and what his condition was.

Further in that regard, Dr. Michael Schwartz (founder of the American Association of Professional Ringside Physicians) observes, "The doctor can always ask the referee during the one-minute break to call a time out immediately after the bell rings to start the next round. Then the doctor can call the fighter over to the ropes and conduct a quick face-to-face examination. We do that sometimes when a fighter is cut. You can do the same thing in a situation like this."

There's no way to know when the bleeding in Abdusalamov's brain began. What we do know is that each punch afterward made it worse. One can assume that, if he hadn't been hit in the head in rounds two through ten, Magomed's brain bleed wouldn't have been as serious as it was. It might not have occurred at all.

If better procedures had been followed, the decision might still have been made to allow Abdusalamov-Perez to continue. But there's no way to know that. We do know what happened in the absence of better procedures being followed.

Here, one can look to the fight that was contested immediately after Abdusalamov-Perez, when Gennady Golvkin defended his middleweight title against Curtis Stevens. After some competitive early action, Stevens took a fierce beating. At the end of round eight, referee Harvey Dock followed Curtis to his corner and told trainer Andre Rozier, "That's it."

"Okay," Rozier responded.

If Golovkin-Stevens had been allowed to go twelve rounds and Abdusalamov-Perez had been stopped after eight, the respective fates of both Stevens and Abdusalamov might have been vastly different from what they are now.

There's also an issue regarding the quality of post-fight medical care that Abdusalamov received.

Let's start with some basic facts: (1) Doctors try to help people; (2) No one in the dressing room after the fight knew that there was bleeding in Magomed's brain.

That said; there's a point at which common sense has to prevail. Abdusalamov had suffered a sustained beating. He'd been punched more than three hundred times by a 235-pound man trained in the art of hurting. There were broken bones in his face, which was bruised and swollen to the point of being disfigured. In any context—whether the beating was administered in a prize ring, on the street, or in someone's home—he should have been taken to a hospital.

As earlier noted, there are conflicting accounts as to whether or not commission doctors told Abdusalamov that he should go to the hospital immediately after the fight. Everyone agrees that there was no offer of help to get him there

A fighter is less likely to go to the hospital on his own than if a doctor says, "We think you should go to the hospital. An ambulance is waiting downstairs to take you."

If New York State Athletic Commission medical personnel thought that Abdusalamov should go to the hospital, they should have facilitated his getting there. The availability of an ambulance would have (1) made it more likely that Magomed would go to the hospital; (2) gotten him there more quickly; and (3) ensured that he was treated in a timely manner once he arrived.

Here, the thoughts of Michael Schwartz (who now serves as chief ringside physician for the State of Connecticut, Foxwoods, and Mohegan Sun) are instructive.

"I meet with the ambulance crew to discuss protocols before every fight," Dr. Schwartz says. "We notify the hospital that a fight card is taking place. We notify the on-call neurosurgeon at the hospital that a fight card is taking place. If a fighter has to go to the hospital, we send him by ambulance, even if it's just for sutures. We give the insurance form to the paramedic before the fights start. That way, if a fighter goes to the hospital, the form automatically goes with him without delay."

At the very least, if New York State Athletic Commission personnel don't want to send a fighter to the hospital in an ambulance, the fighter and members of his team should be transported to the hospital in an on-site motor vehicle reserved by the commission solely for that purpose. Let's assume that a fighter has no facial damage, just a broken hand. Doesn't he deserve that transportation, rather than being sent out onto the streets of Manhattan to fend for himself on a Saturday night?

There are other issues that also have the potential to shade the way a fighter is treated after a fight. One of these issues relates to medical insurance.

As a general rule, boxing promoters purchase several types of insurance. There's signal insurance on big fights in case satellite transmission fails. A promoter who pays a large signing bonus to a fighter might purchase insurance to cover losses should the fighter be injured and permanently unable to fight. But the most common forms of insurance purchased by promoters are:

(1) General liability insurance: This covers personal injury to individuals other than the fighters (for example, fans in attendance at a fight). The per-event coverage limitation on these policies for major promoters is generally between $2,000,000 and $5,000,000.

(2) Cancellation insurance: This coverage is usually in place for major fights. It reimburses the promoter for out-of-pocket expenses should an event be cancelled for reasons other than a breach of contract (for example, an injury to one of the fighters or a natural disaster that renders holding the fight impossible).

(3) Boxer medical insurance: This coverage is mandated by the Muhammad Ali Boxing Reform Act and is purchased by the promoter on a card-by-card basis. Its purpose is to pay a fighter's medical expenses for injuries sustained during a bout, or to pay the fighter's estate if a fighter is killed during a bout. But the Ali Act doesn't specify a coverage minimum. That decision is left to the individual states.

At the upper end of the spectrum, California, Nevada, and Texas require a $50,000 medical insurance policy for each fighter and death benefits ranging from $50,000 to $100,000. Some states require as little as $2,500 in medical coverage with no death benefit.

New York has the highest medical costs in the nation. But the New York State Athletic Commission requires only a $10,000 medical insurance policy for fighters and no death benefit.

Some promoters purchase a $50,000 medical insurance policy and matching death benefit regardless of the state in which a fight card is held. As a practical matter, most insurers won't write a medical policy for more than $50,000. The risk is too great.

K2, which promoted Abdusalamov vs. Perez, purchased a $10,000 medical insurance policy with no death benefit.

When a fighter goes to the hospital, someone has to pay for it. In New York, $10,000 won't cover the cost of an ambulance ride to the hospital, a CT-scan, and fixing a badly broken nose. One has to ask, "Does New York's low minimum-insurance mandate mitigate against a fighter being sent by the commission or going on his own to the hospital after a fight?"

There's also an issue relating to the number of ambulances that were at Madison Square Garden on November 2.

New York law states that a fight cannot begin unless there's an ambulance on site. The promoter is responsible for providing the ambulance, which generally costs between $500 and $750. When a fight card is headlined by an HBO or Showtime bout, the promoter usually arranges for two on-site ambulances to avoid the possibility of a costly delay in starting one or both of the televised fights.

Abdusalamov-Perez was the opening bout on an HBO telecast.

Tom Loeffler (managing director of K2) says it's his understanding that Madison Square Garden arranged for two ambulances to be on site on November 2.

Madison Square Garden did not respond to a request for confirmation on that point.

Two New York State Athletic Commission officials who were on duty on November 2 say they believe that there was only one ambulance on site with a second ambulance "on call." An on-call ambulance in New York generally arrives within twenty minutes.

There's no suggestion that any of the doctors who treated Abdusalamov in the ring or in his dressing room after the fight were influenced by the possibility that sending Magomed to the hospital in an ambulance would delay the start of HBO's main event, thereby adding tens of thousands of dollars to satellite transmission fees and Madison Square Garden overtime costs. But others who were in attendance were likely to have been aware of those contingent costs.

In the aftermath of the Abdusalamov tragedy, NYSAC spokesperson Lazaro Benitez declared, "Our primary concern is the health and safety of all athletes licensed by the New York State Athletic Commission. The Department of State [which oversees the commission] is conducting a thorough inquiry into whether existing health and safety protocols were followed by the NYSAC and its employees and licensees in attendance at the event. Should our investigation reveal a need, DOS stands ready to implement immediate corrective action."

That investigation is now under the control of the New York State inspector general's office.

The inspector general will find that, by and large, New York has more stringent pre-fight medical testing than most jurisdictions. Except for the absence of a serious effort to halt the use of illegal performance-enhancing drugs, the pre-fight testing is pretty good.

But everyone who works for a state athletic commission has a responsibility to the fighters to be vigilant on fight night. That applies to the chairperson of the commission on down. Too often in New York, no one steps in and takes charge to save a fighter when intervention is called for. The classic example of that occurred when Yuri Foreman fought Miguel Cotto at Yankee Stadium three years ago.

Forty-five seconds into round seven, as Foreman was moving laterally along the ring perimeter, his right knee gave way and he fell hard to the canvas. He rose in obvious pain, hobbling when he tried to walk. Forty-five seconds later, again with no punch being thrown, his knee buckled and he fell once more to the canvas. The following round, while trying to move laterally, he staggered and almost fell again.

At that point, following proper procedure, Foreman's trainer asked the New York State Athletic Commission inspector assigned to Yuri's corner to tell the referee that he wanted to stop the fight. The referee inexplicably refused to stop it. Then Foreman's trainer threw a white towel into the ring. Both camps came through the ropes to embrace their respective fighters. But the referee ordered everyone out of the ring and, bizarrely, instructed the fighters to resume fighting. Foreman's knee gave way and he staggered several more times before the end of the round. Finally, Cotto landed a hook to the body. Yuri's knee gave out again, he fell to the canvas, and the referee stopped the bout.

The ringside physician in Foreman's corner should have stopped that fight. The chief medical officer at ringside should have stopped the fight. The commission chairperson should have stopped the fight. But no one stepped in to protect the fighter.

That culture has to change.

Tragedies happen in boxing. It's inherent in the nature of the sport. But when a tragedy happens, it's essential to look back and ask what should have been done differently to minimize the likelihood of future tragedies.

Flip Homansky served as chief ringside physician and medical director for the Nevada State Athletic Commission for more than a decade. During that time, he was widely regarded as boxing's foremost advocate for fighter safety.

Reflecting on Magomed Abdusalamov, Homansky says, "When incidents like this happen, you look at the process, not the end result. The process isn't about, 'We now know that there was bleeding.' The process is about, when someone looks like this and you know he has broken bones in his face, you send him to the hospital. The benefit in going to the hospital is that trained professionals can observe the fighter over time and precious time is saved if medical intervention becomes necessary. That's not a criticism of any specific doctor because I wasn't there. But I doubt that the fighter had anything more important than going to the hospital to do after the fight that night."

Postscript: Christmas Day 2013

Magomed Abdusalamov woke up in unfamiliar surroundings on Christmas morning. Most likely, he was unaware of the change.

On November 2, Adbusalamov suffered a life-altering brain injury in a fight against Mike Perez at Madison Square Garden. He was in a coma for five weeks and at Roosevelt Hospital for fifty-two days.

On Christmas Eve, Magomed was transported to Helen Hayes Hospital in West Haverstraw, New York. The hospital specializes in physical rehabilitation for patients who have suffered catastrophic brain injuries. Russian tycoon Andrey Ryabinskiy has committed to paying for at least two months of rehabilitation. The cost of Magomed's stay at Helen Hayes Hospital will be $51,000 a month.

"Rehabilitation" is a relative term.

The hospital's literature states that its program "treats the complex effects of brain injury, such as difficulty walking, communicating, eating and dressing, limitations in memory and thinking skills, and social, emotional and cognitive issues."

That has led some people to say, "Magomed will live . . . Magomed is in rehab . . . Magomed will be fine."

Magomed won't be fine.

The left side of Magomed's head is grotesquely misshapen. There's a crater where part of his skull was removed during surgery. The visual effect is as if the wax had dripped away from the top of an irregularly burning candle. A sign above his bed at Roosevelt Hospital warned health care providers, "No left bone flap."

Magomed breathes through a tube that has been inserted in his trachea. His eyes gaze vacantly into space. It's unclear how much, if anything, he comprehends.

He is alive.

Some people would choose to not continue living under the current circumstances of Magomed's life. In his present condition, he is not capable of making decisions of that nature. His family has chosen for him.

It's too soon to know what Magomed's condition will be a year from now. His doctors say that, whatever happens, there will be serious neurological deficits. Damage to the brain is more likely to be irreversible than damage to other organs. The younger a person is, the more likely it is that another part of the brain can compensate for the damage. The extent of permanent injury depends on the cause of the damage, which portions of the brain were damaged, and how extensive the damage is.

The hopes and expectations for Magomed are radically different now from what they were two months ago. The arc of his life has been reconfigured. The goal is no longer to become heavyweight champion of the world. The hope—although not necessarily the expectation—is that someday he will be able to think coherently and articulate his thoughts in a way that is understood by others. That he will be able to feed himself and control his bodily functions. That perhaps he will walk again.

This is a tragedy in the truest sense of the word.

Stepping up at the right time saves lives. Referees stop fights. Ring doctors stop fights. Athletic commission chairmen and chairwomen and executive directors stop fights. Cornermen stop fights. When no one steps up to stop a fight, a fighter's life can change irrevocably for the worse.

There's an issue of fact as to whether or not New York State Athletic Commission personnel suggested that Abdusalamov go to the hospital immediately after the fight. Had he done so, he might be on the road to a full recovery today.

Section 213.6 of *The New York State Athletic Commission Laws and Rules Regulating Boxing* references the duties of ring physicians and states, "Such physician may also require that the injured participant and his manager . . . report to a hospital after the contest for such period of time as such physician deems advisable."

In other words, commission personnel could have *required* that Abdusalamov go to the hospital.

Also, New York State Athletic Commission personnel concede that there was no offer of help to transport Magomed to the hospital.

This was a man who had just been beaten up—badly beaten up—as a designed component of a spectacle intended to entertain people. When his part in the spectacle was over, his nose was shattered. The left side of his face was disfigured as a consequence of cuts, bruises, swelling, and the likelihood of more broken bones. Taking NYSAC personnel at their word, he was in effect told, "Thanks; good job. Now go outside, find a cab, and get to the hospital on your own."

Would any football team (high school, college, or pro) tell a player with injuries of that nature to take a cab to the hospital? If a tennis player was injured at the U.S. Open, would the organizers hand him an insurance form and tell him to take a cab to the hospital?

What happened to Magomed Abdusalamov will be used by some as an argument for the abolition of boxing. It's certainly an argument for reform.

Here the thoughts of Bernard Hopkins are instructive.

"After I fought Roy Jones," Hopkins says, "they *made* me go to the hospital. I stayed overnight. And I won that fight. No fighter wants to go to the hospital, lie on a gurney. It's that macho stuff. But I have people around me who watch my back. Most fighters don't have that. Or if they do, the people who are trying to watch their back don't know how."

"You hear how everyone is talking now," Hopkins continues. "'Oh, we care so much about the health and safety of the fighter.' But they don't mean it. They don't care. They—and you know who 'they' are—treat us like cattle. None of these people are thinking about the injured fighter. It's not their kid. It's not their husband or brother or father. The fight is over. The next fight is coming out. They just don't care."